EMPLOYMENT RELATIONS
IN
HIGHER EDUCATION

EMPLOYMENT RELATIONS
IN
HIGHER EDUCATION

Edited by
STANLEY ELAM, Phi Delta Kappa
MICHAEL H. MOSKOW, Temple University

Published by
PHI DELTA KAPPA, INCORPORATED
Eighth Street and Union Avenue
Bloomington, Indiana

Report of a Symposium
Sponsored by
PHI DELTA KAPPA
together with
THE COLLEGE OF EDUCATION
and
THE SCHOOL OF BUSINESS ADMINISTRATION
TEMPLE UNIVERSITY
Of the Commonwealth System of Higher Education
Philadelphia, Pennsylvania

Symposium Planning Committee

MICHAEL MOSKOW (Director), *Associate Professor of Economics and Education,* Temple University

JACK COOPER, *Associate Professor of Education,* Washington State University

PAUL EBERMAN, *Dean, College of Education,* Temple University

STANLEY ELAM, *Editor,* Phi Delta Kappa Publications

WALTER GERSHENFELD, *Associate Professor of Management,* Temple University

JACK LUTZ, *Assistant Superintendent for Instruction,* Norristown Area School District, Pennsylvania

WILLIAM POLISHOOK, *Vice President for Academic Affairs,* Brandywine Junior College

ROBERT WALTER, *Associate Professor of Education,* Temple University

SEYMOUR WOLFBEIN, *Dean, College of Business Administration,* Temple University

Symposium Participants

Chairman, MICHAEL H. MOSKOW, Research Associate
Professor of Economics and Education, Temple University

Presenting Major Papers—HARRY A. MARMION, Director, Institute for
College and University Administrators, American Council on Education; MYRON LIEBERMAN, Professor of Education, City University of
New York City; JOHN W. GUSTAD, Coordinator, Board of Education of
State Normal Schools of the State of Nebraska; WALTER E. OBERER,
Professor of Law and Industrial and Labor Relations, Cornell University; MAURICE R. DUPERRE, Chairman, Division of Teacher Education, Little Rock University, Arkansas.

Session Chairmen—Mr. Moskow; Walter J. Gershenfeld, Associate
Professor of Management, Temple University; Robert L. Walter,
Associate Professor of Educational Administration, Temple University.

Discussion Participants (in addition to Speakers and Chairmen)—
Fred Ambellan, Associate Dean, School of Education, Hofstra
University; Albert A. Blum, Professor, School of Labor and Industrial Relations, Michigan State University; Patrick Carlton,
Education Specialist (Administration), U. S. Office of Education;
Joseph Cronin, Assistant Professor of Education, Harvard University; Seymour Evans, Director, Institute for Staff Relations, New
York University; Richard J. Frankie, Coordinator for Higher Education, Ohio State University; Joel E. Gerstl, Associate Professor of
Sociology, Temple University; Warren H. Groff, Assistant Dean,
College of Education, Temple University; William D. Hayward,
Coordinator of Higher Education, New Jersey Education Association; C. Addison Hickman, Vandeveer Professor of Economics,
Southern Illinois University; Richard A. Hixson, Director, Department of Colleges and Universities, American Federation of Teachers; Robert H. Holtzman, Associate Professor of Philosophy of
Education, Temple University; Herbert J. Horowitz, Assistant to
the Chancellor, Department of Higher Education, State of New
Jersey; Ray Howe, Dean, Henry Ford Community College, Dearborn, Michigan; Van C. Johnson, Associate Professor, Department
of Administration and Higher Education, Michigan State University; J. Joseph Loewenberg, Assistant Professor of Management,
Temple University; J. B. MacRae, Vice President, Pennsylvania
Association for Higher Education; William F. McHugh, Chairman,

National Association of College and University Attorneys, State University of New York, Albany; Robert W. Miner, Special Assistant to the Executive Secretary, National Education Association; Patrick J. Montana, Assistant Dean, Graduate School of Business Administration, New York University; Kenneth Rosenthal, Executive Assistant, Hampshire College, Amherst, Massachusetts; G. Kerry Smith, Executive Secretary, American Association for Higher Education; Jerome M. Staller, University Fellow, Temple University; Alfred D. Sumberg, Staff Associate, American Association of University Professors; William M. Weinberg, Assistant to the President, Rutgers, The State University; J. L. Zwingle, Executive Vice President, Association of Governing Boards of Colleges and Universities.

Preface

The symposium reported herein is in a sense the successor to a series of five institutes on collective negotiations at the public school level sponsored by Phi Delta Kappa, the professional education fraternity, and various collegiate institutions: Rhode Island College (1965), the University of Pennsylvania (1966), Indiana University (1966), Colorado State College at Greeley (1967), the University of California at Berkeley (1967), and Harvard University (1967). By 1968 it was felt that the fraternity's goal of initiating study of the collective negotiations movement at this level had been reached. Other agencies had realized the need for such institutes and were providing them. However, Michael Moskow, who had assisted in planning, organizing, staffing, and directing some of the institutes co-sponsored by Phi Delta Kappa, Dean Paul Eberman, and Dean Seymour Wolfbein saw the need for a new kind of service. Recognizing the development of sentiment for collective negotiations or other new forms of conflict resolution at the college level, they suggested bringing together the most knowledgeable people in this area to conduct a symposium on employment relations in higher education. The object would be to develop a book based on the symposium. With the cooperation of the Temple University Chapter of Phi Delta Kappa, Mr. Moskow secured a grant from Phi Delta Kappa International and further financial assistance from the Temple University College of Education and School of Business Administration. The symposium, which was organized by the planning committee identified on page vi, was held on November 14 and 15, 1968, at Temple University. Most of the credit for assembling the excellent cast of participants whose contributions are recorded in this volume belongs to Mr. Moskow, who served as director of the planning committee. It is his hope and mine that this work will further the rational development of mechanisms and procedures for improving employment relations in higher education.

STANLEY ELAM
Editor, Phi Delta Kappa Publications

June 1, 1969

Contents

•

CHAPTER ONE

FACULTY ORGANIZATIONS IN HIGHER EDUCATION

HARRY A. MARMION

DIRECTOR,
THE INSTITUTE FOR COLLEGE AND UNIVERSITY ADMINISTRATORS,
AMERICAN COUNCIL ON EDUCATION

•

For purposes of this paper only national organizations in higher education will be considered. Emphasis will be given to the issue of faculty-administrative economic negotiations because of their critical importance to the future of higher education. The way in which the issue is resolved on local campuses may give new meaning to institutional cooperation in higher education or it may result in "arms-length" bargaining between the two groups.

ORGANIZATIONAL STRUCTURE

American Association of University Professors

The American Association of University Professors is the only professional organization recognized as performing a truly national role in matters of educational concern to college faculty. Not even the staunchest advocate of the AAUP would suggest that the chapter organization on every campus represents or speaks for that faculty; however, the 85,000-member organization is a strong force on the national level.

1

Although the AAUP has an elaborate national organization with a wide range of committees, "an objective observer would say that the AAUP was Committee A,"[1] on academic freedom and tenure. Certainly, AAUP deserves a great deal of credit for its Herculean efforts in this area. The censure of those institutions not conforming to the standards set by the organization, after careful investigation, have been effective in preventing most administrations from acting in an arbitrary manner. Although academic freedom and tenure cases still exist and new institutions are added to the censure list every year, by and large the issue is under control. There needs to be a monitoring of institutions to assure that hard-won rights of faculty are not abused, but there are other issues of importance. Another important contribution of the AAUP has been the self-grading salary survey, instituted a decade ago and today the most widely utilized barometer of faculty salaries in the field.

"But what have you done for us lately?" many young Turks in academia are asking. What has the AAUP done about regional accrediting of institutions? "We issued this or that statement," says the AAUP national office. Yet in the accreditation process serious decisions are made affecting the future of educational institutions by groups of professional educationalists and administrators, and faculty believe they should be involved.

What about the problems of student unrest? Where does the AAUP stand on this issue? The AAUP participated in the formulation and later adopted the Joint Statement on Rights and Freedoms of Students. The AAUP issued another statement! What about the alarming rise of faculty participation in campus protest movements? Has there been any discernible activity in this area—even a statement about faculty responsibility? What about the serious problem of graduate teaching assistants and their increased involvement in student protest activities? Finally, what about the gut issue of faculty-administrative negotiations on economic issues? (This will be discussed later.) These are just some of the issues being raised by some of those who are AAUP members.

American Federation of Teachers

Whereas the AAUP developed in 1915 out of a need for some organization to protect the academic freedom of college professors, teacher unionism developed first in the lower schools, although some college

---

[1]Israel Kugler, "The Union Speaks for Itself," *Educational Record*, Fall 1968, p. 414.

faculty were members from the beginning. In 1916 the American Federation of Teachers was organized nationally, and in 1919 it received a charter from and became affiliated with the American Federation of Labor. Teacher unionism followed the general development of unions in America, except that during the depression, when union membership generally declined, teachers' unions expanded from 7,000 in 1930 to 32,000 in 1939. In the post-war period the growth accelerated until today teacher unions have approximately 150,000 members.

The significant impact of unions in higher education developed very rapidly. In 1966 the AFT set up a separate college division, indicating the overnight importance of this new area of potential membership.[2] Although there were college locals formed during the depression even at Ivy League institutions, the real impetus has been recent. There are now approximately 70 college locals in the country, most of them in large urban centers in highly industrialized states. I believe that the rapid evolution of college faculty unionism is due to concern over the future financing of higher education and the role of college faculty in determining the distribution of the limited financial resources available coupled with the trend towards statewide senates, extensive layers of control removed from local campuses, and various regional and national compacts in education. These concerns are heightened in urban institutions in areas like New York City which have a strong trade union tradition.

Just as the AAUP has a problem in satisfying its more militant younger members, the union has its own problems. Of the more than 300,000 college faculty members, only about 10,000 belong to unions. When you realize that 85,000 college faculty hold AAUP membership, you recognize that more than two-thirds of the remainder are affiliated with neither organization. Faculty loyalty to a particular academic or professional discipline will undoubtedly continue to ignore any such national organization.

Further, it is difficult for many college faculty even to consider unionism. The position of many is that they oppose trade unionism (for them) because they cannot accept the hired hand, employer-employee relationship upon which the whole concept of trade unionism rests. Yet the typical professor has as the basis of employment a binding personal services contract. Although one may balk at the terms "employer" and "employee," they certainly are not altogether inappropriate. Even if this disposition can be overcome, there is one even more

[2]Walter P. Metzger, "Origins of the Association," *AAUP Bulletin*, June, 1967, p. 236.

serious limitation. The ultimate weapon of the unionist is the right to strike, and this too goes against the professional mores of many college faculty; yet it should be noted that the AAUP at its 1968 meeting in Washington adopted the position that, as a last resort, strikes would be tolerated to correct an otherwise insoluble administrative stance. However, the union still has the problem of overcoming this attitude among the bulk of the nonaffiliated as well as among the AAUP membership if it is to expand with a power block of national substance.

Already trade unionism has indicated one way in which it intends to combat this "status" problem. In March of 1967 the AFL-CIO formed the Council of Scientific, Professional, and Cultural Employees. The plan is for the Council to organize white-collar professionals who, together with those in service industries and public employment, are now the largest sector in the labor force. The fact that the national unions consider that these groups can be organized indicates the power of the economic argument motivating white-collar employees.

Other Organizations

The American Association for Higher Education, an organization of college faculty members and administrators who, regardless of discipline, are interested in higher education, has 24,000 members at more than 1,600 colleges and universities. Its work is primarily informational and is dedicated to the professional development of college and university educators in a variety of ways. Its major drawback is that even though self-governing, it maintains a loose affiliation with the National Education Association. To many college faculty this smacks of professional education; however, despite this supposed limitation, the Association has made many valuable contributions.

In the fall of 1966 the AAHE formed a task force on faculty representation and academic negotiations made up of six faculty members from institutions throughout the country. They began their study with field visits to 34 institutions, running the gamut from junior colleges to long-established universities. The final report of the group suggests the idea of "shared authority" within an institution. Since an institution is a "community of scholars," the functioning of an institution is inseparable from the functioning of the faculty and both should be considered coequals in the process. The task force readily (and realistically) admits that this coequality concept is an oversimplification and that issues will be handled by different institutions in their own way.

The projected solution by the task force for growing faculty unrest, particularly among junior colleges and emergent public institutions, is multifaceted. A need exists to strengthen the *internal* agencies for faculty participation, primarily the academic senate or its counterpart. The key characteristics of a faculty senate should be the expression of individual faculty opinion as well as the expression of opinion within the various disciplines, all accomplished through a body democratically elected with administrative participation but without administrative dominance. These opinions should be concerned with matters of educational importance and not matters of trivia. The task force feels that certain elements of personnel administration, faculty promotion, and similar issues are not those issues that should be considered by this group. The whole gist of the task force's position concerns the faculty senate and its position of preeminence on the campus.

The second part of the task force's recommendations concerns *external* agencies on the college level. Among these external organizations are the AAUP and, in many teacher-preparatory institutions, the NEA state affiliate or the state association such as the interfaculty organizations in Minnesota made up of faculty members within each institution in the state system. These organizations serve a legitimate function, often acting as the conscience of an institution as well as conducting lobbying activities which in many cases it is improper for institutions to do themselves. Unions, of course, are also a kind of external organization. Thus the AAHE has a role to play in these matters.

State associations, mentioned above as one of the external agencies on the collegiate level, may be an important factor in future faculty representation. In New Jersey, for example, roughly 80 percent of the state college faculty are represented by the New Jersey Education Association, which acts as the collective bargaining agent in negotiations with the state. Recently this association publicly censured the chancellor for higher education in New Jersey. Statewide negotiations may happen in some states, but local issues on individual campuses will make the effective role of a statewide organization somewhat difficult, especially on other than economic issues.

Despite some organizational weaknesses,[3] the National Education Association is attempting to play a more important role in higher education. Its role goes beyond loose affiliation with the AAHE. There are strong NEA state organizations throughout the nation made

---

[3]Peter Janssen, "NEA: The Reluctant Dragon," *Saturday Review*, June 17, 1967.

up primarily of professors of education and in-service teachers, and there is a strong student NEA program at most teacher preparatory institutions. Within state associations there has been some movement to increase activity on college campuses. The most striking example of NEA activity in this field is the newly formed National Faculty Association under NEA aegis, which will attempt to interest junior college faculty in membership. This is an attempt to extend NEA influence to those institutions operating beyond the high school for at least a two-year period. At this point it is hard to evaluate the various NEA programs on the college level. It should be noted that the NEA and its state affiliates have significant experience in dealing with the challenges of teacher unionism.

ORGANIZATIONAL POSITIONS—WITH EMPHASIS ON NEGOTIATIONS

The AAUP

In connection with economic negotiations the AAUP position is the traditional one accepted by most faculty and institutions throughout the nation—that of letting the institutions set up their own rules. It must be said, of course, that the AAUP pioneered the report on *The Economics Status of the Profession* and supports the 1957 Committee on Education Beyond the High School proposed by President Dwight Eisenhower which called for the doubling of salaries in the ensuing decade. The same laissez-faire attitude prevails with regard to promotion, merit increments, and tenure—as long as criteria have been established by the institution in consultation with the faculty.

The AAUP, as was said before, fundamentally rejects the whole concept of trade unionism, which is the recognition of an employer-employee relationship. The position of the Association on this matter was reiterated by William Fidler, retiring general secretary of the AAUP, in his address to the 1967 national convention in Cleveland. His view was that an institution is a "community of scholars" in which all faculty members participate in decision making in a democratic fashion.

This approach was carried forward by the recently issued tripartite statement on the "Governance of Colleges and Universities." Formulated over a two-year period through the cooperation of the AAUP, the American Council on Education, and the Association of Governing Boards, this statement was formally endorsed by the AAUP national convention in Cleveland in April, 1967. Both the ACE and the AGB commended the document to their memberships as a significant step toward the clarification of the respective roles of the various components of the educational enterprise, a step that falls far short of endorsement. The document spells out (in necessarily general language) the shared responsibility for institutional control by a community of scholars, administrators, and trustees. Sharing of responsibility is advocated as an alternative to the adversary relationship that would prevail if the faculty segment of the academic community resorted to unionism.[4]

A difficulty with the statement, aside from its generality, is whether the document can accomplish its intended purposes, "to foster constructive joint thought and action, both within the institutional structure and in protection of its integrity against improper intrusions," while relegating the status of students to a cursory acknowledgement at the end of the statement. Representatives of the three organizations responsible for the tripartite statement are considering a further statement pertaining to an expanded student role in governance. There is no indication that this statement will be forthcoming in the immediate future. All the while, this question looms ever larger as the strident tones of student activism increase on campus after campus throughout the nation.

In conclusion, then, the AAUP opposes collective bargaining as an unprofessional mechanism by college faculty, not to be considered under any circumstances, and professes, of course, that the right to strike is rarely to be considered as a potential device to accomplish ends. Yet at its 1968 annual meeting in Washington the AAUP took the position that as a last resort strikes might be necessary. This new position is now consistent with one taken by the organization during the "suspension of services" at Catholic University in 1967, but exactly opposite to the AAUP position taken earlier in the St. John's University case.

The Union Position

The union position is clear-cut, direct, and of course very controversial.

1. The union feels that salaries should be between $10,000 and $30,000 per year. Automatic annual increments should be given to reach this point.

---

[4]The material in this and the following paragraph was taken from Harry A. Marmion's "Unions and Higher Education," *Educational Record*, Winter 1968, pp. 46-47.

2. There should be no merit system as the term is presently understood at most institutions.

3. All promotions should be tied to salary schedules, all of which would be made public.

4. Personnel policies should be written and available to the faculty member.

5. Department chairmen should be elected for definite terms.

The essence of the union position concerning economic negotiations is also clear-cut. All faculty salaries and other conditions of employment should be attained through the collective bargaining process leading to a written contract. The rationale is that only in this way can the faculty as a group redress the imbalance between the individually employed professional and the administration of an institution.

The union is quite specific about conditions of work such as teaching loads—six hours graduate, nine undergraduate, for example.

The other organizations mentioned earlier have positions which are well known. The NEA has achieved a new degree of militancy that includes the support of strikes in some cases. The junior college arm of the NEA is actively fighting the unions for the loyalty of the junior college faculty. A bloodletting will undoubtedly take place.

The main protagonists on the college scene on the issue of economic negotiations are clearly the AAUP and the AFT. Yet the rise of statewide faculty organizations like the NJEA could become a factor in some states. This type of organization might become a national force, especially if the NEA expands its activities in state institutions with strong teacher-training traditions.

There are so many factors to consider in thinking through the problems connected with negotiations that I feel it necessary to divide the discussion into two parts: 1) Analysis of Current Trends in Economic Negotiations and 2) The Future of Economic Negotiations.

ANALYSIS OF CURRENT TRENDS IN ECONOMIC NEGOTIATIONS

Jencks and Riesman in their recently published tome *The Academic Revolution* state that today faculty control over curriculum matters is rarely challenged, that for the most part faculties recommend their colleagues, that they have a hand in the selection of students and a voice in the choice of top administrators. The authors go on to qualify these apparent areas of control by pointing out that the power faculties have is not formal power over institutions that employ them because *ultimately* control is in the hands of the trustees or the legislature. Due to the legal structure of colleges and universities, the situs of ultimate control is clearly understood. From what Jencks and Riesman have said one would gather that college faculties never had it so good. Yet there are danger signals that indicate (to me at least) that all is not well in academia.

Just as students are concerned about the impersonal nature of the educational experience, some faculty also feel lost in an institutional context. To be sure, there are those (currently almost one of every three faculty) who are discipline-oriented and not yet active participants in the administration-faculty struggle. However, events in the form of ever-increasing student enrollment, increased costs of education (some segments of private education being virtually priced out of the market), and ever-expanding external layers of control in the large state systems that add up to a swirl of confusion to faculty people intent, for the most part, on being treated as individuals and distrustful of absentee decision making.

At the present time academicians participate in the affluent society: Scholars in most fields can actually make a reasonable living in academia. Another great advantage college faculty have is their *mobility*. For the most part, faculty do move quite frequently, especially in the junior ranks.[5] The more mobility a scholar has the more significant salary increases he may expect to receive.

Public higher education especially has seen dramatic growth in legislative appropriations for faculty salaries. This has been accomplished with the realization that the student increases have demanded quantitative and qualitative increases in institutional commitments by the various states. Private institutions are hard pressed to sustain the same rate of growth, especially in institutions that are not heavily endowed. The only recourse that private institutions have to keep up with the growth of the public sector is increased tuition and fees. When these increases reach a certain point, to go beyond will, in effect, mean that these institutions will be priced out of the market.

With these generalizations as background, one can now discuss current trends in economic negotiations. Most state legislatures have met the challenges of faculty salary increases. At the same time, however, there have been increasing pressures for closer external control of these institutions because of increased budgetary allotments. As a result, larger classes are the norm and reductions in

---

[5]For an excellent treatment of this issue, see David G. Brown's *The Mobile Professors* (Washington, D.C.: American Council on Education, 1967).

teaching loads are difficult to accomplish. The California system is a typical example of the foregoing analysis. In the face of these external pressures, faculties will become more militant, not necessarily over salaries but over the issue of control of academic matters, which Jencks and Riesman have said they now control. Other state systems will face similar struggles.

In the private sector, the issue may not be primarily economic, but not because private institutions have met all faculty requests for increases. Rather, faculties will recognize the plight of private institutions and continue to staff these institutions as long as a superior environment of academic freedom exists. For example, should these institutions refuse to initiate legitimate reforms suggested by students or renege on any one of several key academic freedom issues, then this could easily motivate faculty militancy. This will be especially true (I think) in Catholic institutions, where the role of the layman has increased dramatically.

In either case, the AAUP chapter may not be the vehicle by which faculties unite, unless on an issue involving academic freedom or tenure, because local AAUP chapters, although they have some autonomy, are subject to some control by the national office. A union or other local faculty organization with more flexibility may provide the degree of militancy these groups feel they need.

Certainly, it is obvious the first battleground will be the public junior colleges, especially in urban areas. These colleges are controlled in many cases by local boards which tend to treat them as appendages of the public school system. The new breed of junior college faculty, experienced after earlier battles with school boards, can be expected to react (or overreact) to any slights either real or fancied concerning control and, of course, salaries.

Next, the public colleges, emerging now as multipurpose institutions from their former teachers college roles, will likewise react to external attempts to control what heretofore have been considered faculty prerogatives.

All in all, the current situations must be viewed as confusing at best, with student unrest lurking around the corner as the one issue not previously discussed that could cause administration-faculty confrontations even before the protagonists reach the economic negotiations issues.

Future of Economic Negotiations

If current trends leave us in a welter of confusion, what about the future? A great deal depends upon the lasting nature of some of our current problems, plus some imponderables.

It is safe to say that expanding layers of control and increased coordination are here to stay. By 1967, 39 states had one or another type of coordinating mechanism. Increased enrollment will continue until at least the mid 1970's. Not only that but automation-increased leisure time, early retirement, and further emancipation of women from the chores of homemaking will increase enrollment even more dramatically than rising birthrates accomplish. The military needs of the nation will be met by some form of service on a "youngest first" nasis. Students will thus be freed from uncertainty about educational interruption at an early age. The name of the education game will probably be megauniversities, with most higher education taking place in large urban clusters of institutions. Shared facilities, use of the metropolitan areas as learning laboratories, massive use of computerized teaching, and other sophisticated gadgets will also free the teacher from the usual six-, nine-, or twelve-hour loads of the past.

The political structure and climate in the nation will change, and the two traditional parties will change beyond recognition. The synthesis could result in a liberal and a conservative party, with the possibility also of a permanent third-party structure. After a brief period of rightist swing (even a bit of repression), the mass of young people, probably voting at age 18, will develop a viable type of economic and political system that will bring the federal government to the point of almost complete financing of all higher education, both public and private, graduate and undergraduate. The attempt of the teacher-scholar to maintain his individuality, to remove the fear of being a minor cog in a megauniversity setting, will certainly tax the ingenuity of a free society and its professorial class. Unions will have a place, but they might be international unions of students, not faculty.

In summary, it would appear that over the short haul the strengthening of internal organizations within collegiate institutions will probably forestall mass defections of faculties to unionism. However, as centralization of decision making increases beyond the perimeters of public institutions, militancy will increase, particularly in public institutions. Then as governmental financing of all higher education increases, militancy may become muted, but no one can say for sure.

A Glossary of Terms

A difficulty in discussing the issue of negotiations on economic matters is the definition of what it is we are talking about. There are those (myself included) who feel that "professional associations" in most cases are types of unions in all but name. I include in´this the American Medical Association, the American Bar Association, and others as well. The difficulty with *educational* associations is that they cling desperately to the clichés of the past in defining the terms necessary to ensure understanding.

1. Collective Bargaining

In the classic sense, "collective bargaining" means that in numbers there is strength. Groups of people doing the same type of work organize in order to negotiate more effectively with their employers. In the United States, collective bargaining received impetus from the Wagner Act of 1935, which made it unfair labor practice for management to refuse to bargain collectively with labor.

a. *Professional negotiations:* In 1962 at the national convention of the National Education Association held in Denver, Colorado, the term "professional negotiations" was first used by this organization. Professional negotiations have been defined as a set of procedures written and officially adopted by the local staff organization and school board and which provide an orderly method for the school board and staff organization to negotiate on matters of mutual concern, to reach agreement on these matters, and to establish educational channels for mediation and appeal in the event of an impasse.

b. *Academic negotiations:* The final report of the task force of the American Association for Higher Education on faculty participation in academic governance coined the term "academic negotiations" as an alternative to the more harsh term "collective bargaining." Academic negotiations means all those steps taken to ensure the presence of adequate means of faculty participation in the operation of an institution. The participation includes negotiations concerning conditions under which college faculty will work.

c. *Representation of economic interests:* As mentioned previously, the most prestigious organization representing faculties of American colleges and universities is the American Association of University Professors. The AAUP, through its Committee on Economic Interests, has its own version of collective bargaining. The position of this committee is that "The Association should oppose the extension of the principle of exclusive representation to faculty members in institutions of higher education and should therefore recommend legislation which would require public institutions to establish adequate internal structures of faculty participation in the government of the institution."

d. *Collective negotiations:* Lieberman and Moskow, in their 1966 book *Collective Negotiations for Teachers: An Approach to School Administration,* blended the positions of both the NEA and the unions to describe what it is that teachers do when they meet with school boards to discuss economic issues. The whole range of activities from negotiating units to final settlement are encompassed in the term "collective negotiations."

2. The Right To Strike

The ultimate weapon of economic reprisal available to union members is the right to strike. This is so emphatic a weapon that it is used, even by militant unionists, only when all other types of negotiation have failed. However, under certain conditions, the right to strike is taken quite literally by members of the teachers' unions. The NEA and the AAUP edge closer to the use of this method in very limited instances.

a. *Sanctions:* A sanction is the withdrawal or withholding of services which does not violate existing contracts. Teachers in a particular school district carry out their contracts for the current year. If at the end of that time no agreement has been reached between the local governing board and the teachers, the teachers are not forced to continue. The NEA issues sanctions and publicizes the fact that these professional sanctions have been initiated. This puts teachers on notice that the particular community or state is not a desirable place in which to teach. National sanctions were imposed in Utah in 1964 and in Oklahoma in 1965. Recently the NEA invoked national sanctions in Florida by urging teachers to boycott the "financially starved" public schools. The Florida case, however, had disastrous results for the NEA.

b. *Censure:* The AAUP has a policy of censuring administrations which, after thorough investigation, are found not to be observing generally recognized principles of academic freedom and tenure. The censured administrations are listed prominently in the *AAUP Bulletin,* and all college faculty who belong to the Association and read the *Bulletin* are put on notice that these institutions have not met their professional obligations with regard to faculty. The most notable action taken by the AAUP in its history was in the St. John's University case. The AAUP not only censured the institution publicly but, because of internal conditions, advised it would seem inappropriate for any AAUP member to accept an appointment at St. John's.

DISCUSSION OF MR. MARMION'S PAPER

MR. CRONIN: One of Mr. Marmion's most provocative sentences is the prediction or the hope that unions will have a place not for faculty but for students. I suggest that if students organize effectively this will be one of the motivating factors for much stronger faculty organization—partly for defense, partly in response to the kind of energy and demands generated by student organizations.

At this time I think it would be folly to predict the long-range impact of the Students for a Democratic Society, but I suspect that as students begin to realize the kind of clout they can muster they will force faculties to coalesce in some more potent way than they've had to in the past. So often the history of faculty organizations has been that of organizing against trustees or against Neanderthal alumni or legislatures. The whole history of the AAUP is in this tradition. But if the students do organize, after they finish getting a number of the reforms that are perhaps quite necessary and then overreach themselves (as is the tendency of so many young groups or groups of young), I think faculty members aren't going to be able to sit back and say, "Isn't it nice that the students are organized. There's no particular reason for us to be." On the contrary, they will build much stronger organizations than we've ever seen. As colleges see what happens at other institutions there will be a growth of the exchange system, the system by which information, tactics, and power are exchanged, so that faculties on different campuses can work in concert.

We can look with horror at two or three campuses closed down, but when it comes to 20 or 30 a countervailing force will emerge.

I have a number of questions, not only for Mr. Marmion but for others. There are many here whose full-time assignment is to develop programs for the National Education Association or the American Federation of Teachers or the AAUP, and these questions are for them also.

Why are there so many faculty members who are unaffiliated with any of the three major organizations discussed in Mr. Marmion's paper? We need some data on this. We need some hypotheses on why at certain types of institutions there is a tendency to affiliate with the NEA, why at others there is a tendency to affiliate with the AFT. Why is the AAUP strong in certain universities or colleges and not elsewhere?

Is it, for example, because of organizational inertia that none of these groups has launched any kind of broad-based recruiting or organizational drives except in certain pockets? Does it have something to do with the reward systems in institutions of higher learning, a high level of satisfaction with working conditions and with compensation? Or has it something to do with the culture of higher education, which might be characterized as individualistic and indeed almost entrepreneurial in the 1960's?

Or, looking at the same question from a different angle, what incentives and rewards are there for membership or participation in these various organizations? What are the perceived rewards and what kinds of persons are likely to respond?

The AAUP has a long history of defense of academic freedom and concern about tenure issues. Does this attract certain types of academics? What program is there in the realm of economic negotiations or economics relations? There is certainly a classification system of salaries, but what is there for those who seek the kind of benefits that, say, the AFT might offer?

What incentives or what rewards does the NEA offer? Is it true that some of the teacher-training institutions are more likely to attract people to the NEA, in part because they perhaps have had experience in elementary and secondary education and have been members of the NEA, and because their students (at least in rural and metropolitan settings other than the city) are likely to spend most of their professional lives in the NEA? Or is it because the NEA offers some services to state colleges, to teachers of education? Is it because the NEA traditionally has been responsive to the needs of rural educators? Is it because there are programs reaching for federal aid of certain kinds that makes the NEA more attractive than, say, the AAUP?

Is the AFT appeal mainly to the professor in the urban setting? Is there appeal in the AFT in terms of its link with the rest of the labor movement and to the working class in particular? Does the strong tradition of civil rights activity in the Union constitute motivation for a number of persons to join, and has this been true in the past? Will it be true in the future, after the 1968 strikes in New York City? The answers are hard to find, but it certainly will be useful to know what are the incentives and to what groups these various organizations have appealed. It will be useful in part to enable these groups to engage in intelligent self-analysis and decide how to broaden their appeal, if that's what they wish to do. Otherwise they may default and allow others to move into the areas we are talking about.

I think we need also an analysis of the functions of membership in each of the groups, a kind of organizational analysis. Do these groups exist to increase the benefits accruing to the individual or to a class of individuals? Do these organizations exist to improve working conditions? Do they exist to reform the system or just to point out abuses that deviate from norms? Are these organizations there to build alliances with other groups? Both the NEA and the AFT relate to other groups in a kind of coalition form.

I have to agree with Mr. Marmion that the ferment among young faculty, the radicalization of faculties, is going to have a major impact on the various employee organizations. It may well be that those professors who have made it and who were used to hard times in the 1930's or 1940's are now delighted with all that they have won and all that they have accumulated. I can't be that sanguine about the younger faculty members. Already some of them are graduates of the Peace Corps, and we're going to have more graduates of SDS. Such persons are going to seize various organizations and use them for a variety of purposes, including social reform, including the reform of universities. They're going to use the existing organizations to try to make universities more relevant to the communities around them. This has already happened in the organized social science groups, first among the sociologists and now in political science. There are other instances where the Young Turk groups are moving out and are trying to change dramatically the nature of their organizations. This movement is going to extend, at least to an extent, into some of the other organizations.

I would predict that this will not be a long-term movement, however. If you read Clark's volume on the French Teacher Union, which is by our standards a fairly radical union in terms of wanting to have broad policy impact, not merely on all of education but on society in general—you find a strong pull to exist mainly for the welfare of the membership. The major energies of teacher groups are going to be expended on that. I think we will find that neither the NEA nor the Union will be a major force for social reform, that some other organizations may serve that function better. But there will be some experimentation in the next five or ten years in pursuit of ways to make these organizations serve as vehicles for social reform generally; and such efforts will reshape, to an extent that it's hard to predict right now, the nature of these organizations.

In looking ahead we also must take into consideration the supply and demand factor. The professional market at the moment allows for a good deal of individual wheeling and dealing and therefore there is less reliance on an organization to negotiate collectively. But that's a function of a number of social and demographic forces, including the shortage of young men in the age group of which I am privileged to be a member. But as I look ahead 10 years and see the hordes of highly trained and highly intelligent young men coming behind me, I know it's going to be very, very different. It's going to be very different for those already established and it's going to be very different when the market becomes more competitive. It's especially dependent upon what federal policy is in the next four or eight years in terms of graduate school fellowships and research and the like.

The fact that we've been living in a very pleasant situation in terms of availability of grants for the last ten years does not mean that the next ten years are going to be the same; and this kind of factor could very well influence the collectivization of faculty members at a variety of universities.

I'm also not so sure that the junior colleges are going to be the frontier of collective negotiations. I'm much more intrigued with what is happening in the city colleges. Mr. Marmion mentioned San Franciso State. I think the state and urban colleges and universities are going to be where we see most of the action, at least in the next five years. There are others here who might want to comment on that.

CHAIRMAN MOSKOW: Thank you very much, Mr. Cronin. The floor is now open for discussion.

MR. HAYWARD: I represent a segment that in New Jersey at least is the controlling organization with regard to faculty, and I would like to elaborate on the brief mention in Mr. Marmion's paper.

MR. MARMION: You mean the state teacher organizations with local units in public institutions of higher education?

MR. HAYWARD: Yes, and I'll clarify exactly what I mean. The thing that I'm concerned about has not been discussed anywhere in the professional literature. Jencks and Riesman haven't written about it and neither has Peter Janssen in the *Saturday Review*. Even Moskow and Lieberman ignored it, though to be fair I should note that the subject is outside of the scope of their book on collective negotiations.

The truth of the matter is that in New Jersey, and in other states too

(Michigan and a few others), the state education association is in higher education with both feet. We have an Association of New Jersey State College Faculties. Approximately 80 percent of all faculties in all six state colleges are members of this organization. Last year it negotiated a statewide personnel policy and salary guides. This organization now has signed faculty authorization cards designating it as sole bargaining agent. The state association is demanding to be recognized under our public laws as the sole negotiating agent for faculties.

Mr. Marmion says, "The main protagonists on the college scene on the issue of economic negotiations are clearly the AAUP and the AFT." I challenge that, at least for the state of New Jersey, as being completely and totally untrue.[1]

Understand, too, that many of the people who have joined the Association are also members of AAUP, because they clearly recognize that the AAUP is not in the business of negotiations. The AFT also has some members among our ranks, but the Union as such in the entire State of New Jersey has a membership of no more than two percent of the total faculties. Quite frankly, then, I laugh when I see them listed as being a protagonist.

MR. MARMION: I do say in my paper, "There are strong NEA state organizations throughout the nation made up primarily of professors of education and in-service teachers, and there is a strong student NEA program at most teacher preparatory institutions." I maintain that these organizations in certain states can become militant trade-union type organizations as opposed to NEA- or AAUP-style organizations.

MR. HAYWARD: I beg to differ. We're NEA-style. I'll support Bob Miner and the NEA staff right down the line.

There is one other point that I think is very salient, and it affects the NEA, too. You may recall a reference to the NEA as "the reluctant dragon" by Peter Janssen in the June, 1967, *Saturday Review.* Pete is guilty of something that I'm afraid many people are guilty of, and that

[1]On May 10, 1969, faculties at five New Jersey state colleges voted overwhelmingly for representation by the ANJSCF and the local campus faculty associations. The associations had been challenged by both the AFT and the AAUP. Newark, Montclair, Paterson, Trenton, and Glassboro State College faculties piled up an 80 percent organizational plurality statewide for ANJSCF, which is a New Jersey Education Association affiliate. At a run-off election a week later between the associations and the AFT, the former also won at Jersey City State. The May 10 vote gave the associations a total from all six campuses of 1,147 votes. The AAUP received 123, the AFT 194.—*The Editors*

is assuming that NEA membership represents the total association membership in the country or in a given city; also, he compares NEA membership with the total AFT membership. When you join the AFT you join the national as well. However, at the moment only 50 percent of our college faculty members and teachers in the state of New Jersey are members of NEA, so here's a block of 30,000 who are "association" who are not NEA; but in a hands-down battle they'll be behind NEA 100 percent.

CHAIRMAN MOSKOW: Mr. Miner, correct me if I'm wrong. The NEA membership now is about one million?

MR. MINER: 1.1 million.

CHAIRMAN MOSKOW: And the membership of all the state affiliated associations is about 1.8 million?

MR. MINER: I think it's probably very close to two million.

MR. ROSENTHAL: I'd like to ask a rather simple-minded question of Mr. Hayward. In New Jersey the NJEA organization is attempting to become a negotiating agency. What is it that you want to negotiate? What do you want to represent your faculties for?

MR. HAYWARD: Last year, with the help of the State Department of Higher Education, we published a personnel policies guide that we had in effect negotiated over a three-month period—not officially in terms of there being a recognized agent, but we did produce this document.

Here is a worksheet consisting of some 60 items which we want to negotiate. These items include a whole section on salaries (with subareas), summer schools, 12-month pay options, personnel policies, fringe benefits, rank promotion, teaching load—with specific points thereunder.

The interesting thing is that in addition to the state-level items there is also a list of items which will be considered at the local faculty level. These will be negotiated with local boards of trustees.

MR. ROSENTHAL: Aside from salary scales, what kinds of working conditions are concerned? Are you concerned with the number of hours taught?

MR. HAYWARD: Absolutely. We're concerned about teaching load, overload and compensation for overload, definition of contact hours, load reduction, sabbatical leaves, rank and promotion.

MR. ROSENTHAL: Have people argued with you that you really can't compare contact hours and teaching hours at one institution with those at another? Do you feel that all your institutions are so similar that this becomes readily comparable?

MR. HAYWARD: I think for the most part many of them are readily comparable, although there may be special departments wherein you would have to make separate evaluations.

MR. OBERER: One of the major problems of collective bargaining in public employment is who is the employer. One of the things you said, Mr. Hayward, touches upon that. You suggested that your faculty organization was going to be negotiating both on a statewide level as to what might be called statewide issues and at the local campus level with regard to local issues. Who will be representing the teachers at the local level?

MR. HAYWARD: The local campus faculty association: the Montclair State College Faculty Association or the Newark State College Faculty Association.

Under state law the money comes from the legislature (that organization from whom all the blessings flow), and everyone is, therefore, legally employed by the state. However, when you get into personnel policies there may be differences between the overall state policies and those prevalent on the local campus.

CHAIRMAN MOSKOW: Are these local faculty associations affiliated with the New Jersey Education Association?

MR. HAYWARD: Yes. Not directly, but through their own Association of New Jersey State College Faculties, which is an affiliate of NJEA.

MR. HOROWITZ: I represent the organization Mr. Hayward wants to negotiate with. I was just wondering what you do, though, if, for example, one of the local faculty groups decides that it wants to be represented by the union at that level.

MR. HAYWARD: We already have the authorization cards.

MR. HOROWITZ: I'm talking theoretically. We don't know what's going to happen tomorrow. But how does this work out? Let's say a Union man shows up and says, "We feel that we represent a majority and we want to hold an election." Let's say this is at Newark State College. Then an election is held and the Union wins at Newark State; but the State Faculty Association wins at the other five places. So at each campus you have the representative organizations negotiating with the local boards of trustees, but then you have the State College Faculty Association negotiating with the Board of Higher Education, according to the scheme you proposed. What happens with the faculty at Newark State?

MR. HAYWARD: I have a letter from the Union attorney stating Union policy which indicates that the Union doesn't stand for that.

MR. HOROWITZ: For what?

MR. HAYWARD: For challenging once there has been a duly appointed organization, with signatures and authorizations and membership.

MR. HOWE: Mr. Hayward's remarks raise a very interesting question. He seems to suggest that Mr. Marmion's emphasis on the *distinctions* between organizations may be the wrong direction. It appears to those of us on the firing line facing faculty militancy that as the question of economic representation approaches, the distinctions between organizations diminish rapidly. Thus it couldn't matter a tinker's dam from the administrative point of view which organization it is facing across the table, because the techniques are essentially the same, the ambitions and aspirations are essentially the same, the demands are virtually predictable.

I would ask Mr. Marmion to comment on this. Even the AAUP, after its firm declaration of preference, says that should a local decide to go for economic bargaining it is perfectly appropriate for the AAUP to be the vehicle.

MR. MARMION: I think New Jersey may be atypical. I don't think any organization anywhere else has 80 percent of faculty, and I think this fact lends credence to what you're saying. On economic issues, Mr. Hayward may wake up some day and find that he has a union, whether one calls it by that name or not.

MR. LIEBERMAN: Nobody has really responded to Mr. Horowitz' question. If one organization is negotiating a statewide master agreement, and at the local level the faculty choose a different organization, it is hardly responsive to say that the differences between organizations don't count. They count to the people at the local level.

This same problem will emerge with public school teachers. We will have negotiations at the state level for all public elementary and secondary school teachers.

However, within a particular community the teachers may choose one organization to represent them locally despite the fact that another organization with a statewide majority is negotiating some conditions of employment (e.g., the retirement contributions) on a statewide basis. Personally, I don't know of any cases in private employment where one group negotiates an industry-wide agreement and yet a different organization is responsible for negotiating supplementary agreements at the local level. Are there such cases?

MR. BLUM: You'll find that procedure used in Europe where the federation will negotiate concerning common demands, such as wages, while the separate unions will negotiate concerning the specific issues at the more local level. Denmark is an example.

MR. LIEBERMAN: I think that this would tend to be an exceptional situation. In any case, we haven't really answered the question of what would happen if one organization had a statewide majority while a different organization had the majority on a particular campus.

MR. HAYWARD: The card that the individual signs has an "A" and a "B" section. Each college had its own cards printed up. Section A says, "I hereby designate and authorize the Newark State College Faculty Association." That's the local side of it. Section B says, "I also hereby designate and authorize the Association of New Jersey State College Faculties."

MR. LIEBERMAN: What if they change their minds? Assume that they designated the state organization and then wanted to change their minds about the local.

MR. HAYWARD: To continue with the cards. They say, "This authorization and designation shall remain in force until such time as I shall submit to the named association a signed statement revoking this authorization and designation."

MR. MacRAE: I gather from what Mr. Horowitz is saying in response to Mr. Hayward that Mr. Horowitz as the representative of the chancellor's office is going back and stir up the AFT—and he'll divide and conquer!

MR. McHUGH: This problem of overlapping jurisdiction referred to by Messrs. Lieberman and Horowitz may come up in a representation proceeding now before the New York Public Employment Relations Board involving the State University of New York.[2] The AFT says that the uniting should take place on a campus-to-campus basis. The University's position is that it should take place on a statewide basis.

I don't think the question raised by Mr. Horowitz is easily answered. One of the traps is to say that there are easily identifiable local and statewide issues. Given a unified multi-campus institution such as the State University of New York, when you really get down to the specifics of separating local from statewide concerns there is going to be a large gray area of joint issues.

Concurrent campus-to-campus negotiating rationalized on the basis that some issues are statewide and some local would lend, in my

---

[2]In the Matter of State of New York (State University of New York), et al., v. State University Federation of Teachers, Local 1733, AFT, et al., PERB, 1969. There should be a decision in this case by early fall of 1969.

opinion, instability to the collective bargaining relationship. The prospect of dealing with a number of different unions representing identical employees on different campuses on "local issues" is alarming to me. I don't preclude the possibility of a "local" negotiating local issues under the aegis of the statewide organization.

The tendency for a statewide union would be to try to draw the local issues away from the campus, if there is a competitor union on the campus. This would create friction between unions during both the bargaining process and the administration of the contract. This friction may in the short view be tactically desirable from a management point of view, but in the long view it is undesirable.

Bill, what is your reaction to the local-statewide issue bit?

MR. HAYWARD: I don't for one minute imagine that anything we negotiate this year would be the final answer, any more than the personnel policies guide we negotiated last year would be, and that next year and the year after and the year after that there would be more refinements. Those of you who are expert in the field of national labor relations know that labor relations law decisions have been coming out in volumes year after year. So it will be a progression settlement.

MR. WEINBERG: This discussion is on a pretty high theoretical level because there are very few facts involved. In New Jersey, the public Employee Relations Commission has not yet been appointed, so it has not decided the recognition and unit issue in the state colleges.

Another point is that the New Jersey law is as vague as possible. For example, in discussing unit determination it simply uses the concept of "community of interest." So Mr. Hayward was merely expressing his hope. We have no way of knowing yet whether he may effectuate his hope in terms of a Commission decision. Our discussion on New Jersey is a case study limited to a small cluster of state colleges. The colleges were state teachers colleges and have recently been retreaded into multi-purpose state colleges. There are many colleges in New Jersey, both public and private, that do not quite fit this pattern presented by Mr. Hayward.

I would guess that the Commission will make a decision on the unit based on the "community of interest" and an identification of the effective funding agency rather than the original authorization cards.

MR. BLUM: As I listen to the comments both about the New Jersey experience and also about the student revolts and what they may mean to unions, I can't help but remember Santayana's statement that those who forget the past are condemned to repeat it. Thus if you're going to use the private sector as an indication of what will happen in unit determination, may I suggest that either the union or the NEA will ask for whatever size or type of unit they think they can win. Managers will try to promote a unit in which they think they will win. Both will then develop a philosophy to explain what they do. I think philosophy is relevant, but not always as a predicter of the future, if the past is any indication.

Concerning students as the motivator of unionization, let me just point out that Sidney Hook was once a communist, then a socialist. Now look at his attitude toward student revolts! A lot of the people who are the senior professors (I guess I'm now on that level) used to be on picket lines. There was a left wing among students in the 1930's and 1940's and teacher unions didn't develop as a result. In fact, if you look at the history of unionization in general, unions were frequently created by the skilled, the best, and the most autonomous workingmen. The spark had to come from people who felt some sense of conflict and recognized some feeling of unity.

Are professors going to wait for the students to be their guides in establishing organized collective behavior? By the time students become well organized they'll be senior professors—and perhaps as inactive as senior professors now.

My whole point is that one shouldn't depend upon the students to motivate faculty to organize for collective action. If there is an argument in favor of organization, it should be an argument in favor of it— not of waiting, patiently or impatiently, for the kick in the shins from the students.

MR. CRONIN: Mr. Marmion said it was more likely that the students would unionize than the faculty. The point I made was that one factor which faculty members couldn't ignore would be students acquiring more power than faculty in bringing about certain types of drastic changes. Then, I said, the faculty would coalesce. But I think much more relevant is the coming economic squeeze. As I talk to governors and other people who have to raise the money for both elementary and secondary education and higher education, and as I look at the other soaring costs of state and local government (not just for education but for welfare and other services), and as these other sectors of the public economy organize to "get theirs" too, I think we can look ahead five to eight to ten years and see some kind of attempts to hold down the costs and also to hold down the salaries, which have been increasing nicely. I think at that point the "skilled craftsmen" of higher education are going to begin to organize in their own interest, but I would quite agree that it's going to be the economic and not simply the student forces that are going to precipitate this change.

I don't think we're going to have this long, 30-year honeymoon wherein a young radical can become a conservative, affluent senior professor. The ferment at Harvard 18 months ago, which was neatly nipped by John Dunlop, had to do with the instructors making noises that they were rather unhappy at spending three years after the Ph.D. in a position that was not yet that of assistant professor. A very elaborate survey resulted in the decision that that position should be abolished and abolishing it would prevent instructors from organizing a union at Harvard University.

MR. BLUM: Would they get more money?

MR. CRONIN: The institution would just wipe out that particular position and move new people more quickly to the somewhat higher paying assistant professor step.

That solution may work right now, but if that's where the pressure is and if that's where somewhat larger numbers are in the next ten years competing for scarce spaces, there may be some ferment at the assistant professor level then.

MR. MARMION: The things that are going on on the campuses now—the degree of militancy, violence, and turmoil, college presidents and chancellors of state systems having police protection—present a very serious problem. I think this is a somewhat different left than the '30's left or the post-World War II left.

MR. BLUM: But it may not be the kind of left that engenders unionism. The left of the '30's and '40's was a left organized in terms of economic reform and sympathetic to unionism.

MR. MARMION: Look at the statement of Prime Minister Trudeau of Canada recently. He said he's not concerned about Germany; he's just concerned about armed revolt in the United States. I do think there is a difference.

MR. BLUM: Yes, but I don't know whether the difference will lead to unionism or anarchy.

MR. SUMBERG: Before we all sing "Solidarity Forever," may I just bring us back to the path that we started on long ago with Mr. Marmion's article. I do represent the AAUP and I regret sincerely that we start a conference on such an important subject from the standpoint of organizational differences. I would much prefer to talk about what is being done in higher education in response to the problems of public employment collective bargaining rather than blowing our individual horns about what we are doing or perhaps what we are not doing.

I regret that Mr. Marmion feels that the AAUP is not responsive to collective bargaining as a need, and I equally regret that instead of writing this article in Connecticut he hadn't been back at his office, which is only two floors below us, and he might have stopped up and talked with us to find out what goes on in the AAUP these days in regard to collective bargaining. What is true in April may not be similarly true in November. There are people who loved us in May and don't love us in November, and there are some people who did not love us in May who now do.

I think it is not true that the AAUP is not responsive to collective bargaining, particularly in view of the statements issued beginning back in the 1950's relative to the AAUP's concern for economic interests. Indeed this concern goes back to the '30's, even back to the original declaration of principles in 1915.

To return to the contemporary scene, I think it is extremely important to recognize that the AAUP is a bargaining agent at a college in Illinois. Its affiliates today are seeking bargaining status with the assistance of the national association. On Saturday evening of last week, in a smoky hotel meeting room in Albany, New York, our State University of New York's affiliated chapters voted to go beyond their present status of intervener and become an agent in the collective bargaining negotiations in the State University of New York.

We have very responsible statements, approved by our Council and at our annual meetings, which place the AAUP very much in the mainstream of collective negotiations or collective bargaining.

What I think is really important is not so much the way in which one announces his concern for collective bargaining as the way in which an organization or a group of organizations approaches the question of public employment collective bargaining. All of us have much in common in dealing with this very peculiar situation; and I say "peculiar" because legislatures have drawn their models from industrial legislation, legislation affecting the private sector. They have not taken into consideration very serious problems that exist in higher education and which may very well create still more serious problems as the bargaining agents are chosen and begin their operation.

Mr. Hayward is extremely optimistic. I hope his optimism has some basis, because a couple of weeks ago I spoke to representatives of all the AAUP chapters in New Jersey by telephone and I didn't quite find the same optimism. He hasn't taken into account the situation at Rutgers, which is equally affected, or at the community colleges.

Again, the organizational structure is not as significant in this basic issue as the problems of how to approach the issue of public employment collective bargaining and how to approach the commissions or the boards which have been established, how to educate trial examiners whose experience is primarily in the private sector, and how to determine what approach in terms of a bargaining unit can be more meaningful than statewide or local bargaining units.

If I may now make a couple of corrections to Mr. Marmion's statement I'll be glad to rest my case. What has the AAUP done about regional accrediting of institutions? I'll be glad to send Mr. Marmion a copy of the approved statement on accreditation which the AAUP has had in operation only since April, but which has really been the basis of our work with accrediting institutions for a number of years.

Where does the AAUP stand on student unrest? I'll be glad to send him the student section of the Tripartite Statement, which he evidently feels is inadequate. We do also, and therefore we are working more successfully, I think, than the ACE at this point on that. I'll also send the statement on rights and freedoms of students, which, as you realize, has a very wide appeal to students because they were involved in drawing up the document.

Generally speaking, I think any attempt to characterize national organizations today is fraught with danger. They change so rapidly, as we've noted here. But I think even more important is the necessity for realizing that they are not so concerned with their own ends as organizations as they are with the problems confronting all of us in higher education.

MR. HIXSON: I want to say, going back to another point, that my association with emerging AFT locals in the colleges leads me to believe that they cannot be characterized any more in terms of left and right. I suppose the best thing you can say about them is that they are very much center. There are still a few old ideological locals left, but they remain small elitists. The new, emerging locals understand that to take an ideological position is to thwart their growth and their ultimate success. And I'll use this very much overused term: They are pragmatic in the extreme.

MR. DUPERRE: There are two or three points that have emerged in the discussion which I would like to follow up, but I want to get back to what Mr. Marmion said about the radicalization of young faculty. I think I know what he means by that, but I'd like him or other people to elaborate on it, as I will. Perhaps—and only perhaps—somebody like Harry Edwards is a real honest-to-goodness radical, and we should scratch our heads a little bit about him. He's a Black Power activist. But I very much favor other activities which Mr. Marmion might lump under radicalization (though I hope he doesn't), those of the young faculty members who are exceptionally concerned with the social issues of the day, are involved with their students, are not aloof, are very much a part of what is going on. I hope you didn't intentionally try to slur these efforts.

MR. MARMION: Mr. Cronin mentioned the rank of instructor. In my opinion, for many reasons the rank of instructor is fast disappearing from college faculties and is being replaced by graduate assistant or teaching assistant, whatever the term. These assistants have a much closer relationship to students than they do to faculty or to the departments in which they teach. They may have a loyalty to their advisor, because he's the guy who is going to get them through. Young non-tenured faculty members are in the same boat. Before tenure they are as concerned and uneasy at Harvard as they are at Montclair State.

I am glad to see that they are involved with social issues and with teaching and with students as students. But their involvement really goes beyond that in some instances; in some cases young faculty people are not only aligning themselves with students, but they are apparently trying to bring down institutions. I don't want to say that this is a national trend. It's very spotty. But I'm concerned about the degree of radicalization which results when young faculty are aligning themselves with most outrageous student conduct. At one Midwestern college several students took off all their clothes in class, protesting "man's inhumanity to man." Just yesterday the papers reported the decision of the faculty-student committee at that institution. The students involved were denied permission to participate in campus activities for the rest of the academic year. In my opinion, as a result of this decision, the president was left with no options.

MR. DUPERRE: I'm somewhat familiar with that institution. I haven't been there for several years, but I believe it is quite a conservative sort of institution. I don't know the immediate causes for people to strip their clothes off, but I would imagine it would take quite a buildup of pressure to cause them to take such action.

MR. ZWINGLE: What I have to say is rather dull after that! I think it's useful, however, to round out the record.

Mr. Marmion's comment on the Tripartite Statement is well put, but if one remembers that the statement was brought up for completion in 1964-65, one recognizes that it might have been foolhardy to try to take a clear position about the student dissent issue at that early date. The debate then was whether to say anything. There was some question whether a statement now would be worse than no statement. Perhaps the judgment of the group was wrong. It was concluded, however, that in view of the amount of effort that had gone into this much of a statement it should not be delayed further; and it was also emphasized that this was intended as an opening statement intended for further revision.

Our own office had just been opened. Our Association* was just beginning to find its way. I take some satisfaction in having originated the language commending the statement rather than for formal adoption. It would have been foolhardy for us to have adopted the statement. An association such as ours cannot pretend to represent the great variety of boards of control in the country at large.

Thereafter there was some hesitation to go vigorously into the field of the student position in the matter of governance, partly because the statement on student rights was then being developed. It has since been adopted by a number of organizations.

Meanwhile, however, our own association has taken its own course, trying to illuminate the question by successive public discussions and publications. All these are intended to encourage and stimulate boards of trustees to see that policy positions are prepared in the light of their own circumstances as contrasted with taking a uniform position.

One must recognize that despite the stereotypes of boards of trustees so widely held, there is relatively little information behind these stereotypes. For that reason we have engaged in some cooperative researches. Among them will be the first complete roster of trustees. We then will at least have a data bank available for questions that are now merely a matter of opinion. I am not espousing or defending the Tripartite Statement. I only suggest that it is much better than nothing.

MR. OBERER: To get back to our subject, which is faculty organizations in higher education, it seems to me that we've ignored one fundamental facet of the topic, and that is what tactics or techniques given organizations are willing to apply. I remember, as a member of the AAHE task force examining a state college in the State University if New York system, talking with a fellow who was a member of

*Association of Governing Boards of Colleges and Universities

the Executive Board of the AAUP and had also been one of the charter members and founders of an AFT chapter at the local campus. He was a very interesting fellow, and I asked him how he explained the latter in view of the former. He said he wanted the AFT present because of its "superior weaponry."

Those of us who have had anything to do with collective bargaining in the private sector know that its essence is the strike or the threat of the strike. That's the motive power for collective bargaining. So my question for Mr. Sumberg is whether when the AAUP gets into the contest for representation as collective negotiations or bargaining agent is it ready to go sled-length.

MR. SUMBERG: I'll be glad to answer it.

MR. LIEBERMAN: Could I throw in another question on that point? In Mr. Marmion's paper there is a statement that the AAUP is opposed to collective negotiations under any circumstances.

MR. SUMBERG: I pointed that out as—

MR. LIEBERMAN: Wait a minute. I think you pointed to some locals of the AAUP that have come out for negotiation, but you have not pointed to the national policy. Just as the NEA (or the AFT) may have a national policy and some locals may differ, so may the AAUP. Now, is that statement of Mr. Marmion's simply his editorial interpretation of national policy, or what is now the national policy of the AAUP concerning the desirability of collective negotiations?

MR. SUMBERG: The policy as adopted at the annual meeting in April refers to the availability of collective bargaining. We're not talking about the desirability of collective bargaining under any circumstance. We're talking about the availability of collective bargaining as a desirable means to the solution of problems on campuses where the concept of shared responsibility is inoperative.

As a national policy, collective bargaining is a desirable means where shared responsibility does not operate. I think Mr. Marmion is still in error where he says, "In conclusion, then, the AAUP opposes collective bargaining as a mechanism by college faculty as unprofessional." He makes that as a completely categorical statement. Also, they are "not to be considered under any circumstances" and, finally, "the right to strike is rarely to be considered as a potential device to accomplish ends."

That isn't in keeping with our policy at all. The REI statement talks about the availability of collective bargaining for faculty senates and for local chapters of the AAUP. Let's put it on a democratic, permissive basis for a faculty. If collective bargaining is the desire of a faculty, then a faculty senate which may be recognized as a legitimate bargaining agent by a public commission is desirable; also an AAUP chapter is desirable.

MR. MARMION: I stand by the statement because I know what happened: The AAUP found out that a junior college in Illinois had been designated as a collective bargaining agent. The local chapter people called up the national office and said, "We're going to bargain with the board. We're an AAUP chapter, so what are you going to do?" Then the AAUP took a position on that matter.

Then there is the Catholic University situation—the cessation of activities. That was a strike.

MR. SUMBERG: That's right, and we supported it.

MR. MARMION: Yes, but you didn't support a similar situation at St. John's University. I guess what I'm trying to do here is to push. The question was asked here whether you were going to go all the way on this. I wish that you would say it is the national policy of the AAUP that under certain conditions collective bargaining can take place; but you haven't issued a statement that makes it clear-cut.

MR. SUMBERG: Have you read the REI statement?

MR. MARMION: Sure.

MR. SUMBERG: It's clear. All of our chapters understand it—

MR. MARMION: So in a local chapter you'd support a strike under certain conditions?

MR. SUMBERG: Under certain conditions, yes, that's right.

CHAIRMAN MOSKOW: Is the answer to Mr. Oberer's question that if the local chapter wants to go on strike you will support it?

MR. McHUGH: Be careful. That's outlawed in New York State.

MR. SUMBERG: Even in Pennsylvania they won't allow it.

If conditions are such that a faculty finds it must do what we call suspend services—you call it a strike and there's very little difference— if a bargaining agent feels that it must go out on strike because of certain conditions that exist—

MR. MARMION: Who is going to determine that? The local chapter?

MR. SUMBERG: The local chapter and the national—in terms of our support for it. Every other organization does the same thing.

MR. MARMION: Not in collective negotiations.

MR. SUMBERG: Oh, yes indeed.

MR. OBERER: My purpose was not to put Mr. Sumberg and the AAUP on the carpet by any means. I am really reflecting upon what we've seen happen in public education at the elementary and secondary levels. What has happened is that what was originally a choice—that is, between the Union and the Association—has now become in big-city confrontations the choice between Union A and Union B; and I was just wondering what that portends with regard to higher education. Will the AAUP, and maybe some of the organizations, continue to give an alternative of a different sort from that of the AFT, or because of competition will they feel they're going to have to become as militant as the Union and fight fire with fire?

I think that's an interesting question and an important one.

MR. SUMBERG: I think part of the answer to that, Professor Oberer, is the availability of such devices as sanctions or a form of censure which is not quite the academic freedom censure but still is what the AAUP uses. What we really need in collective bargaining (and we have a number of people who are available, all types of groups) is some creative collective bargaining which at the same time will search for the alternatives that are available and which industrial labor has been successful in finding.

MR. WEINBERG: I think one of the most interesting types of literature in the labor movement is the fiction that comes out of the international headquarters that has almost nothing to do with what is actually happening in the locals and in practical collective bargaining. The phenomenon we are observing here is similar. Different organizations make official statements and take positions, but it is their local organizations that are setting policy. The headquarters must adapt to the local policy as best it can.

It is fruitless to try to pin down these organizations. All of them are in a state of flux. They are changing as rapidly as the situations change on campus. They are doing their best to bridge documents between the old stale policies of last year and what they know exists now and what they think may happen in the future. The odds are they have been wrong in all three stages.

What is happening on the local level is important. There seems to be a general pattern of faculty members being increasingly involved and having more to say about their own destinies. The pattern is similar, whether it is the AAUP, or locally in New Jersey under the New Jersey Education Association. Whatever the organization may be, professors want a greater say in determining their economic and professional destinies. Because they are articulate, they fall into the same trap as public school teachers and social workers. They make it much too complex. Their focus on professional issues makes it more difficult to identify the key issues in bargaining. The key issues usually are income and basic work issues. It happens that in education basic work issues are complicated.

MR. GUSTAD: My only reservation about Mr. Marmion's paper is that I think he left out very largely a discussion of a set of organizations which I think are at the moment very largely controlling, and I'm talking about the professional societies, the disciplinary societies. While the AAUP might search for certain kinds of sanctions against an institution, the disciplinary societies now do exercise such sanctions. Several years ago, for example, Ohio State virtually imported en masse the mathematics department of another university because the other university wasn't treating the mathematicians properly. This sort of thing goes on rarely with respect to whole departments, but surely with respect to individuals.

What effect the change in the marketplace in the next decade is going to have on the disciplinary societies I don't know, but I do know that they do exert all kinds of serious pressures on the administrations and boards of trustees of individual institutions.

CHAIRMAN MOSKOW: Did the disciplinary society play a role in this particular case you alluded to?

MR. GUSTAD: I'm not sure what part the society as a whole played. The disciplinary grapevines are terrible and wonderful things, and I know that this is in part how we became aware that most of that department was ready to pick up and move and that they wanted to move as a unit because they had some research groups, and so on. Whether the disciplinary society as an official body played a role I don't know. The fact of the matter is that in my own discipline, psychology, the American Psychological Association grapevine is great. I'm sure the APA wouldn't go on record and say, "Don't take a job at Newark State College because their salaries aren't so good," but the word gets around.

These are not well-organized groups in the same sense as those are that Mr. Marmion was talking about; but the fact is they exert an enormous amount of influence, which may be why the AAUP, the AFT, and other groups are encountering a little less enthusiasm than might otherwise be the case.

MR. GERSTL: As merely a parenthetical addition to the comment just made, I wonder whether Mr. Marmion would care to comment on whether it makes any sense at all to consider professional societies union in any way, in the same way that he has suggested that the AAUP is for many intents and purposes union-oriented.

MR. MARMION: I think we have a semantic difficulty. I think some of the professional associations—for instance, the medical associations—but not necessarily the discipline societies, are like unions.

MR. GERSTL: I meant specifically discipline societies.

MR. MARMION: No, I think they're professional in character. Concerned with their own disciplines. I don't think they attempt any punitive sanctions, and I don't think Mr. Gustad was inferring that they did. In his illustration, professors of one discipline just didn't like it at the one institution and they left.

I don't see them as a factor in this situation, except, as I point out in my paper, loyalty to a particular discipline will undoubtedly keep numbers of faculty out of the AAUP or the AFT.

MR. GUSTAD: When a faculty member at X college gets unhappy, if it's a matter of salary, let's say, he's not likely to go to the AAUP. He'll write to the national headquarters or to some friends somewhere and say, "Help! Get me out of here." And this works remarkably well.

CHAIRMAN MOSKOW: I'd like to pursue this a little further. In my particular field I'm not sure he writes to the national headquarters of the professional society. He writes to friends he has in his discipline in other schools.

MR. LIEBERMAN: That's a great indictment of the AAUP.

MR. SUMBERG: You haven't read the want ads in the *AAUP Bulletin*.

MR. LOEWENBERG: The hiring hall function of the disciplinary society is, I think, abominably done. (Of course, I speak from my own limited knowledge.) I think it's a very irrational and inadequate mechanism, but it's probably at least as successful, if not more so, than the AAUP or any other organization.

MR. LIEBERMAN: Mr. Marmion pointed out that the AAUP organizes only a minority of professors, and I want to suggest some reasons why this is the case.

Mr. Marmion states that "an objective observer would say that the AAUP was Committee A," which deals with academic freedom and tenure. I suggest the very narrowness of the program of the AAUP is a factor in why people don't join it. Professors, like other people, are less likely to join organizations with very limited programs and objectives. I happen to believe that the AAUP is not particularly effective even in academic freedom and tenure cases partly because that's where so much of its emphasis is. It would be a more effective organization even in academic freedom and tenure matters and would enroll more people if it had a broader program.

Significantly, the AAUP has never made an all-out effort to organize the disciplinary societies as departments of the AAUP. In other professions, the organizations of specialists are departments of the comprehensive organization that enrolls all of them. In the American Medical Association there are affiliated organizations of anesthesiologists, surgeons, and so on. In contrast, the professors are fragmented organizationally. It would be very helpful if the key disciplinary organizations were affiliated in some functional relationship to the AAUP so that one organization would serve both the disciplinary and the common needs of professors.

CHAIRMAN MOSKOW: Would you like to respond, Mr. Sumberg?

MR. MacRAE: Mr. Chairman, before he responds could I put another question to him along the same line? It's a question and possibly a prediction also.

Just as the AFT has forced the NEA into professional negotiations (and that's a pseudonym for collective bargaining), isn't the AAUP going to be forced (maybe "forced" is a bad word) to serve its clientele better by adopting some sort of collective bargaining statement? It probably won't be called that, but it would be somewhat similar to what the AFT is forcing the NEA to do.

MR. SUMBERG: Basically, the problem of the AAUP is, I think, that it doesn't have as much visibility as some people would like. I've been a member of the AAUP now for over 12 years and a member of the staff for two years, and the thing that has interested me is that so much of our work goes unnoticed because we attempt not to give it any public view. Most of our mediation work in the academic freedom area is done quietly. The cases you hear about are the cases that have not been resolved; these are the cases that frequently lead to censure. But the mediation work of the AAUP largely goes unnoticed because we operate in the confidence of the faculty and the administration.

I know what bothers Mike Lieberman because I read his article here and have talked with him before. He seems to me to want a single monolithic organization in academic life which essentially will take care of all the problems that face the academician, and I just don't see academic life in that context. It's far more pluralistic, as is our society, with the result that to ask each of the disciplinary organizations to become departments of the AAUP essentially defeats the purposes of both the AAUP and the disciplinary organizations.

The cooperative efforts that exist among organizations—among the organizations represented here, by the way—prove to be extremely effective on local, state, and national levels. Interestingly enough, many of the disciplinary organizations—60 of them, in fact—have endorsed the 1940 statement on academic freedom and tenure, and many of them advertise in their journals the names of organizations which are on censure. The American Historical Association puts an asterisk beside the names of those institutions which advertise positions and which are on the censure list.

To ask them to become a department of the AAUP, then, doesn't quite solve their problems or indeed solve our problems, or suit the objectives they have. Many of them are in the field of accreditation. The American Historical Association today is accrediting professional historical graduate programs. Also, many of them are as deeply concerned with the issues of academic life as the professional organizations tend to be.

The question which Mr. MacRae asked—whether the AAUP will be forced into collective negotiations at the college level as the NEA was at the public school level, is quite current in academic life.

I don't think the AAUP responds to the pressures of other organizations per se. I think it responds largely to what the constituency that it represents, which is all of academic life, is talking about. There are some who are talking about collective negotiations. There are some who are talking about nothing at all, which is of greater concern to us: the great apathy that exists in academic life today among professors.

That comes as a surprise to you, perhaps, but nevertheless there are very serious problems of apathy at schools throughout the country. You hear about the situation at San Francisco State College, but you don't hear about the situation at Kutztown State College. You hear about Slippery Rock because it's first on the football list, but you don't hear about the conditions existing at a community college in Massachusetts where there are very substantial problems, including apathy on the part of the faculty and the administration with respect to those problems.

MR. MacRAE: Our AAUP chapter has difficulty finding something to talk about. We all belong, as they do in many other colleges, because it's a prestige organization.

MR. SUMBERG: There are a lot of things they can talk about if they want to. Committee T is on governance, college and university government. There we don't have the same concept of censure. There we're talking about sanctions.

MR. MONTANA: Mr. Marmion's paper indicates that two-thirds of college faculty members are not affiliated with either the AAUP or a union. Mr. Cronin in his remarks raises the point: Why are so many faculty members not affiliated and what incentives are there to belong to any of these organizations?

Has it been because of ineffective efforts of the unions in their approach to faculty members? There are other vital issues here. In the case of the non-tenured faculty member the designation of employer-employee is very strong, and he would be ripe for unionization for improvement of hours, wages, and conditions of employment rather than this shared responsibility concept permeating many of the statements of the AAUP representative.

In my experience, many professors do not care to share in the governance of a university. It's not their job. As union contracts designate, management has the right to run the business. The administrators run the college business and the faculty members are interested in other things. They are motivated differently. We should recognize this fact as we proceed.

MR. SMITH: I wanted to make the same point, that Mr. Cronin raises some very key questions. To be sure, we left out some other key questions. But just for the record I'd like to suggest that they be followed up (perhaps by some of the 75,000 members of Phi Delta Kappa who are looking for research problems). I should like to know not only how many college faculty members are affiliated, but with what organizations. We need further definition, because a great many are affiliated with their disciplinary organizations and with other groups.

The other question is, what incentives and rewards are offered, or, to turn it around, what rewards and satisfactions do faculty members and administrators want to take from their experience.

These are very important questions that obviously can't be answered in the next three minutes, but they need further study.

MR. BLUM: You can always focus on who isn't unionized or organized or why some are and some aren't. After all, in the industrial sector not everybody is unionized. Most white-collar people aren't unionized. I've been doing research in that area for 10 years now and I still don't have the answer explaining why the rest aren't unionized.

Under some conditions in certain institutions, they will become unionized. One has to separate the groups and analyze the issues and analyze the organizations, and what they're doing and what they're not doing. It seems to me that if there are a lot of apathetic teachers or professors who don't belong to unions the organizations ought to ask why not, why they don't belong. If they can't be organized in one place, perhaps they can in another. It may be that the organization of teachers may have to start in the state colleges, and, as a result, professors at universities may even learn some lessons from other institutions.

MR. MINER: I'd like to respond to Mr. Weinberg's statement. I may have misunderstood part of what he said, but at one point he indicated that he does not think it wise or important for us to look at the kinds of policy statements which in fact have been issued by national organizations, or that we ought not try to pin down organizations to the development of these statements.

For the purposes of this symposium this may be really the central issue. We learned a lot of lessons in Florida, as I'm sure all of you people are aware. It is true, certainly, that state and local organizations within a structure that has state and local affiliates do not necessarily have to agree with national policy; but I believe those national postures have to be established in an area, for example, as critical as collective negotiations today.

It would seem to me that to dodge that issue or refuse to look at the kinds of national postures which have been established would be really to beg the entire issue. I see it from this standpoint. It may be that every faculty in this country is not going to adopt negotiations; I think it would be naive to assume that they will. But there are some faculties right now who are saying, "We believe that collective negotiations is in fact the only route to shared authority."

What this means is that while in a sense policy is certainly made at the local level, it must be in line with the national posture; the effectiveness of the program carried out at local and state levels will depend to some degree upon taking a strong national position and then gearing the machinery to adhere to that position.

With regard to what Mr. MacRae said about the NEA in 1961 having been forced into a position of accepting collective negotiations, there is certainly some truth in that statement. But I would like to look at it at this point as being, in a sense, an admission of the fact that if faculties are going to be involved and indeed if they are going to share authority, then the vehicle by which this must be done to be effective is certainly going to be professional negotiations or academic negotiations.

At any rate, if we're talking here about faculty organizations in higher education and if that does involve collective negotiations, then we must examine national postures. As for the AAUP's position at this point, Mr. Marmion, you've made it pretty clear that they would do anything to avoid collective negotiations. That fact says to me that if in Illinois a local does decide to go into negotiations, the AAUP is really admitting paralysis, because they are involved now at the local level in a process which at the national level they have not consistently endorsed. It would indicate to me that the very necessary machinery for carrying out policy at the local level probably doesn't exist.

ADJOURNMENT

CHAPTER TWO

REPRESENTATIONAL SYSTEMS IN HIGHER EDUCATION

MYRON LIEBERMAN

PROFESSOR OF EDUCATION
CITY UNIVERSITY OF NEW YORK CITY

•

The objective of this paper is to assess the major representational systems, in existence or proposed, for higher education in the United States. This objective is developed as follows: First, the paper sets forth the purposes and types of representational systems in our economy. It then outlines the characteristics of representational systems in higher education, including those proposed by various organizations and agencies active in higher education. The analysis then focuses upon some major issues characterizing representational systems in higher education. Then concluding sections are devoted to the implications of the analysis for faculty representation systems and for the leading organizations seeking to organize faculty members.

At the outset, certain limitations should be noted. Perhaps the most important is the lack of comprehensive data on the nature, number, and effectiveness of representational systems in higher education. For example, "faculty senates," under a wide variety of titles, constitute a common type of faculty representational system. Nevertheless, this observer was unable to locate research data providing both a feasible definition of academic senates and a count of their frequency. Systematic research into their operations was also not available, although there are many case studies on the subject.[1] Typically the case studies deal with situations wherein the academic senate has failed to operate effectively. For this reason, the studies do not necessarily provide a balanced view of the extent or effectiveness of academic senates. The same conclusion would apply to the available material on other representational systems in higher education.

The lack of evaluative data is particularly evident. Regardless of the structure of a representational system, the results obtained under it are affected by other factors such as the ability of the persons exercising leadership roles in the system. Of course, the tendency of representational systems to produce outstanding leadership is a legitimate basis for evaluating the systems, but it may be very difficult to ascertain what is due to the system and what is due to other factors. In any case, this observer was unable to discover useful studies along these lines.

The analytical problem is to identify a basis for evaluation which is practically defensible even though limited to very gross data which may not illuminate the relationships between crucial variables in specific situations. The approach adopted here has been to assume that representational systems for professors share some of the goals of representational systems in other fields. The specific content of these goals, such as professional autonomy or enhanced professorial welfare, may vary from field to field, just as they vary from institution to institution within the field of higher education. Nevertheless, the goals will be similar if not identical in some respects. For example, any representational system, regardless of whether it applies to professional or nonprofessional employees, or public or nonpublic ones, is supposed to strive for the prompt resolution of grievances. Thus although all objectives of representational systems may not be similar, effectiveness in achieving those that are seems like a reasonable if imprecise basis for evaluation. If this is so, perhaps we can draw some valid conclusions about the effectiveness of representational systems in higher education despite the lack of detailed data on many important issues.

---

[1] For example, see Archie R. Dykes, *Faculty Participation in Academic Decision Making* (Washington, D.C.: American Council on Education, 1968). In a sense, the reports of Committee A of the American Association of University Professors often constitute case studies of academic senates, or of other types of faculty representational systems.

PURPOSES OF REPRESENTATIONAL SYSTEMS

Professors typically participate in several representational systems. As citizens, they participate in a system of political representation. Those who own stocks participate in a system of economic representation. If professors find it necessary to employ lawyers, they participate in still another representational system, and so on.

A representational system in higher education must serve the purposes appropriate to groups of employee professionals. Despite some interesting disclaimers, professors are employees of institutions of higher education. Therefore, their representational systems at the institutional level include, but are not limited to, the broad purposes of employee organizations. These purposes include improving the terms and conditions of employment for the employees.

In mentioning this purpose first, there is no intent to prejudge the priority it receives or should receive in practice. At the same time, professors are a particular kind of employee, at least in their own eyes. Professors are concerned about their field of study, their subject-matter organizations, the goals of their employing institutions, and a wide variety of factors which are not terms and conditions of employment. These aspects of professorial concern are summed up for many by the concept of "professionalism."

For present purposes, the point is that representational systems at the institutional level can and should also be analyzed in terms of their effectiveness in serving "professional" as well as "employment" purposes. In practice, the two types overlap and are often closely interrelated. Smaller classes are an improvement in working conditions; they may also be a defensible objective strictly from the "professional" standpoint of improved student performance. Thus although our main concerns here are the representational systems relating the professors to their employing institutions, the overall effectiveness of such systems must take into account their effectiveness in relating professors to other components of higher education, such as national scientific and academic organizations, students, and so on. We shall not, for example, consider here the way in which history professors are represented in the American Historical Association or medical professors in the American Medical Association; nevertheless, we should recognize that representational systems at the institutional level are not the only ones in higher education.

Employee representational systems (as well as employee organizations) are typically initiated by the employees. Analytically, the organization is only one element in a representational system, but both system and organization are meant to serve the same broad professorial purposes. Within this context, the AAUP's statement of its organizational purposes is adequate as a statement of the purposes of representational systems in higher education:

". . . to facilitate a more effective cooperation among teachers and research scholars in universities and colleges, and in professional schools of similar grade, for the promotion of the interests of higher education and research and in general to increase the usefulness and advance the standards, ideals, and welfare of the profession."

TYPES OF REPRESENTATIONAL SYSTEMS

The effectiveness of any representational system in higher education will ultimately depend upon the specific circumstances prevailing there. What prevails successfully or otherwise, in private enterprise, municipal employment, or other sectors may be helpful in higher education, but only to the extent that the relevant conditions in these other fields are similar to those in higher education.

Some professors insist that there is no similarity between employment conditions in higher education and in other fields. This is an ideological preconception, not an empirical fact. Reasonable men can differ about the extent to which higher education can or should differ from other fields of employment, but higher education is not a *completely* unique area of employment relations. This does not mean that other experience is to be copied; undoubtedly, some of it at least is to be avoided. But to make intelligent judgments on this issue, we need to know what other representational systems have been tried and what experience has been pursuant to their use. With this in mind, a few comments about representational systems outside of higher education may be in order.

In private employment, especially such as is governed by federal legislation, the predominant representational system is collective bargaining through an exclusive bargaining agent designated by a majority of the employees in an appropriate unit. As defined in federal law, and as used here, collective bargaining (or collective negotiations) is ". . . the performance of the mutual obligation of the employer and the representatives of the employees to meet at reasonable times and confer in good faith with respect to wages, hours, and other terms of employment, or the negotiations of any agreement, or any question arising thereunder, and the execution of a written contract incorporating any agreement if requested by either party, but such obligation does not compel either party to agree to a proposal or require the making of any concessions."[2] Although each of these elements raises a number of significant issues, the basic structure of this representational system is fairly clear.

Collective bargaining is in part an adversary process. Nevertheless, the rationale for it assumes that the parties involved in bargaining have common interests which outweigh their conflicting ones. The parties are not required to agree or to make any concession but to follow a procedure requiring sincere effort to reach agreement. The rationale is that if the parties follow the procedure, they will in practice arrive at a mutually satisfactory agreement because of the predominance of their common interests.

For a variety of reasons, the adversary element in collective negotiations is frequently stressed. Attitudes toward the procedure often depend upon whether one sees collective negotiations as an appropriate response to a pre-existing conflict of interest, or as a procedure which creates such conflicts, or both. Regardless, the agreement-making and community of interest aspects of collective negotiations are also essential elements of its theory and practice; inability or unwillingness to recognize this serves no scholarly purpose. Nor is any such purpose served by assuming that a rejection of invalid criticisms or assumptions about the process commits one to the proposition that it is feasible or appropriate in higher education.

For several very practical reasons, collective bargaining requires employee representation through an exclusive bargaining agent. The bargaining agent (typically but not necessarily a union) is authorized to negotiate a binding agreement for the employees in an appropriate unit. Under federal legislation and some state statutes, the bargaining agent must be designated as exclusive representative by a majority of the employees. The employees retain the right to change their bargaining agent or to go without one under specified conditions; however, once certified as the exclusive representative, the majority organization has the exclusive right to negotiate terms and conditions of employment for all the employees in the unit for a specified period of time.[3]

---

[2]Labor Management Relations Act, 1947, Sec. 8 (d).

[3]For a more detailed analysis of collective bargaining as well as the other representational systems discussed in this paper, see Myron Lieberman and Michael H. Moskow, *Collective Negotiations for Teachers* (Chicago: Rand McNally & Company, 1966).

The vast majority of employees covered by federal labor law are represented as employees through an exclusive bargaining agent. However, such representation is an employee initiative, and this initiative is not always exercised. The reasons vary from fear of employer reprisal (though such reprisal is illegal) to the belief that exclusive representation is undesirable or unnecessary in a given situation.

State and local employment relations, including public employment relations not under federal jurisdiction, present a variety of representational patterns. In addition to exclusive representation in negotiations by a majority organization, other types of representational systems include employee councils, joint representation, and multiple representation systems. A few brief comments about each type may help to clarify the subsequent analysis.

Employee councils are representational systems in which the employees elect one or more fellow employees to represent them. Employees are thus not represented through external organizations. Only individual employees of the same employer represent their fellow employees concerning terms and conditions of employment. Employee councils are thus "internal mechanisms"; neither individuals who are not employees nor organizations serve as employee representatives in employee councils.

Under joint representation, employees are represented by organizations on the basis of membership. Unlike exclusive representation, where one employee organization represents all the employees in an appropriate unit, organizations represent their members only under a system of joint representation. The rationale is that an organization should have the right to represent its members but not the right to represent nonmembers, including those adamantly opposed to the organization.

Sometimes a system of joint representation is qualified by a requirement that an organization enroll a minimum number of employees before it is entitled to representation rights. Without any such qualification, an employer could be faced with the prospect of negotiating with a tremendous number of small organizations. To avoid such an outcome, organizations may be required to enroll a certain minimal proportion of employees before they are entitled to representational rights.

Proportional representation is a form of joint representation in which employees are represented by representatives from different employee organizations. Representation is in the form of a committee (or council). Organizations have membership in the joint committee in proportion to the number of employees enrolled by each organization; thus if organization A enrolled twice as many employees as organization B, the former would be entitled to twice as many representatives as the latter on the joint committee. Again, a minimal number of members may be required for representational rights. The procedures for allocating places on the joint committee vary, but it is not practicable to adjust such places to small variations in organizational membership.

Finally, there are situations in which two or more representational systems coexist. There may be an employee council coexisting with some system of organizational representation. Multiple representational systems present many theoretical and practical inconsistencies, but there is no doubt that such systems do exist; in fact, this appears to be the predominant pattern in higher education.

ORGANIZATIONAL POLICIES ON FACULTY REPRESENTATION

Let us turn next to organizational policies on faculty representation. The policies of the AAUP will be considered first.

The most recent statement of AAUP policy is set forth in the Association's "Statement of Policy on Representation of Economic Interests." This statement was approved by the Association's Committee on the Representation of Economic Interests in January, 1968, and by the AAUP's Council and the Fifty-fourth Annual Meeting in April, 1968. This policy statement clearly places the AAUP on record in support of internal mechanisms (i.e., employee councils) for faculty representation. Because the representational system faculties want is the one they are most likely to get, and because the AAUP is the largest professorial organization in the United States, this recent statement is worth quoting in some detail:

> . . . Two main kinds of approach [to faculty representation] have been developed: (1) collective bargaining by an exclusive bargaining agent, patterned after union procedures in industry, and (2) professional self-representation by an internal faculty agency, based upon faculty authority of the kind which the Association supports for the handling of all kinds of faculty interests.
>
> The Association recommends that faculty members, in decisions relating to the protection of their economic in-

terests, should participate through structures of self-government within the institution, with the faculty participating either directly or through faculty-elected councils or senates. As integral parts of the institution, such councils or senates can effectively represent the faculty without taking on the adversary and sometimes arbitrary attitudes of an outside representative. . . .

. . . statutory models of general application may be ill-suited to the situation of the faculty member in higher education. As stated above, he has, or should have, access to avenues of self-government and of shared authority and responsibility. Because of these special characteristics of the academic community, professors should be especially concerned to avoid dependence on external representative agencies that diminish the opportunities of the faculty for self-government. B. The Association will therefore oppose legislation imposing upon faculty members in higher education the principle of exclusive representation derived from models of industrial collective bargaining. When legislation of this character exists or is proposed, the Association will rather support measures that will encourage institutions of higher education to establish adequate internal structures of faculty participation in the government of the institution. . . .

. . . 1. Any statute authorizing collective bargaining for public employees should permit, for faculty members of colleges and universities, some system of joint representation. In such a system, collective bargaining might be conducted by a committee composed of delegates from each of the organizations which represented a substantial number of faculty members and which were willing to take part in the system of joint representation.

2. Any such legislation should make it clear that, in higher education, a faculty-elected council or senate is eligible to represent the faculty, since such an internal representative can have the requisite autonomy and independence of the administration to carry out its functions. . . .[4]

Significantly, the Association's policy statement goes on to state

[4]"Policy on Representation of Economic Interests," *AAUP Bulletin*, Vol. 54, No. 2 (June, 1968), pp. 152-53.

that "if the faculty is considering representation through an outside organization, the Association believes itself by virtue of its principles, programs, experience, and broad membership, to be well qualified to act as representative of the faculty in institutions of higher education."[5] Thus although opposed to collective bargaining through an exclusive representative, the AAUP believes that it ought to be selected as the bargaining agent if a faculty should disregard this advice.

The American Council on Education is another organization deeply interested in faculty representational systems. The ACE is formally composed of institutions, organizations, and agencies concerned with higher education; in operation, it is controlled by college and university presidents.

The ACE's position on faculty representation is embodied in a 1966 statement formulated and issued jointly with the AAUP and the Association of Governing Boards of Universities and Colleges. The statement thus reflects the views of the major organizations of administrators and lay boards in higher education. Despite some language which could be interpreted otherwise, it seems clear that the ACE and AGB endorse faculty representation through internal mechanisms. This is not surprising, since such mechanisms typically strengthen the position of the employer *vis-à-vis* the employees; what may be more significant is that the statement was jointly formulated and approved by the AAUP as well. As a matter of fact, there is nothing in this joint statement to indicate that the AAUP, or any external organization, should exist or play a significant role in the government of colleges and universities. Perhaps one reason for the omission is that the statement urges that rather broad responsibilities be delegated to the faculty:

> The faculty has primary responsibility for such fundamental areas as curriculum, subject matter, and methods of instruction, research, faculty status, and those aspects of student life which relate to the educational process. On these matters the power of review or final decision lodged in the governing board or delegated by it to the president should be exercised adversely only in exceptional circumstances and for reasons communicated to the faculty. . . . Faculty status and related matters are primarily a faculty responsibility; this area includes appointments, reappointments, decisions not to re-

[5] *Ibid.*, p. 153.

appoint, promotions, the granting of tenure, and dismissal. . . . Determinations in these matters should first be by faculty action through established procedures, reviewed by the chief academic officers with the concurrence of the board. The governing board and the president should, on questions of faculty status, as in other matters where the faculty has primary responsibility, concur with the faculty judgment except in rare instances and for compelling reasons which should be stated in detail.

Agencies for faculty participation in the government of the college or university should be established at each level where faculty responsibility is present. An agency should exist for the presentation of the views of the whole faculty. The structure and procedures for faculty participation should be designed, approved, and established by joint action of the components of the institution. Faculty representatives should be selected by the faculty according to procedures determined by the faculty. The agencies may consist of meetings of all faculty members of a department, school, college, division, or university system, or may take the form of faculty-elected executive committees in departments and schools and a faculty-elected senate or council for larger divisions or institution as a whole.[6]

The American Federation of Teachers is composed predominantly of teachers below the college level. Nevertheless, the AFT has recently created a staff position to implement its interest in enrolling college and university personnel. At present, about 10,000 college and university faculty belong to the AFT, including a considerable proportion of junior college personnel.

The AFT supports collective bargaining through an exclusive representative for college as well as for elementary and secondary school personnel. AFT locals have occasionally gone on strike to secure such a representational system, and in the immediate future, the success or failure of AFT college locals in achieving bargaining rights, and in negotiating good agreements from a professorial point

[6]American Association of University Professors, American Council on Education, and the Association of Governing Boards of Universities and Colleges, *1966 Statement on Government of Colleges and Universities*, in Louis Joughin (ed.), *Academic Freedom and Tenure*, a Handbook of the American Association of University Professors (Madison, Wis.: University of Wisconsin Press, 1967), p. 98.

of view, may be a crucial factor affecting the rate at which collective bargaining becomes accepted in higher education.

One other position on faculty representation should be mentioned here, even though it is not the official position of a major national organization in the field of higher education. This is the position set forth by a task force established by the American Association for Higher Education enrolling both administrators and faculty members in higher education.[7]

In many respects, the report of this task force is the best (i.e., the least confused) statement on faculty representational systems currently available. This is undoubtedly due to the fact that the task force included several members with considerable professional background and experience in employment relations; two nationally recognized authorities in public employment relations served as counsel to the task force.

The AAHE report states "a clear preference for the development of effective internal organizations as the primary instrument of faculty participation in campus government. In most cases this will mean the academic senate or its equivalent."[8] The report goes on to outline some of the requirements which an effective academic senate should meet. It then goes on, however, to support the principle of exclusive bargaining rights for any organization which gains the allegiance of a majority of the faculty. The report also urges that regardless of their legal freedom to avoid a test of faculty interest in exclusive representation, institutions of higher education follow the same basic procedures concerning representation elections and recognition that are embodied in the National Labor Relations Act and in the state statutes which follow the NLRA pattern for state and local public employees.

FACULTY SENATES: AN INTRODUCTORY ANALYSIS

Of all the representation systems listed, it is probable that some type of faculty senate is currently the most common if not the prevailing type on U.S. campuses. This is only to be expected in view of the organizational positions previously mentioned. Given the fact that the AAUP, ACE, and AGB (the preeminent organizations of faculty, ad-

---

[7] *Faculty Participation in Academic Governance,* Report of the Task Force on Faculty Representation and Academic Negotiations (Washington, D. C.: American Association for Higher Education, 1967).
[8] *Ibid.,* p. 39.

ministration, and governing boards respectively) officially support the use of faculty senates, it would be surprising if they were not a common pattern of faculty representation.

Faculty senates vary a great deal. For example, faculty representatives may be elected on a departmental or a college basis or some combination of these. In some institutions, the administration appoints certain persons to the senate, or administrative appointees may preside at certain senate proceedings. Faculty below a certain rank may be unable to vote or hold office in some senates. The legal or constitutional base of the academic senate also varies widely from institution to institution.

These variations can be very important, but no attempt will be made here to explore them. Instead, let us consider faculty senates chiefly with regard to their salient characteristics as representational systems. In doing so, the analysis will consider at some length the question of whether special factors in higher education justify or require a representational system generically different from those prevailing in other areas of employment, including professional employment.

In theory and practice, faculty senates are a type of employee council. Employee councils were fairly common in private employment before the Wagner Act. In operation, they failed to provide effective employee representation for the following reasons:

1. Employee councils lacked funds needed to pursue an aggressive campaign of employee representation. Employers provided the funds, and they naturally did not wish to subsidize a strong employee representation system.

2. Employers typically regulated the internal affairs of employee councils. The more serious an issue became, the more likely that the employer would exercise his control over the representation system to impose his will on the employees.

3. Under an employee council, there is no employee appeal from an adverse decision by the employer. This is because employee councils are not organically related to higher echelons of employee organization, such as a regional or national organization. There is nobody outside the employing agency to whom the employee can appeal, at least without calling into question the basic adequacy of the employee council itself. An adequate employee representation system would envisage the possibility that employer action may have to be vigorously resisted by resort to outside assistance and that such resistance should be available within the representational system.

4. Employee councils typically put the employees at a psychological disadvantage. Under a council system, employee representatives are employees under the direction and control of the employer. Whereas the employer is or may be represented by persons who devote full time to the problems of employment relations, the employee representatives tend to be more inexperienced since they do not work full-time at representing the employees. Because the task of representing the employees is superimposed on their full-time work, the employee representatives are handicapped in preparing for representational activities.

5. If the employee representatives on the council are chosen from subgroups of employees, there is no employee representative whose constituency includes all the employees. This weakens the moral authority as well as the practical ability of the employee representatives to represent all the employees.

These and other deficiencies in employee councils are not simply matters of conjecture. They are the reasons why employee councils are, in effect, prohibited by federal labor legislation from representing employees on terms and conditions of employment. As a matter of public policy, federal law supports the principle that employees shall be represented by organizations free of employer domination. Since employee councils are likely to be employer dominated, they are prohibited, *even if the employees are professionals and desire such a representational system.*

It seems hardly debatable that faculty senates are characterized by at least some of the objectionable features of employee councils. For example, faculty senates typically lack funds independent of those provided by the administration. For this reason, the senates are gravely handicapped in securing the services needed for effective representation. Faculty senates are not likely to have the expert negotiating, actuarial, accounting, legal, and other experts needed to maximize faculty benefits. This weakness is not routinely overcome by the expertise available from within the faculty.

In the first place, many faculties with academic senates simply lack the expertise needed for effective representation. Most faculties will not include a lawyer specializing in employment relations or an expert on pension and retirement systems. Most will not have experts in public finance or public personnel administration. Furthermore, faculty members with an expertise useful for representation do not necessarily participate in the academic senate. The individual faculty member may be unable or unwilling to devote the time to securing benefits which are diffused to the entire faculty; the effectiveness of a representational system that relies upon volunteers to perform all the specialized services required for effective representation is open to serious question.

As in private employment, it is typical for employers (i.e., administration or governing board), to regulate the internal affairs of faculty senates. In many institutions, faculties have worked diligently to get their trustees to incorporate a faculty senate into the official statutes of the institution. Such incorporation is usually regarded as a victory for a "faculty self-government." Surely, however, a strong argument can be made that faculty senates have precisely the opposite effect.

Suppose a board of trustees has approved the structure of a faculty senate and the senate is now recognized as an official component of faculty government. Suppose further that the faculty subsequently desires to change the representational system. It may want to exclude administrative officers or have faculty representatives elected at large instead of by department or college. If such changes must be approved by the trustees or by the administration, the "self-government" is obviously a matter of sufferance, not of right. Its inherent tendency is to be authorized or tolerated only to the point where it threatens no crucial interest of governing boards or administrators.

Of course, if one assumes that there is not and cannot be a conflict of interest between the faculty and those who must approve the structure of "faculty self-government," there is no problem here. In that case, however, it is difficult to see the need for a representational system in the first place. Paradoxically, a union of common laborers can change the way it selects its representatives without consulting the employers of common labor. Professors represented through academic senates cannot change the way they select their representatives without employer approval. Nevertheless, the professors supposedly have more "self-government." This is a curious conclusion, to say the least.

Perhaps the argument is that laborers have more control only over their organizational affairs, whereas the professors have more control over occupational affairs even if they are subject to employer control in ways that laborers are not. Still, it is at least as reasonable to suppose that an employee organization which operates independently of employer approval or support will press more vigorously than one which is not for joint decision making in employment relations.

Academic senates are not part of any state or national structure which can bring pressure to bear upon a recalcitrant administration. When an administration finally rejects a senate recommendation, the faculty's options are to accept the rejection or to appeal to an external organization. On its face, this situation is clearly inferior to the procedures prevailing in private employment under exclusive representation. In the latter situation, the exclusive representative negotiates a binding agreement on terms and conditions of employment. The employer administers the agreement, but he is effectively precluded from interpreting or applying the terms and conditions of employment in such a way as to deprive the employees of their rights under the agreement. This is so because the employees typically have the right to appeal to arbitration of such disputes by an impartial third party. Such appeals are part of the structure of employment relations, hence they are relatively expeditious in practice. By contrast, a faculty member or organization wishing to challenge an adverse decision by an employer must activate local and national organizations which have no legally or operationally recognized place in institutional employment relations.

Although faculty senates are clearly subject to some of the disabilities of employee councils, perhaps they are not so subject to others. For example, a major weakness of employee councils is that the employee representatives must prepare for their dealings with the employer after the normal work day or on weekends. Apart from the physical burdens involved, the employee representatives find it difficult to communicate with appropriate persons or locate appropriate resources at these times.

This weakness probably does not apply to faculty members to the same degree that it does to employees in private enterprise. Some institutions of higher education provide released time for representational duties, much as an industrial company releases union shop stewards for union duties on company time. Even without this arrangement, however, faculty members typically have more time to prepare their case than employees operating under an employee council in private enterprise. Faculties are also more likely to include personnel who would not be at a disadvantage psychologically in negotiating with institutional management. Nevertheless, on balance, it appears that the major criticisms levelled against employee councils are valid as applied to faculty senates.

Why do faculties support a representational system characterized by such basic deficiencies? The belief that faculty senates constitute a "professional" (as distinguished from an "employee") approach to faculty representation is undoubtedly part of the explanation. "Employee" is a dirty word in academe; in fact, academicians frequently assert that they are not "employees." One example of such an assertion may suffice to indicate its widespread acceptance among faculties. In the spring of 1968, Bertram H. Davis, the newly appointed general secretary of the AAUP, stated that:

"Faculty members have rightfully complained when boards or administrators have treated them as employees, and it would be ironic if they were now themselves to perpetuate the employer-employee concept through an industrial style of collective bargaining."[9]

Such professional overreactions to their employee status (including the delusion that they are not employees) is based upon the conviction that professors are professional persons and that professional status is inconsistent with employee status. This conviction is clearly fallacious, but it underlies much academic support for faculty senates.

The reason is that most professors fail to understand the distinction between an employment problem and a professional one. Employment problems should be resolved within the context of employer-employee relations; professional problems are those appropriate for action by professional organizations independently of employer action. To illustrate, suppose a physician appears late for his appointments. What is the patient's recourse—to report this to the local medical society? Ordinarily such tardiness is not handled this way. If a patient is aggrieved for this reason, he seeks an adjustment from the physician; if he does not get it, he changes physicians. But whatever he does, the matter is not ordinarily referred for action to the physician's professional organizations. It is an employment, not a professional, problem.

Suppose, however, that the physician has been supplying a dope ring at great profit to himself. In this case, the professional organization would be concerned with the physician's right to practice at all; the problem would be clearly a professional one.

A problem can be both an employment and a professional problem. For example, a physician who operated recklessly might give rise to legal action by his employer, i.e., the patient. Such reckless be-

---

[9]Bertram H. Davis, "Unions and Higher Education: Another View," *Educational Record*, Vol. 49, Spring 1968, p. 144. The fact that an individual can become the full-time executive officer of the AAUP while denying that professors are employees surely has some implications for the effectiveness of the AAUP as an employee organization.

havior might also justify disciplinary action by his professional organization. Without attempting a precise categorization, we can say that some actions are clearly employment problems, some are clearly professional problems, and some are both.

In higher education, however, the problem is not where to draw the line. It is the lack of awareness that there is a line to be drawn. As a result, faculties are apt to insist upon "professional autonomy" or "academic self-government" on problems which should be handled as employment problems.

For example, suppose a faculty member habitually appears late for his classes. For a faculty to regard disciplinary action, if any, as within the scope of their "professional autonomy" is to be confused. Such confusion probably stems from the fear that if jurisdiction over such matters is not "professional," i.e., within the faculty's domain, it must be an unbridled administrative prerogative. It would be possible for the faculty and the institution to negotiate a binding agreement which (1) would include the grounds and criteria for disciplinary action and which (2) would be administered by the administration with ample safeguards against administrative violation of the agreement. But this possibility simply has not occurred to most professors.

We may put the matter this way: Failure to understand how employee representation systems can and do work to serve professional employees leads many faculty members to deny that they are employees at all. Having abandoned any claim to protection as employees, these faculty members seek such protection as a professional prerogative. In doing so, however, they have thoroughly confused both employment relations and professionalism on the campus.

The idea that persons should not be appointed to administrative positions (president, dean, etc.) without professorial approval is strongly supported by many professors as an appropriate step toward "professional autonomy," "faculty self-government," and "democracy." Realistically, the idea illustrates the pervasiveness of professional confusion concerning their status as professionals and as employees.

In the first place, there is a conflict of interest on the part of faculty members who recommend persons for administrative positions (in this context, meaning those that involve making decisions or effective recommendations concerning faculty employment, retention, promotion, discipline, and so on). Professors are not likely to recommend candidates who advocate curtailing their courses or programs. Nor can we assume that a professor would knowingly recommend anyone known to harbor sincere doubts about the competence or promotional merits of the recommender. As a rule, faculty members on appointment committees tend to support candidates known or likely to have a favorable view toward the individuals on the committees or their particular academic projects and objectives.

The conflict of interest does not disappear if, as happens, the appointment committee recommends someone whose views on these matters are not known to the committee members. A college president or dean or chairman will find it more difficult to make objective personnel decisions about faculty members who vigorously supported or opposed their appointment than about those who did not participate in it.

Stripped of its academic rhetoric, a faculty appointment committee involves all the contradictions inherent in having employees choosing the representatives of the employer. The dangers inherent in this procedure extend far beyond the likelihood that faculty members will recommend on the basis of the expected impact on their own interests. The procedure itself maximizes the possibility that a managerial appointment will be made on the basis of employee interests which are not laid on the table.

It is doubtful, to say the least, whether a faculty appointment committee provides as much faculty protection as a negotiated collective agreement covering terms and conditions of faculty employment and negotiated consultation procedures on other matters of mutual concern. Theoretically, faculties might enjoy the benefits of both procedures although they are ideologically inconsistent. The selection committee approach to college administration puts great reliance upon choosing a "democratic" individual. Faculty rights are not secured by a written agreement on terms and conditions of faculty employment, regardless of the individuals occupying administrative positions at any given time. They are supposedly secured because the faculty, in its wisdom, will choose administrators who will render adversary procedures unnecessary. Because of their confusion over professional autonomy, faculty members assume that they should choose, or at least have a veto power over the selection of, employer representatives.

Apart from the fact that such participation is subject to unhealthy resolution of various employer-employee conflicts of interest, it does not provide adequate protection for the faculty. Adequate protection requires adherence to certain procedures *regardless* of who occupies particular administrative positions. To put one's faith in whoever is appointed to administrative positions while simultaneously failing to insist upon the incorporation of appropriate administrative procedures in an enforceable contract is a questionable order of priorities.

A representational system should not be evaluated solely on the basis of its effectiveness from the standpoint of the employees represented. The interests of the employer are also important, and those of the public may be decisive. For this reason, the public policy implications of faculty appointment committees cannot be ignored.

As previously pointed out, it would seem contrary to public policy, at least in publicly supported institutions of higher education, to permit public employees to select the representatives of the public employer. To whatever extent procedures permit or encourage this, they increase the probability that hidden conflicts of interest will play an unhealthy role in the selection process. Beyond this, there are additional and perhaps even more important issues to be raised.

Assume that a faculty senate exists and that a board of trustees has agreed to appoint as president only a person recommended by the faculty. Assume also no administrative interference or pressure but ample support for whatever the faculty needs to arrive at a recommendation. Assume, therefore, that the trustees pay all the expenses of faculty participation without stint while agreeing to appoint from a list submitted by the faculty. On most campuses, such an arrangement would be cheered as a great step forward.

Suppose, however, the faculty members on such a presidential appointment committee do a very poor job. Perhaps they do not work hard at it. Perhaps they work their heads off, but their judgment is poor. What happens to them as a result?

Obviously, if they have recommended a person who turns out to be a disaster, the president so recommended is not going to press the matter. He is not going to say, to the faculty or trustees or to anyone else, that the faculty selection committee flubbed the job. Nor is it likely that the trustees on their own will cite the disastrous recommendation as a reason to deny the faculty members who made it any advances in rank or pay or privilege.

By contrast, a department chairman is held responsible for the quality of his recommendations to deans and presidents. If a chairman recommends weak persons for appointment or promotion, this fact is legitimately cited against him in evaluating his own performance and setting his own future level of compensation. We are, therefore, confronted by a most anomalous situation. At the lowest administrative levels there is accountability for personnel recommendations; one clearly expects the quality of staff recruited by a chairman to be a significant factor in the evaluation of the chairman. But not so for the faculty committee to recommend a president. Whoever heard of a board of trustees or university president citing the poor judgment of the faculty presidential selection committee as a reason to withhold rank or pay to the committee members?

In short, faculty appointment committees constitute an irresponsible approach to appointment, since there is no accountability for the quality of the work done. As a practical matter, it would be extremely difficult, if not impossible, to inject accountability into the procedure. Who would implement the procedure? The president who was appointed as a result of the shoddy committee performance? The trustees who accepted and acted on the recommendation? The rest of the faculty? Absurd.

It is indeed remarkable that the AAUP, which has never allowed active membership to persons whose duties are mainly administrative, should nevertheless support procedures whereby the faculty, as employees, participate in the selection of employer representatives. Perhaps some board of trustees should propose that the officers of the AAUP be selected from a list submitted by the trustees to the faculty. This would make as much—or as little—sense as having the trustees choose the president from a list submitted by the faculty. In any event, the surprising thing is not that professors confusedly support the procedure—after all, it is difficult to resist the temptation to be a president maker. It is that so many governing boards have taken this academic rhetoric as seriously as they do.

Efficiency is not a very popular concept in academe, but it is important from a public policy standpoint. With this in mind, I would like to turn next to some comments about faculty senates from the standpoint of faculty efficiency.

It is an article of faith on most campuses that professors want to share, to participate, in decision making. The very vagueness of this objective suggests the desirability of careful analysis of its operational use and implementation.

How do professors "participate" in decision making? Typically, participation means that a faculty committee must be established to deal with a problem. If there is no faculty committee, there is no faculty participation.

The upshot is a tremendous diffusion of faculty energies to administrative matters, e.g., parking or scheduling. However, the function of faculty representation should not be faculty administration of an institution. Rather, it should be to ensure that administration is equitable and efficient. The way to achieve this objective is not to have the faculty choose the administrators or to administer the institution but to incorporate equitable and efficient administrative procedures in a contractual agreement between the faculty and the governing board. A grievance procedure culminating in binding arbitration by an impartial third party should be available to process a claim that the administration has violated or misapplied these procedures. Under such an agreement, the faculty would undoubtedly devote less of its time and energies to administration than it does now under faculty senates.

In other areas of employment, the employee representation system is neither designed nor intended to shift the burden of administration from the employer to the employees. On the other hand, the rights of the employees are protected because they are spelled out in a contractual agreement with impartial arbitration as the terminal point of the grievance procedure. If, therefore, the issue is whether a dismissal was for just cause, the employees' protection is not that his fellow employees process the charges and sit in judgment on them. It is that the employer must follow the standards and procedures embodied in the collective agreement; if he fails to do so, his action can be challenged through a grievance procedure in which the employer must ultimately prove his case to an impartial third party. Similarly, the function of a faculty representation system and of faculty organization should not be to administer the institution but to achieve agreement with the employer on how administration should be carried on and to enforce such agreement where enforcement is necessary.

Despite all the talk about faculty self-government, professionalism, and so on, the vast majority of professors have not more but less protection against arbitrary and unfair employer action than the vast majority of employees under contractual collective agreements. One reason is that contractual agreements provide greater protection than delegated authority, which can be revoked or ignored under pressure. Another reason requires that we reexamine the mystique of faculty participation.

The prevailing philosophy is that faculty protection lies in faculty self-government and faculty participation in personnel decisions. However, faculties and faculty organizations and academic senates are hardly immune from prejudice and self-interest and error; these are not administrative monopolies. The issue, then, is this: If the faculty exercises final authority on personnel decisions, how are faculty members protected against unjust action by the faculty?

Under a faculty senate, such protection is virtually nonexistent. The logic of the faculty senate approach is that a decision is right because it is made by the faculty. If this interpretation seems unfair, the answer is simple. If the rightness of a decision depends upon the standards and procedures involved in making it, then those standards and procedures should be binding upon *anyone* who has to make the decision, regardless of how that person or group is selected. But this view logically leads to a contractual approach through an exclusive representative, not to a faculty senate.

The point here is simple but fundamental. If the role of a faculty organization is not one of administration but of ensuring that administration is equitable and efficient, there is, at least in theory, an organization in being whose *raison d'être* is the protection of faculty rights from arbitrary or unjust administration. But if the faculty itself is responsible for the administrative action, faculty rights are practically without protection from administrative abuse.

Because faculty members are employees, their organization should serve protective functions. These should not be its only functions, but they are important ones. However, if a faculty senate assumes the functions of the employer, where does the aggrieved faculty member go for assistance? Surely not to the AAUP, since the Association's test of due process and equity in employment relations is whether the faculty made the decision being challenged. Beyond this, the AAUP merely recommends that "the terms and conditions of every appointment should be stated in writing and be in the possession of both institution and teacher before the appointment is consummated." The Association does not, however, recommend that these terms and conditions of employment include the teacher's right of access to his personnel file, that evaluation reports about him by administrators be routinely made available to him for his information and reaction, and that complaints and criticisms about him from any source that may bear upon his status be brought to his attention. Thousands of public school teachers have these and other protections as contractual rights; meanwhile, unless a personnel decision involves tenure, the AAUP has no rationale for involvement, and not even then if the faculty made the decision challenged.

Thus far, most of our attention has been paid to faculty senates because their viability is the major issue in faculty representation now, and will continue to be in the next few years. However, there are other important issues in faculty representation which should be mentioned.

One major issue is who should be represented in a faculty representational system. Are department chairmen, deans, and central office administrators to be included among those represented by the same system that represents nonadministrative personnel? Significantly, this issue arises sometimes with respect to a faculty senate. Some faculty members believe that administrators should not be constituent members or officers of the senate; others feel differently.

It appears likely that this issue will be fought out mainly over the status of department chairmen. It is difficult to believe that deans (or higher administrators) will, ought to, or want to be represented by faculty organizations, internal or external, concerning the terms and conditions of employment for deans. On the other hand, we can expect growing controversy over the status of department chairmen. One reason is that the title actually encompasses a widely disparate group of positions from the standpoint of employment relations. One chairman may have only three members in his department and receive no time or compensation for his administrative duties; another may have a department of 25 and serve chiefly as an administrator.

There is widespread inconsistency on this issue, even on the part of those who advocate collective negotiations through an exclusive representative. For example, a proposed contract[10] between the State University Federation of Teachers and the State University of New York being disseminated by the Federation includes the following:

A. *Administrative personnel.* The hiring, retention, and separation of division heads, associate deans, deans, vice presidents, and presidents shall be done with the advice and consent of the faculty. . . .
B. *Department chairman.*
   1. *Election.* The department chairman shall be elected by full-time faculty of the department.

These proposals may be intended mainly for their propaganda value, but the fact that they were made at all suggests the popularity of the view that faculty members should choose employer representatives in institutions of higher education. Furthermore, even if the AFT strategists who propose this are doing so only for tactical reasons, the tactics themselves will reinforce the view that faculties ought to choose

---

[10]The proposed contract is available from the New York State AFT College and University Council, 300 Park Avenue, New York, N.Y. 10010.

administrators. All such propaganda will tend to obscure the issues, including the issue of administrator membership in the faculty's negotiating unit and organizational representative. Eventually, administrative personnel above the chairman's level will be recognized as employer representatives, hence not to be chosen by the employees; in both the short and the long run, there will be widespread variation concerning the place of department chairmen in the representational structure.

Another aspect of unit determination may prove more troublesome than administrative roles, especially in the larger institutions. A college faculty includes an extremely wide range of talents. Many of these talents are in great demand outside academe; many faculty members, such as professors of medicine, tend to identify more with the organizations in their field such as the AMA than with faculty organizations interested in academic governance.

In large organizations enrolling a wide variety of occupational talents and levels of compensation, organizational leadership must respond to the wishes of its largest constituent groups. In higher education, these groups may not accept the view that faculty compensation should be geared, partially at least, to market factors. Thus a faculty representational system composed largely of faculty members in the social sciences and humanities—fields in which the nonacademic demand for personnel may not be strong—may object to large differentials for faculty in such fields as medicine, engineering, mathematics, or law, where the nonacademic demand is very strong indeed. It is difficult to visualize English and history and speech professors dying on the barricades for $25,000 salaries for their colleagues in professional schools, even though such salaries may be rather modest for the kinds of persons who teach in them.

Thus there may be tremendous heterogeneity within faculties at a single institution, in terms of (1) their identification with organizations which are primarily nonacademic, (2) the nonacademic demand for their services, and (3) their conditions of employment, such as load, research facilities, administrative organization, and level of instruction. This heterogeneity raises serious questions as to whether a single organization, internal or external, can effectively represent all the faculty.

The problem is complicated by the fact that some conditions of employment, such as retirement benefits, are institution-wide, and it would be practically impossible or extremely difficult to change this. One possible solution is institution- or even system-wide negotiations on matters that should logically affect all faculty. Yet even here there will be major difficulties if faculty from some areas conclude that they can do better apart from an institution-wide representational system.

In technical terms, this is the community of interest problem. Should all faculty members, regardless of subject or function, be part of one faculty representational system at their institution? Do all share such a community of interest that effective representation, efficient administration, and stable employment relations are maximized by a single system? Or will there be constant friction as various specialized groups come to feel their interests are being sacrificed in such a system?

At the present time, this issue is important chiefly in the smaller public institutions which have salary schedules applying to all faculty. The main effect of such schedules is to introduce rigidities in the compensation structure, but the problem is not typically regarded as an especially serious one. If faculties at larger institutions turn to collective negotiations, however, this issue will become more important to both administration and faculty. The administration will normally want to avoid negotiating with several different faculty groups. Apart from the increased demands on administrative time resulting from such multi-unit negotiations, there are some tactical advantages in requiring major faculty groups to agree among themselves on their proposed allocation of institutional funds. Under a unitary system, the administration can also avoid being whipsawed by organizations representing different faculty negotiating units.

Probably these advantages to the administration will outweigh the real disadvantages of multi-unit negotiations (e.g., by a different faculty organization representing each of the major professional schools or institutional divisions). Nevertheless, it seems safe to predict that some smaller groups within the faculty, especially in areas of highest nonacademic demand or least academic identification, will become increasingly unhappy with institution-wide representational systems. These groups may not be dissatisfied with current institution-wide systems, such as faculty senates, because these systems do not really prevent the administration from making a separate deal with subgroups within the faculty.

SUMMARY AND CONCLUSIONS

Let me now try to summarize the preceding analysis and suggest some issues and trends of future concern. Essentially, the analysis has been devoted chiefly to academic senates. Its major conclusion is that faculty senates are subject to the deficiencies of employee councils for these reasons:

1. Faculty senates rely upon the employer for funds and facilities. Thus they have inherent limitations on aggressive representation of faculty interests.

2. The structure of faculty senates is subject to approval by institutional governing boards and/or administrators. Faculties should not permit the mechanics of their representational agency to be subject to employer approval.

3. Faculty senates lack accountability. Faculty members assert that teaching and research competence should be the standards of personnel administration. Nevertheless, they wish to exercise personnel functions that vitally affect the integrity and effectiveness of their institutions. It is practically impossible for faculty senates to provide for faculty accountability in matters of personnel administration.

4. Faculty senates tend to place faculty representatives at a psychological disadvantage in dealing with institutional administrators.

5. Faculty senates increase the probability that faculties will lack experienced full-time representatives supported by the wide variety of supporting services and personnel needed for effective representation.

6. Faculty senates make no provision for appeals outside the structure of the institution. Since the senates are not part of any larger representational system, any such appeals are inherently outside the scope of institutional representation.

7. Faculty senates which exercise personnel functions tend to deprive faculty members of protection against abuse in the exercise of such functions. An employee organization is needed to protect faculty against certain kinds of employer action. If the employer delegates such action to the employee organization, no agency serves the protective functions of an employee organization.

These criticisms of faculty senates are not exhaustive. What is needed is not so much a critique of their inherent weaknesses, but an explanation of their persistence in spite thereof. The analysis has touched upon some reasons, such as befuddled faculty leadership and the large numbers of faculty who identify with, and find their greatest support in, nonacademic organizations and pressures. An additional reason for the representational vacuum in higher education relates to the organizational dynamics of the AAUP.

In electing faculty members to serve on the AAUP's Executive

Council, its major governing body, there is a natural tendency to nominate and to vote for the better known professors at the most prestigious institutions. Unfortunately, employment relations for leading professors at prestigious institutions may have little in common with employment relations in other institutions, especially state college systems and struggling private institutions. The faculty at the prestigious institutions are employees, but their income levels and perquisites are so high that collective negotiations seem irrelevant, even dangerous to them. On the other hand, the faculty at state college systems are in a much different situation. The individual faculty members tend to lack bargaining power and urgently need to utilize their collective strength to improve their conditions of employment. Unfortunately, the AAUP's national leaders are more apt to be the leading beneficiaries of the status quo than the apostles of change. Eventually, pressures from the rank and file will make themselves felt, especially as the increasing size of the professoriate forces it to seek more effective ways to exert collective pressure upon the employing institutions.

This pressure will inevitably lead to an upsurge of collective negotiations in higher education. Such negotiations are advocated most vigorously by the AFT; however, professors typically do not desire identification with public school teachers or with organized labor. The present interest in collective negotiations in higher education, despite its unattractive auspices, suggests that a breakthrough may be near. One good agreement, negotiated at a moderately prestigious institution, could well set off a chain reaction that will affect a number of institutions in the near future.

In a 1967 vote at 18 state colleges in California, the combined faculties narrowly rejected a proposal for an exclusive bargaining agent (by 274 votes out of 5,756). Indeed, had eligibility to vote been determined on more rational grounds (administrators were permitted to vote on many campuses), it is quite possible that the proposal would have carried. As it was, the proposal carried in four of the six largest institutions in the state college system.

These changes will inevitably result in organizational realignments and reorientations. At present, the organizational situation in higher education is extremely fluid. A crucial issue is whether the AAUP will modify its opposition to collective negotiations before rival organizations capitalize on such opposition on a large scale. The AFT, however, is not the main national threat to the AAUP. The AFT has too many handicaps in the organizational sweepstakes, and it may merge with the NEA within the next few years. The near future will provide the NEA with its greatest opportunities in higher education; much depends on the NEA's reactions to these opportunities.

In competing with the AAUP, the NEA has some important advantages as well as disadvantages. Most faculty members are in state-supported institutions, hence representation at the state level is essential. Nevertheless, the AAUP has never been organized effectively at the state level; there is not a single full-time leader of the AAUP at the state level. By contrast, the state associations of the NEA are well organized and could use such organization very effectively in a contest for professorial membership.

More importantly, the NEA has learned some invaluable lessons regarding faculty representation in the past few years. In the early 1960's, the NEA was adamantly opposed to collective negotiations through an exclusive representative. Today, the Association provides a broad spectrum of negotiating services for its state and local affiliates. The NEA has been through all of the arguments against collective negotiations—the Association advocated them to the point of disaster. It therefore has no illusions about the rhetoric of the current debate in higher education. Also, both NEA and AFT leaders have had invaluable experience in representation elections. They are far better equipped to conduct such elections than either the weak local chapters of the AAUP or its somnolescent national office.

The major handicap confronting the NEA would be the greater prestige of the AAUP in higher education. This handicap is substantial but not insuperable, provided the NEA were to make an all-out (and sophisticated) effort to organize professors. The Association may be too preoccupied with other problems to launch such an effort. If it is not, and if it does not delay until more realistic leadership emerges in the AAUP, it could become the majority organization in higher education in the United States. After all, less than one-third of all the professional personnel in higher education are AAUP members now. This reflects something less than smashing success in organizing professors.

Recent representation proceedings at the City University of New York City are equally significant. The City University includes over 10,000 faculty members on 17 constituent campuses, including the city's highly regarded city colleges. After protracted hearings, the New York State Public Employment Relations Board divided the faculty into two separate bargaining units. One unit consisted of faculty in tenured positions or positions leading to tenure; the other unit consisted of faculty holding part-time or other positions not leading to tenure status. The organizations seeking representation rights were the United Federation of College Teachers, a higher education affiliate of the AFT, and the Legislative Conference, a faculty organization not affiliated with any state or national faculty organization.

In the first election, the UFCT won bargaining rights for 6,060 nontenured faculty. The vote was 1,634 for the UFCT, 731 for the Legislative Conference, and 350 for no bargaining agent. The result in the tenured unit was inconclusive. With 5,647 eligible to vote, the Legislative Conference received 2,095 votes, the UFCT 1,680 votes, and no bargaining agent 656 votes. Subsequently, the Legislative Conference won the runoff election by a vote of 2,067 to 1,774. It appears, therefore, that the UFCT would have won bargaining rights for the entire faculty had there been only one bargaining unit. The low vote for no representation and the absence of an AAUP affiliate from the ballot are other noteworthy aspects of this election.

Recent developments in New Jersey are especially significant. In 1968, the New Jersey legislature enacted legislation providing bargaining rights for state and local public employees. In vetoing the bill, New Jersey's Governor Richard J. Hughes stated, "I have been asked by administrators and by organizations representing college professors to exclude faculty members from the coverage of this act so that the evolving pattern of college senates, in which elected representatives of faculties participate on an equal basis with college administrators in developing policy, not be impeded. In view of this apparent unanimity, I am recommending such an amendment." Nevertheless, the legislature overrode the governor's veto by substantial margins, so that professors in public institutions of higher education in New Jersey now have bargaining rights. In May, 1969, the New Jersey Education Association, which conducted a vigorous campaign to achieve bargaining rights for its local affiliates in the New Jersey public colleges, was designated as the bargaining agent by almost 80 percent of the total faculty in these institutions. Developments such as these indicate that we are on the verge of widespread changes in faculty representation systems.

In fact, the organizational situation in higher education today bears a striking similarity to an earlier situation in education below the college level. In 1961, the AFT was urging collective bargaining for public school teachers. The NEA and its affiliates, which enrolled most of the country's teachers, opposed it. The NEA's reasons were identical to those urged now by the AAUP. Collective negotiations was appropriate only in the industrial sector. Teachers dealt with persons and ideas, not inanimate objects. Since public education is not carried on for profit, and there are no profits to be divided, there is nothing to negotiate about. Collective negotiations is inconsistent with professional status. The relationships between teachers and administrators would be impaired by the advent of collective negotiations, which would replace a collegial and cooperative relationship with an adversary one. Strikes or the threat of strikes are an essential characteristic of collective negotiations; since strikes by professors (at least in public institutions) would be illegal, collective negotiations would be futile.

The NEA barely averted organizational catastrophe by its belief in these pronouncements and anathemas. When the need for a more effective representation system at the local level could no longer be avoided, except at the risk of losing hundreds of thousands of teachers to the AFT, the NEA embraced collective negotiations, albeit under its own label and with never a word to indicate that its previous opposition was misplaced. Today, persons not publicly committed to collective negotiations cannot realistically aspire to a top leadership position in the NEA; a few years ago, open support for negotiations would have destroyed a person's chances for Association leadership.

All of this experience, as well as the history of employment relations in the private and other public sectors, seems completely lost on the AAUP. Its leadership does not appear to take seriously the possibility that AAUP objections to collective negotiations may turn out to have as little merit as NEA objections to it in 1961. This view does not require any uncritical view of collective negotiations or insensitivity to real differences between higher education and other fields.

Collective negotiations, culminating in a contractual agreement which is binding on the parties to it, has certain advantages to employee groups. The very fact that such negotiations are virtually always an employee initiative certainly strengthens the presumption that there are some advantages to collective negotiations. Granted, collective negotiations also involves disadvantages which may outweigh the advantages. In that case, however, the critics should explicate these disadvantages. They should be able to identify the specific conditions in higher education which render negotiation inappropriate there; generalized appeals to the notion that "higher education is different" are not enough.

Most assuredly, professors do differ from steelworkers, airline pilots, doctors, lawyers, public school teachers, and sanitation workers, to mention just a few groups which negotiate collectively. But it could also be said of any one of these groups that they differ in some important respects from others which negotiate collectively. If opposition is to rise above the cliché level, it must focus upon specific differences which are relevant to the appropriateness of collective negotiations.

It is precisely at this point that the AAUP's opposition to collective negotiations through an exclusive representative falls short. For instance, to oppose collective negotiations on the ground that it would create an adversary process where none exists is a rather pitiful argument at this stage—one expects that faculty leaders would by now understand the distinction between recognizing a conflict of interest and creating one. Similarly, other AAUP policy statements do not respond to the real issues; the Association's arguments ignore rather than respond to the basic issues in representation systems. As much as anything, its failure to confront the issues indicates that the AAUP will experience severe strains in the immediate future.

One of the most striking illustrations of the AAUP's failure to understand the issues is its policy toward legislation authorizing collective negotiations in institutions of higher education. The AAUP opposes "legislation imposing upon faculty members in higher education the principle of exclusive representation derived from models of industrial collective bargaining." As a practical matter, no one has proposed legislation that would "impose" collective bargaining on a faculty; the latter need only vote for no representative to avoid this outcome. But to oppose legislation that would authorize faculties to decide for themselves whether they want to bargain collectively is another matter.

It is doubtful whether the vast majority of AAUP members realize fully what the AAUP is doing, both in its stated policies and in the activities of its staff associates. In effect, the AAUP supports any kind of representation system except collective bargaining as long as it is chosen by the faculty; the collective bargaining alternative is so bad, however, that faculties must not be permitted to choose it.

I do not believe that the AAUP can or should survive if it adheres to this policy for very long. The NEA learned through bitter experience that it could not actively oppose the right of teachers to negotiate collectively while simultaneously urging them to vote for NEA affiliates in representation elections to choose an exclusive representative. It will be interesting to see how long it takes the AAUP to learn the same lesson.

DISCUSSION OF MR. LIEBERMAN'S PAPER

MR. BLUM: I was very much impressed with Mr. Lieberman's severe and, I think, generally justified attack upon the senates of most universities in that they do not represent professors as employees. Yet as I read his paper, and then the one by Professor Oberer, I was struck by the either-or approach of both.

Let me start by disagreeing with Mr. Lieberman's comparison of the faculty senate with the employee councils prior to the Wagner Act. I think his comparisons are just, but I would like to offer a different comparison of the faculty senates. It may be a little more relevant to our own experiences and my own hopes for developments on university campuses.

I would like to compare the senate with the works councils in many European countries. Works councils exist in the European countries at the same time that many unions exist. Their function, at least theoretically, is to discuss various problems with the employers. (The employers belong and they meet together with employees.) In addition, many of these saw employers negotiate with a union. Sometimes the union has representation on the council. Sometimes it has representation only because the workers vote for individual union members. The union continues to represent the workers as employees.

It strikes me that if we use this analogy in looking at the role of the senates and of other organizations on a university level we have some basis for hope about the senate. If one compares a senate to a union, obviously the senate is a failure; frequently, I admit, it is a failure on its own ground. If one compares a departmental committee with a grievance committee, one is being foolish; it doesn't solve that problem. And on those grounds I am in complete agreement with Mr. Lieberman.

But to accept the union or collective bargaining to represent college professors on all grounds is, I also think, a mistake. A faculty committee to choose a president may, I grant, be wrong in terms of accountability, but a president of a university is not the president of General Motors. He's a president of a university and as such he is supposed to be the leading educator at that university. He doesn't only make decisions concerning my wages and hours and working conditions as a professor. He also makes decisions concerning educational policy, and I, unlike most tool and die makers, am concerned with the educational policies of my employer. If I'm the tool and die maker at Henry Ford's I don't really care what Henry Ford's philosophy of management is. But as an educator, I am concerned with the overall educational philosophy and therefore want a voice in who he is.

There are many matters on which I would like to be able to confront the administration as an employee, and I think *there* is the role for a collective bargainer. But there are other things concerning which I would like *not* to confront my administrators but rather I would prefer discussing the issues with them, and this is the role for the senate. In fact, I would like to define collective bargaining differently from Mr. Lieberman. My definition is a process by which management and employee representatives negotiate agreements which the respective parties will accept.

I believe that the respective parties in the university will not accept a union determining curriculum in negotiations with administrators. If there were a problem involving whether a speaker could speak on the campus, I would not leave it to the union to make a decision with the administrators. These are educational issues and to discuss these issues is the main role of the senates.

On the other hand, I think there is a role for an outside group to act for professors and employees. The fact that there isn't such an outside group is one of the reasons why faculties frequently are demanding that no administrator be present at the senate meetings, that no administrator participate in advisory committee meetings, and as a result there will be a decline in the dialogue between administrators and faculty at many of these senates. But if there were an outside group ready to fight for faculty on some of these issues I think it wouldn't matter if administrators were present at senate meetings.

I would argue, then, that in the university there should be a role for faculty senates in arguing professional matters and there should be the role for a collective bargaining agent to argue and fight for many of the rights which (as Mr. Lieberman has very justifiably said) faculty do not have and, what is even worse, do not even recognize that they don't have.

I don't think university unions will be enough for the faculty professor. We should use both the union and the senate.

MR. HOROWITZ: You define those two entities, Mr. Blum, in nice neat little packages. After Mr. Hayward pulls out his list of 60 demands I wonder if they'll fall into such neat categories. How do you place them into such neat categories? It's a beautiful model, but how do you do this?

MR. BLUM: Of course, there are not neat packages. You fight about it as you've fought historically in America in industrial relations about what, for example, are management prerogatives. Why should there be a neat package? This is why you're on one side of the bargaining table and he'll be on the other. If you think you're right you fight and don't give in, and if the faculty think they're right on what should be bargained they'll fight. I don't see any problem. The whole process is a part of learning. The process of collective bargaining, as I tried to suggest in the definition, is a process of communicating also. There is no neat package and I didn't mean to imply there was. I just suggest it as a goal.

MR. HOROWITZ: Can you really break up these issues at all? That's really what I'm suggesting. You're saying that it can be hammered out. If you're talking about curriculum, for example, there is a part of curriculum which affects the legitimate interests of an outside agency fighting hard for certain curriculum conditions, and yet a lot of professors don't want to have an outside agent dabbling in curriculum questions. There is a very gray area by definition. I don't know if it can be hammered out.

MR. BLUM: What I'm suggesting is that in some places one area is appropriate for negotiations and in other places it will be another area.

MR. SUMBERG: I'm really sorry, Mr. Lieberman, that you turned off against the AAUP some years ago and in doing so distorted your whole intellectual objectivity towards higher education. That's a mouthful, but I hope you will appreciate it in the context of a paper which I read hoping that I would see at least some objectivity in the area of collective bargaining. And I said this morning that I think what is needed now in the field of collective bargaining is some creative thinking, some imaginative thinking, and not the sort of thing in which you engage.

You have directed a charge toward me personally and I would not want to see a paper published which included that charge unless you believe it and you have some evidence for it. You say: "Thus I have heard AAUP staff members argue before public bodies that the Rhode Island Board of Trustees of State Colleges had no right to conduct a representation election among the faculty because there was no specific statutory authority for such action. Yet these staff members made it clear that the AAUP would not support legislation authorizing faculties to negotiate collectively even if every faculty member wished to do so."

You know that I was in Rhode Island in support of our chapter at Rhode Island College at the time the election was held in your college. You and I both attended the hearing on February 6. It was not a hearing before the Rhode Island Board of Trustees of State Colleges. It was a hearing before the Rhode Island State Labor Relations Board. You know that I did not say at that time that there was "no right to conduct a representation election among the faculty because there was no specific statutory authority for such action." There was statutory action. The Michaelson Law had long since been passed in Rhode Island, and our position in regard to that in behalf of our chapter was this: We were asking on the basis of a legal question that had been raised by the Committee of Concerned Faculty and the Board of Trustees. The question was one of the legal right or the autonomy of the college, and the question was to be adjudicated by the State Labor Relations Board.

I certainly am very disturbed over a misrepresentation on the part of a person such as you in a situation such as that, and I hope that you will correct it.

In the overall, I would say there are many places in which you carry on your diatribe against the AAUP. You enjoy doing it and have enjoyed it for years. I wouldn't want to interfere with that enjoyment on your part, except I think when it comes to the point of actual misrepresentation.

You do the same thing at another point. You say: "The AAUP opposes 'legislation imposing upon faculty members in higher education the principle of exclusive representation. . . .'" As a practical matter, no one has proposed legislation that would impose collective bargaining on a faculty member. What you have failed to recognize is that here is our concern over the issue of exclusivity and not over the creation of legislation. We have appeared before a number of governmental agencies. Most recently I appeared before the Governor's Task Force on Public Employee Labor Relations in Maryland in support of legislation and asking for recognition of certain types of provisions in that legislation which would protect the faculties of the state colleges and the University of Maryland. This has been our position throughout the United States. This is our reason for discussions with George Taylor and the Taylor Committee over the Taylor Law in New York State, where there is a good deal of concern over the nature of that law.

On the whole, I personally have a deep concern over the position which you express here, but it is certainly your right to do so. You don't like faculty senates. You find them anathema, and in so doing you begin to compare them with the industrial models; and then where they don't quite fit you begin to turn them into something a little different.

Your concern over the AAUP is, I think, most noteworthy, and I shall certainly take back to my colleagues in the office your concern as to what the policies should be.

But let me say this: Having just reviewed all the collective bargaining agreements that are now in existence in higher education, I am not impressed with anything that has been done along this line, particularly in those institutions that you're talking about. Where we have collective bargaining agreements I think the truth of the matter is that in most cases up to this point they have done nothing more than institutionalize the powerlessness of the faculty or permanentize, if you like, their storied condition; and putting it all down in contract form is not going to resolve their problems. They have substantial problems which need considerable concern on the part of many groups, and having put it on paper hasn't cleared the confusion by any means. Indeed, it may very well at times have added to the confusion.

I'll be glad to continue at a later point.

CHAIRMAN GERSHENFELD: Mr. Lieberman has graciously consented to comment on your remarks.

MR. LIEBERMAN: It's very easy to get diverted from the key issues here. Is it or is it not the case that faculty senates lack resources of their own? Wouldn't any such lack be a weakness of a senate? Forget the analogy with private employment and ask yourself the question: Is that a weakness or isn't it?

I'm not saying that the presence or absence of independent resources is the only thing to be considered. My point is that the issues have to be examined in context. To illustrate further, don't faculty senates preclude representation by full-time faculty representatives? And if that's the case, isn't it a weakness of the senates? References to industrial models do not resolve the specific issues relating to faculty senates.

Another issue: If a department chairman makes poor personnel recommendations, that fact is taken into account in evaluating his performance as a chairman. If you're going to have the faculty make these recommendations and the faculty does a poor job, you ought to be able to remove the faculty that does this. Otherwise, there's no accountability for these decisions.

MR. SUMBERG: Why do you say it's always a poor choice?

MR. LIEBERMAN: I don't, but there must be accountability for faculty who exercise these recommending functions. I can't accept a system where the faculty makes decisions that are normally made by the employer and then escapes accountability for them. I have never seen a faculty recommendation for promotion or tenure that said to the average faculty member who sat in on a selection committee: "Over the past five years you've recommended X, Y, and Z for positions and they've turned out to be dogs, so we're not going to give you a promotion."

Internal mechanisms eliminate responsibility and accountability, and unless faculty members focus on these specific aspects of faculty senates and forget all this talk about analyses—

MR. SUMBERG: You made them.

MR. LIEBERMAN: Only as a way of getting into the topic. The crucial question is whether there are factors in higher education that remedy the weaknesses of employee councils. They may be worthless in private employment and work out in the university setting. However, in the last analysis, we can't avoid analyzing how a council works out in higher education. If it's all right for faculty senates not to have funds of their own, then that particular weakness of employee councils elsewhere doesn't apply in higher education; we would have overcome one objection to them. But unless we can show why a specific objection to employee councils does not apply to faculty senates, then the objections will remain.

MR. ROSENTHAL: Funds to do what? What do you want them to have the money for?

MR. LIEBERMAN: You want them to publicize their program, to put pressure on the employer, to gain recruits.

MR. ROSENTHAL: What if they can do all this without funds?

A PARTICIPANT: They can't.

MR. LIEBERMAN: If they could, fine; we would have removed that objection.

MR. SUMBERG: Mr. Lieberman, would it be all right with you if a collective bargaining agreement said, "This exclusive bargaining agent shall receive $100,000 to carry on its activity"?

MR. LIEBERMAN: From management?

MR. SUMBERG: From the company.

MR. LIEBERMAN: For the company to do so would be illegal.

MR. SUMBERG: It would not be illegal. In a state without unfair labor practice laws it couldn't be illegal. Why would it be illegal?

MR. LIEBERMAN: Then I would consider it dangerous from the standpoint of public policy.

MR. SUMBERG: Policy is one thing.

MR. LIEBERMAN: To have an employee organization, public or private, be dependent upon managerial resources and still be an effective organization would be highly unlikely. The reason is that the support would disappear in a crisis. When the chips are down, faculty senates are helpless because they're dependent upon the employer.

MR. BLUM: The real hang-up in dealing with your paper, Mr. Lieberman, and the whole problem of teaching unionization in general, I guess, is that really there are three separate phenomena at work here. One is the teacher as a professional; another is the teacher as an employee; and another the teacher as a citizen.

In 1968, there was a dispute going on in New York which was a mixture of all these things. It was not simply a strike for a raise of 20 cents an hour. The teacher by the very fact of being in a business of extending the social values of our society is not merely an economic animal.

It's in trying to look at how professors can work in these three areas that I think we should develop new formats. I'm not sure what they should be, and I think we have to work at them. This is why I suggested this other work council model—not because I think it's the answer, but I feel there can be a combination of systems which would reconcile the dynamics of all these three phenomena.

MR. OBERER: Let me observe first that I think you get no more out of a premise than you put into it, and if your premise is one of inherent conflict between the administration and the faculty you're the captive of that premise. I don't feel that way about my situation. Indeed I can't even tell you who my employer is. It's certainly not my dean. It's certainly not President Perkins of Cornell University. It's not the Board of Trustees. I don't know who it is and I don't think any of them know who it is. It's a unique kind of relationship.

On the presidential and faculty selection front Mr. Lieberman's assumption seems to be that poor selections will be made or at least that faculty selection committees are extremely fallible. My concern is that good selections be made, and if the faculty has something to contribute on this front (it has knowledge and it has contacts), it ought to contribute to the hilt because it makes one hell of a lot of difference to me who is president of Cornell University or who is dean of the Cornell Law School or indeed the School of Labor and Industrial Relations.

Now, on the accountability of a faculty selection committee front, I've been on such committees. Indeed I've been chairman of our faculty selection committee and I'm accountable to my faculty. When my committee comes in with a recommendation, the rest of the faculty puts us on the stand. They go out and read the stuff that the person we recommend has written. They double check with their friends and contacts with regard to classroom performance and general horsepower.

Finally, on the dollars front, the contribution of funds in private enterprise collective bargaining agreements frequently entails re-leased time for union functionaries, time spent in processing griev-ances, for example, rather than in the production process for the em-ployer; and indeed over a period of time it might add up to a lot of money. A hundred thousand dollars was mentioned here. I don't know how much G.M. pays the UAW a year, in effect, for this released time of UAW committeemen, stewards, and what-have-you who aren't working—at least not in the usual sense—but are paid their regular wages nonetheless. It's a lot of money.

Finally, I have a question for you: Where will the money come from if you have a collective bargaining representative for the faculty? The faculty is going to have to dig it out of its own pocket, is it not? And indeed if a faculty senate is in such a jam as you suggest it typically is, let them dig it out of their own pockets if they need money to publicize their position. The dues money of the union is what pays for union representation, and the union isn't going to linger long over a situation which is a losing one for it. It may subsidize an organizing or representation operation at Campus A out of dues col-lected at other campuses, or out of dues collected in other lines of work. It may do this for a while, as the Industrial Union Depart-ment of the AFL-CIO did under Reuther in support of the AFT, which is one of the reasons the AFT got off the ground the way it did. A lot of money was put into that operation, the point being that the unions were having a hard time organizing white-collar workers and still are; they were losing blue-collar workers and they saw the handwriting on the wall.

I was executive director of the Public Review Board of the United Auto Workers for a two-year period. The union leaders were very much afraid of that handwriting on the wall. They were losing members and they had to break through somewhere. They saw in teachers a prestige group which might enable them to make the breakthrough into the white-collar area.

In any event, the faculty can ante up out of their pockets, whatever the scheme of representation is.

MR. LIEBERMAN: My paper recognized that faculty members do have more time than the average employee in private employment and that some institutions do provide released time that could be counted as equivalent to the time off for the shop steward in private employment.

Your comment about your own accountability to the faculty for your service on a selection committee raises some doubts. How are you accountable to them? What can they do *to* you?

MR. OBERER: What they can do to me is think less of me and that's a hell of a lot.

MR. LIEBERMAN: That's not accountability.

MR. OBERER: That's the ultimate accountability in my scheme of things.

MR. LIEBERMAN: Maybe you don't care whether they think less of you. Professorial approval is a different thing than taking the quality of your recommendations as a factor in personnel recommendations concerning you. To equate what some group thinks of you as equivalent to the latter kind of accountability is confusing the issue.

MR. OBERER: Let me add a point here in response to that comment. I want the Cornell Law School to be the best damn law school in the country if possible, and my colleagues have the same aspiration. My dean has the same aspiration. President Perkins and the Board of Trustees have the same aspiration. In this we're all working together. That's why I say your premise of conflict is just utterly inapplicable in my case. I don't mean to say there aren't tensions, human tensions; my wife and I have those, but I don't need a collective bargaining arrangement with her.

MR. LIEBERMAN: But just because you want it to be the best law school doesn't mean that the recommendations you make are good ones. You can't say that because we all want this to be good, we're exempt from accountability on the quality of our recommendations.

MR. OBERER: How else can we get the best law school we can get?

MR. LIEBERMAN: By making people accountable for the quality of their recommendations.

MR. HAYWARD: I agree almost 100 percent with Mr. Lieberman.

In New Jersey we are living side by side with the faculty senates. We see the senates as having one particular function and the Association as having another. We're not competing. We're not trying to wipe them out. We're working with them. We have our job to do and they have theirs. We do not want to be encumbered with their responsibilities.

When our public employee negotiations law was passed the Governor tried to veto it, and he tried particularly to veto out the college faculties. He said, "I've noted the extreme importance of having employee confidence in whatever procedure is set down for redress of their grievances. The other side of that same coin is that where a group of employees and their employers desire to pursue non-adversary procedures for the solution of grievances they should be permitted to do so.

"I have been asked by college administrators and by organizations representing college professors to exclude faculty members from the coverage of this act, so that the evolving pattern of college senates, in which elected representatives of faculties participate on an equal basis with college administrators in developing policy, not be impeded."

The Governor received his advice from AAUP representatives in the state of New Jersey, and I know this to be fact.

In the September, 1968, *AAUP Bulletin,* in an article entitled "The California State College's Adoption of a Statewide Grievance Procedure," it is pointed out that "in 1961 Chancellor Gallagher's procedures provided for submission of a grievance to successive levels of administrative authority. After seven years of negotiation by the academic senates of the California State Colleges a procedure was adopted on June 27, 1968. Final decisions under these procedures provide for either administrative or peer-group judgment."

I submit that could not work with us. During the past six months I have had 11 grievance appeals from faculty through the New Jersey Education Association, and in each one of these cases it was either administrative decision or peer-group judgment which was responsible for the specific grievance.

It will take an external organization—outside of the internal faculty organization controlled by the administration. It will take an organization with money, with resources. If we need mediators, negotiators, and paid employees to do this job, it will cost possibly hundreds of thousands of dollars in New Jersey alone over the next two or three years, or maybe even the next year. The only organizations that can do this are organizations that have the staff, that have the money, that have the will, that have the respect and support of the faculty.

MR. HICKMAN: As long as we're choosing up sides and in order to maintain some semblance of equilibrium, I would like to note that I agree almost 100 percent with Mr. Oberer.

It seems to me that there are two pervasive assumptions or premises that run through Mr. Lieberman's paper. One Mr. Oberer has noted, namely, the assumption that there is a chronic, endemic, inescapable conflict situation in higher education. The second assumption is a pervasive analogy between industrial and academic life, an analogy that I grant may have historically been understated and underplayed. It seems to me in this paper it is overstated and overplayed.

This pervasive assumption is relevant because it leads directly to some specific positions that are at least arguable. Let me take one of these positions and indicate how this underlying assumption has directed the conclusion. Mr. Lieberman opposes allowing faculty to be involved in the selection of administrative officials and apparently even in the appointment of their own colleagues. His opposition to this involvement is apparently a direct result of drawing an industrial analogy. I would argue that his position on this issue also rests upon three specific premises, each of which I think is wrong.

. First, this position rests on the premise that the faculty member is exclusively an employee. That he is an employee I would not argue for a moment, but he is also a professional. Whatever the difficulties of defining "professional" may be, there is a reality here. When we use the term "colleague" we are also dealing with a reality. I would argue that in his role as a faculty member the faculty member is dealing with deans, provosts, and presidents not only in their role as employers but in their role as academic colleagues, in their role as fellow professionals. This is evidenced by the fact that in most instances I know about administrative officials have to have at least minimal academic credentials as well as administrative qualifications. If part of the faculty-administrative relationship is professional and scholarly, the faculty member certainly has a legitimate stake in the quality of the men with whom he must work.

A second premise that I think underlies this position is an adversary relationship and the existence of a collective bargaining contract. It is argued that it scarcely makes sense for you to be allowed as an employee to pick the representative of the employer with whom you must bargain. This assumes that a collective bargaining context exists (which it may or may not). Even if a collective bargaining situation does exist, and there is a contractual arrangement, faculty members must still deal with administrative officers over a wide range, an almost infinitely wide range, of issues, many of which are not conventionally found within any collective bargaining agreement that I know about. If only in terms of the kinds of issues that are not resolved in agreements, again the faculty member has a stake in the quality of the man that he must deal with outside the contract as well as inside.

The third premise underlying this position is that in practice faculty members will tend to choose as administrators their cronies or potential cronies. I would argue that presidential experience with appointing Supreme Court justices suggests that it is difficult to be sure who will turn out to be a crony and who will not. But, more important, a faculty of any quality will find its own long-run self-interest better served by choosing a good man than by choosing a crony. In my experience you usually get a better man with active faculty involvement in administrative appointment that you get without it.

MR. WEINBERG: I would like to continue with some of the points raised by Mr. Hickman and Mr. Oberer. It is always a pleasure to hear Mike Lieberman present a paper. The room gets filled with debris as he demolishes some of our cherished shibboleths. Missing from his paper was a comparison of the faculty member as a professional with other professionals such as engineers, doctors, and lawyers. The professor does not fit easily into the niche we may use for professionals when we build models based on the private industrial world.

MR. LIEBERMAN: We have to be careful about confusing the situation of the fee-taking professional with that of the professional who is employed on salary. The reason why physicians don't typically bargain is that they don't have a common employer, so there is never any reason for them to negotiate collectively. When their situation is comparable to that of the professors, they do negotiate collectively. For example, doctors in some Canadian provinces are paid fees set by the provincial government. In this situation doctors must negotiate collectively what fees they will be paid, and they use the same tactics that other salaried groups use.

The problem here is to make sure that, in whatever analysis we make of professors and other groups, we take into account the real differences in their employment situations.

I think, for example, that professors *as a group* exercise relatively little control over entry into teaching. I don't want to open that up now, necessarily, but the point here is that we do not exercise the same controls over entry that some of the professions do. I think we could better advance ourselves economically by exercising those controls, because we would then have shifted the balance of power in negotiations. We almost wouldn't need collective negotiations if we could exercise tighter control at the points of entry.

MR. HICKMAN: Isn't control of the doctorate that kind of control?

MR. LIEBERMAN: No, because that control is largely control on an institution-by-institution basis. Some of the institutions with doctoral programs have practically no standards whatever.

MR. SUMBERG: You want licensing of teachers?

MR. LIEBERMAN: I haven't said I want licensing of teachers.

MR. SUMBERG: Certification of college teachers?

MR. LIEBERMAN: No, I don't think so. I haven't advocated that at all.

MR. SUMBERG: What do you want as a means of control?

MR. LIEBERMAN: In analyzing the situation of professors and other professionals, I was trying to make two points. First, where professionals as a group are on salary, they bargain. To say we don't bargain as professionals is to overlook the fact that the reason other professionals do not bargain is that they don't have a common employer. Such reasoning justifies not bargaining for a reason that is not applicable to the professional situation.

The other point is that professional groups typically exercise more control at the point of entry than professors do, and this strengthens their position more. As for whether college teachers *should* be licensed, I took no position on that. I think I'd probably be against it.

MR. McHUGH: In publicly supported education, when we talk in terms of conflict and adversary relationships we have to make a distinction between conflicts within the academic community and conflicts arising from its relationship with other functionaries. Relationships between the academic community and the executive branch of state or local governments can well give rise to conflict situations. That leads to my second point.

I have to agree with what Mr. Oberer says about "accountability" to his colleagues. As a lawyer and as a professional person, I fully sympathize with what he's talking about. But then I must ask a question of the faculty member: Does he feel similar "accountability" to a local or state official where he is in an institution supported by public funds? Put differently, does the faculty feel a collective accountability to the public?

The quest for excellence in publicly supported institutions may raise conflict situations between a faculty and public officials involved in the availability and allocation of resources for academic programs, including resources with which to hire faculty.

The third point I'd like to raise specifically with Mr. Blum is: How do you make the distinction between the economic interests and the academic interests of faculty members, if there is indeed a difference? Is faculty-student ratio as an issue an economic interest or an academic interest or a combination of both?

When you get down to sitting at the bargaining table, is it feasible to have two employee organizations (in the general sense of the term) —one there to negotiate economic interests and another (not at the bargaining table, but figuratively in the academic community) to be concerned with academic interests?

MR. BLUM: The problems that you have raised don't disturb me very much because I'm at the professor end. Therefore, if I create pressures on you from the union bargaining position or from the senate, that's your problem. If I don't like your decision I may switch my allegiances.

MR. McHUGH: Let's assume you're the AFT and you have certain interests and you want to advance certain positions relative to the faculty-student ratio. The faculty senate, on the other hand, considers this issue an academic matter and not the subject of negotiation. Is there such an adversary relationship between your two organizations as to foster instability in the relationship? Is it more practical (aside from "management" tactics) to have only one organization advance the faculties' collective interest?

MR. BLUM: I think it would depend on the institutions we're talking about. It's very interesting to note that those faculty members here who have been focusing on faculty senates teach at universities where the faculty has tremendous power—for example, at Cornell.

This is why I can't generalize. If I were teaching at a community college in New York where I once taught, I would want everything spelled out in a contract—everything. We had to have time-cards at that place at one time. So I really can't generalize concerning this problem. Engineers have unionized at times and at other times have used sounding boards—which is a faculty senate kind of thing. It really depends upon the situation in a given setup.

In short, I don't really disagree with Mr. Lieberman. I think he chose bad examples, for example, this issue of selecting a chairman. This is the wrong issue on which to fight for collective bargaining rights. There are enough other issues which justify collective bargaining without focusing, I think, on those even at Cornell, Southern Illinois, or Michigan State.

MR. LIEBERMAN: My reference to selecting the chairman was not directly an argument for collective negotiations. It was a criticism of faculty senates and the other ways in which faculties make employer decisions.

There are arguments that if faculties negotiate, they inject a conflict of interest where none existed before. There is a long history to this argument. It arose, as I am sure everyone here knows, in private employment. We've heard it in public education and we've heard it in a lot of other places.

Mr. Hickman, would it be in your interest to get $25,000 more than you now get?

MR. HICKMAN: I suppose.

MR. LIEBERMAN: You're not sure?

MR. HICKMAN: I don't think it would be the overriding consideration.

MR. LIEBERMAN: I'm not asking you that. Would it be in your interest to have $25,000 more a year than you now get?

MR. HICKMAN: I suppose.

MR. LIEBERMAN: Would it be in your institution's interest?

MR. SUMBERG: It certainly would.

MR. LIEBERMAN: I'd like to hear Professor Hickman's answer.

MR. HICKMAN: I don't get the gist of your intention.

MR. LIEBERMAN: I just wanted to illustrate the point that your interests and those of your institution don't always coincide. There is a difference between recognizing a conflict of interest and creating it. It is really surprising that there are people here who still take seriously the notion that there is no conflict of interest between professors and their employers.

There are many issues which should not be negotiated, but you don't invalidate the case for negotiation by choosing issues which are not negotiable, even in the outlook of those who support negotiations.

As a matter of fact, I have vigorously and publicly criticized the notion that "everything is negotiable." There are many very important matters that shouldn't be resolved through the negotiation process. For example, we shouldn't negotiate certain aspects of curriculum or program. This doesn't invalidate the case for negotiating other issues, such as terms and conditions of employment.

To take the position that there is no conflict of interest between professors as employees and their employing institutions—well, I think I'll go back and ask mine for $10,000 more to see if we have nothing but common interests.

MR. HICKMAN: I think Mr. Lieberman is dichotomizing again. My reaction was against any schema that seems to assume total, unremitting, pervasive conflict of interest. It is not my position that there is never conflict of interest; I couldn't have been in this game 30 years and believe that. But if I had to choose between models based upon lack of conflict of interest or upon total conflict, I think I would opt for the lack of conflict of interest. Realistically, there are conflicts of interest, but I wouldn't build a system of government on the assumption that these are perennial.

MR. LIEBERMAN: They're perennial, but they're not pervasive.

MR. HICKMAN: That is a better word.

MR. LIEBERMAN: But on those items where they do exist I think we ought to have a representational system that is appropriate.

MR. HICKMAN: Yes, but then we get into the argument as to what the best form should be.

CHAIRMAN GERSHENFELD: Before you proceed I think it's worth observing that Mr. McHugh has done us a valuable service. It seems to me that most of the remarks—or polemics, if you will—have been offered from a particular vantage point, emphasizing either professionalism or employee relations and the consequent needs encompassed by the function. The service that I think Mr. McHugh has done for us is to point out that there are many issues—such as class size—that become at once professional and economic issues. This brings the problem to a head, I think, for all of us.

MR. DUPERRE: I think it's probably working out well that we often have to wait before we get to make our comments. I won't have to take sides now, as I was going to do a moment ago. I will take the occasion, though, to endorse Mr. Oberer, who very ably presented some of the points I proposed to make; let me take over from there.

As you pointed out, Mr. McHugh has put his finger on something significant, and perhaps Mr. Blum has provided an escape hatch for all of us with his advocacy of a pluralistic or at least a dualistic system.

One of the beliefs that I hold dear, for instance, is academic freedom; I should not like to see this become negotiable. I think Mr.

Lieberman said, pretty much in these words: "Why shouldn't academic freedom be negotiable?"

Is this correct?

MR. LIEBERMAN: Absolutely.

MR. DUPERRE: I should not like to see this principle involved in an antagonistic relationship, so that each year one wonders, "Are we going to have tenure this year or not?" As somebody mentioned, maybe 10 years from now we will have a labor surplus and a board is going to be able to say, "This year we don't think we'll put academic freedom or tenure into the contract. What are you fellows going to do about that?"

I think this is conceivable and I should not like to see it happen.

MR. LIEBERMAN: In that case what will your protection be?

MR. DUPERRE: My protection will be, I think, the dualistic system, where an organization such as either a faculty senate or an AAUP chapter will champion this right and keep it as an ideal, not an issue. I'll go along with you that perhaps we sometimes have employers and employees in higher education, but we don't, by God, have higher education as a business. I won't buy that.

Let me make one more point and I'll let you have your reaction.

MR. CRONIN: What do you mean by that last statement?

MR. DUPERRE: Mr. Lieberman said that anybody who argues that you don't have employees in higher education is all wet. I'm inclined to believe this. We are employees in a sense. There are some issues, such as salary, working conditions, etc., which are employer-employee issues. But there are some things which are not employer-employee issues, and we don't run a business. You should not use this model and say that a college or a university should be run like a business. There are, of course, many business ideas you should adopt—careful accounting procedures, etc.

MR. CRONIN: Are you saying there shouldn't be a budget or there shouldn't be wages or support services?

MR. DUPERRE: No. I put that escape hatch in there and said we should have accounting and payroll procedures—there are many things which we have to adopt from business. But we're not making cars.

MR. LIEBERMAN: You don't have to negotiate on every item. You don't have to negotiate on academic freedom if you don't want to.

I've negotiated for school boards where the teachers have proposed contractual clauses that provide that teachers shall have freedom in the classroom to teach as they see fit, subject only to questions of competency; and the boards have agreed to this. Academic freedom thus becomes a contractual obligation of the board. Under those circumstances, the teachers have more academic freedom than professors do where their board unilaterally adopts a policy protecting academic freedom.

Academic freedom is more secure where it is a contractual obligation of the institution than where it is merely a policy unilaterally adopted by a board.

MR. DUPERRE: Let me try to point up my objection to contractual agreements for all sorts of matters in higher education. When you set up a contractual agreement (again, this is based on personal observation and thinking, and you have already said at the beginning that this basis is subject to criticism), you tend to set the minimums, and these then become not only the minimums but the maximums.

For instance, I've noted in at least one or two schools that when you have a contractual agreement arrived at through an antagonistic relationship between a board and a union, constructive change is very often aborted. A faculty member's suggestion is met with, "You had better take that up with your grievance committee." It may very often be a constructive suggestion. An administrator may like it, but he'll say, "Why don't you take it up with your grievance committee?"

An administrator may come up with a bright idea and then hold himself back and say, "Wait just a minute. Why don't we just save this for the next bargaining session? We'll use it to sweeten the pot. We'll make a concession with it."

Unless we have at least the dualistic arrangement Mr. Blum has suggested, we're in trouble.

MR. HOLTZMAN: Three quick points. This gentleman got a good laugh with, "Shall we expect academic freedom this year or not?" But that starts from the assumption that you have it to start with. If you didn't have it, it would be an important question to know whether you were going to have it this year or not. I think we want to have our cake and eat it too. We want every year to be able to raise that question if we don't have it, and once we've got it we don't want it to be negotiable any more. If you can find a way to do that, I suppose a lot of us will look to you.

Second, on this other issue that has been ricocheting around for some time now, whether Mr. Lieberman's concern with collective negotiations doesn't rest on the notion of pervasive conflict of interest: It seems to me it doesn't rest on it any more than an interest, let's say, in world government rests on the supposition that war is the natural and continuing state of mankind (which it may be). Or take domestic relations: To say that the set of laws covering marriage relationships, including some specifications about divorce or about when you can or can't beat your wife, rests on the notion that the steady condition is beating your wife is, I think, a mistake. The fact that this is sometimes the case and can be the case is enough reason to be concerned with these things, it seems to me. But the principle of collective negotiations doesn't rest on the assumption that that conflict is the steady condition.

Finally, I have been puzzling ever since I read Mr. Lieberman's paper in preparation for this session over this business about faculty selection of administrators, because I've been one of those who for a long time thought this was a pretty good idea. I've been puzzling over why I thought it was a good idea and how I was going to take account of this attack, in effect. I don't really have a solution, except that I just want to say this: Faculty selection of administrators is indeed inappropriate as accountability arrangements stand now. I think Mr. Lieberman has made that pretty clear, and I may have to yield on that. But there is an alternative to his solution, namely, to make the administrators agents of the faculty rather than of the board; and the way to do this, it seems to me, is to make not only the administrator's selection but also his salary, retention, and removal a faculty prerogative.

That doesn't solve the problem, because it still leaves the board with the necessity of going out to get its agent, rather than the faculty being left trying to find an agent. There is nothing inherent in the notion that faculty would pick the administrators that makes it stupid, except the fact that once we've picked them then we lose the initiative here. The continuance in office becomes somebody else's right to decide, not ours.

MR. HOWE: As a chief administrative negotiator in a college that has collective bargaining, and as the chief executive officer of a college that has a viable faculty senate, and as a person who performs both those functions by virtue of a recommendation of the faculty that I hold my administrative office, I am not bothered by many of the things that concern people at this table. My concerns are on an entirely different plane.

As to my preferences, which have been quite extensively expressed here, I reserve those to the cocktail hour at home, where unfortunately I have to associate with a union member who is also in her spare time my wife.

I do, however, have a concern that I think is legitimate here. There is some confusion resulting, I think, from an apparent assumption that the difficulty in distinguishing between the province of the senate and the province of a bargaining agent rests upon the divergence in the constituency of the senate and the constituency of the bargaining agent. They are the same. The constituency of the faculty senate at my institution is total. The constituency of the bargaining agent at my institution is total.

There is one additional complicating element I would wish to put forth. Presumably, within their constituency—which has two natures and two interests—faculty can agree on their version of where things should be allocated. But may I point out that with a bargaining situation the administration has also to agree as to where they should be allocated, because we have, due to the bargaining situation, the unquestioned right to come to the bargaining table with negotiable items not defined. We can bring any item under the sun that we consider of significance to us. So in the final analysis the faculty will determine its own version of what should fall where, and questions will be resolved in conjunction with the administration's determination of how it feels regarding them.

CHAIRMAN GERSHENFELD: I'd be very much interested in hearing your comments, Mr. Howe, about the analog from the private sector. The thing that we've all observed is, of course, the expanding scope of collective bargaining through the years. Do you anticipate that the same phenomenon will occur with the collective bargaining representative at your institution, that it might grow to encompass issues not now within its ken but which could be presumably in this other area?

MR. HOWE: I know of no practical limits upon the negotiability of any items affecting the college. The determination of what is negotiable is itself negotiable.

MR. MOSKOW: My comment would have been more appropriate about half an hour ago, but I'll go on anyway because this is probably the only chance I'll get.

I read your paper very carefully, Mr. Lieberman, and tried to figure out where you went wrong. I think it's really a question of emphasis more than anything else. I personally think that collective negotiations or bargaining is going to grow, probably at the junior college level and among some other unfortunate institutions. There is no question that it will grow. I wouldn't hazard a guess as to how many institutions will be affected; but I'm sure there will be a large number of high quality institutions which will *not* have collective negotiation arrangements.

You and Mr. Oberer started out by saying very similar things: that faculty members are both employees and professional persons. Mr. Oberer goes off in one direction and emphasizes the professional side of it; you go off and emphasize the employee side of it, but you never mention anything at all about the professional side. The complete exclusion of this factor is an implicit assumption that it's so unimportant that it does not contradict anything you've said about the employee side. I think possibly that might be where you went wrong.

For example, you talk about conflict of interest. Certainly there is conflict of interest. Unless I've misunderstood the discussion, I think everyone here agrees that there are some possible potential conflicts of interest in a faculty member's relationship with the administration when he is employed by an institution of higher education. However, it is possible that this conflict of interest may not be important to him, maybe because of his own individual bargaining power or maybe because of his psychological makeup. It just may not be too important to him.

You say late in your paper: "An employee organization is needed to protect faculty against certain kinds of employer action." It may be necessary to protect faculty members against certain types of employer action, but you should also make a statement to the effect that if, however, the faculty members do not want to have an employee organization represent them, then this is their prerogative. The cost of having an outside organization represent them may be too great. It may be that the additional utility they would gain from having this organization may just not measure out when compared with the actual cost. The cost may be in terms of some psychological loss or something else. I think this fact explains why a number of people here disagree with you.

I think something you said about the AFT and the NEA applies. You said you thought the NEA was really going to grow and become very important in higher education; it could become the majority organization. You thought the AFT would not grow at this level. You said faculty members don't seem to want to be affiliated with labor. You also said you weren't going to discuss the merits of whether they should be affiliated with the labor movement. The reaction here may correspond with these reactions of faculty affiliating with the labor movement.

In many institutions it may be the most "logical" route for faculty to have an outside bargaining agent, but they may just not want it, because the costs are too great for them. That point has to be emphasized in order to balance out your paper.

I would like to consider this question of participation in the selection of administrators. I've done some research on nonprofit organizations and boards of other organizations and I'm very much interested in the question. Do you think that the faculty should participate at all in the selection of a president and department chairmen? Should there be any means at all by which it might participate in this determination?

MR. LIEBERMAN: The means could be a negotiated agreement, I think, spelled out in a contract.

MR. MOSKOW: I said participation.

MR. LIEBERMAN: I think part of our confusion here is over what we mean by participation. I think negotiating a collective agreement is participation. I think the faculty contributes to what they want in the agreement and their representatives try to get this; that's a form of participation.

MR. MOSKOW: But in the selection of a president of a university— should a faculty participate at all in that?

MR. HICKMAN: How do you do that by a bargaining agreement?

MR. LIEBERMAN: I personally do not recommend it.

MR. MOSKOW: In other words, the expertise that the faculty would have (since they all know something about educational policy, and so forth) is really not too important in the selection of the person who serves as the president of a university. What about a department chairman? Would you say the same thing about department chairmen?

MR. LIEBERMAN: At the chairman level, we have to know what the functions are. In some situations, the chairman of a large department is as much an administrator as a dean in a smaller institution. In that case, he would clearly be a representative of the administration and should be chosen by it, not by the faculty.

MR. MOSKOW: In the departments where I have worked the chairman had a great deal to say about curriculum and about the selection of new members in that department. He was an *ex officio* member of all committees of the department.

MR. LIEBERMAN: I think you're absolutely right in suggesting that some faculty members will just do without effective representation; they'll feel no need and won't push for it. But the fact that a faculty happens to be satisfied with an arrangement is not the last word on whether that arrangement should prevail as a matter of public policy. I do not believe that what is good for the professors is necessarily good for the country. On many campuses the professors as a group are recommending who should be hired and who should be promoted, and so on, and there is no accountability for their recommendations or decisions. The fact that they are satisfied and the administration is satisfied, or even that the board is satisfied, isn't enough to satisfy me in some cases.

MR. McHUGH: One further comment on the economic-academic issue, and this is relative to Mr. Howe's remarks. I can appreciate where, in a smaller community of scholars, the union and senate could work as a collective whole, and there would be no basic dissension. Nevertheless, in larger, more diverse institutions the leadership of the senate may well disagree with the union on fundamental issues affecting academic matters such as recruitment and retention of faculty. Thus, the senate may advocate merit increases and the union across-the-board increases.

There is the difficulty of making the distinction—at least it's a difficulty I have—between economic and academic; maybe coalition bargaining can be considered.

MR. BLUM: May I ask a question? How many faculty senates have ever taken a position on merit versus across-the-board increases? I don't know of any faculty senate that has anything to say about economic issues.

MR. HICKMAN: I've been a member of three senates that have taken positions.

MR. BLUM: But it's not very common, at least.

MR. McHUGH: Mr. Blum, I'm just posing this as hypothetical.

MR. BLUM: I recognize your issue is a good one.

MR. LIEBERMAN: There is nothing in my paper that suggests that all faculty senates, regardless of their function or how they are established, should be abolished. It would be quite appropriate to have a faculty senate whose function would be to make decisions or advise on certain matters which are not properly subject to negotiation.

Mr. Moskow, in answer to your question concerning my objection to certain kinds of faculty participation: I object to the notion that a faculty should have a right to designate the individuals or have a veto power over the designation of individuals who will perform employer functions.

MR. MOSKOW: It's very hard to speak about specific forms of

participation, but shouldn't faculty have some say in the selection of administrators?

MR. LIEBERMAN: The easy answer would be yes, but that doesn't advance us one bit. "Some say" can mean anything.

MR. MOSKOW: But the impression you're leaving is that they should have no say, that they have nothing to contribute in this area. The impression you're leaving is that the expertise of the members of a particular department is completely unimportant in choosing a chairman for that department.

MR. LIEBERMAN: It may well be that way in some cases.

MR. HICKMAN: This, again, is because you're looking at a chairman or dean exclusively as an employer, and they're not exclusively that.

MR. MacRAE: Mr. Chairman, some years ago I took a course with the Englishman Harold Laski. He was speaking about an institution which was electing its president, and he said that all they were doing was substituting the politics of maneuver for the politics of power.

That's item one. Item two is: Mr. Lieberman thinks that the NEA is much more likely to become the bargaining agent than the AFT. Using the same premise he has stated, I suspect it's the other way around. I suspect that the horror of being identified with organized labor is much less than the horror on the part of college professors of being identified with elementary and secondary school teachers.

MR. CARLTON: One of the problems I'm having has to do with the question of economic inequality. I think individual frustration tends to thrive on inequalities in the educational economic sector, whether at the college level or at the elementary and secondary level. The institutions that I serve from day to day don't seem to have a very severe problem at this time.

Mr. Marmion pointed out that there is considerable current difficulty at the junior college level. I haven't been aware of this, so it's a revelation for me to see these tensions surfacing. I know that the fellows I graduated with in 1966 accepted senior college and university positions at salaries of from $9,500 to $10,000 for nine months, which is quite adequate. I certainly wouldn't have struck to obtain more and certainly I wouldn't elect a bargaining agent to protect myself under such circumstances.

Another concern of mine is the fact that conflict tends to thrive on what you might call status differences. While there are certainly status differences on the campus, I do feel that these are considerably less pronounced than those found in other sectors of the economy. It saddens me to think that as we start institutionalizing the conflict model we may see manifested the divisiveness that is now present in the secondary schools.

I just came down from Detroit where the National Academy of School Executives conducted a seminar on collective negotiations. The participating superintendents were talking about "the enemy." They believe their teachers are the enemy now. They were sitting there and chortling over little ploys they can use to beat their fannies in Michigan—in all seriousness.

I'm sorry that this has to come. Perhaps it's inevitable, but I regret it.

I was a little worried that Mr. Lieberman felt the necessity of stressing the accountability issue so much. I think that the tyranny of the majority is a time-honored concept; as a result I fell into Mr. Oberer's intellectual camp. I agree that one's appearance in the eyes of his fellows is of supreme importance. Maybe I'm naive on the issue, but I'm thinking of Lyndon Johnson's famous statement: "Don't pee in the trough, boys; we've all got to drink." I think we do need a protectionist organization on the campus to try to deal with the situation; hence I favor faculty participation, accountability or not.

If I were offered the opportunity to express my best judgment I would just let the logic of events carry us along. I hate to see opportunistic groups rushing in an organizing everybody. Of course, I'm sure I would do the same thing if I were employed by one of these groups.

Let me make one last point. I can speak here with somewhat more authority, perhaps. I think, Mr. Lieberman, that you ought to take a look at the question of what is going to happen with the advent of extensive stoppages on campuses which depend upon the federal government for large sums of money. At this point, I would argue that it becomes a question of who the employer really is. If professors can be construed to be government employees, then the federal government may take it upon itself to move into the breach—legislate and start taking some sort of direct action.

I have it on good authority that there will be legislation introduced by private interest groups to establish some sort of impasse resolution machinery on the federal level to work in elementary and secondary education. This very likely presages a later move in higher education.

Now let me put in my disclaimer. I am required to state that I am speaking as an independent professional, and even if my opinions are eminently reasonable—and I have every reason to believe they are—I cannot claim to speak for the Office of Education.

MR. HOWE: In the circles in which I travel, which may geographically coincide with where you've just been, we do for nine months of the year indulge in the fancy of "whipping their fannies" and for three months of the year in the reality of dealing with teachers across the table. The fancy and the reality are distinctly different. But we have to find some sort of psychic compensation.

MR. CARLTON: It worries me when we discuss professional capital punishment as related to the accountability issue. Mr. Lieberman was emphasizing it to the extent that it's almost like saying, "We're going to fire this individual if he doesn't do the right thing—if we hire the wrong man we're going to remove him from his position at the first mistake." That's almost like excising the gonads. I don't think we have to go that far.

MR. HOWE: You don't go that far. When I mentioned earlier that I reserve my preferences for the cocktail hour, I didn't mention that my best friend is happily a guy that I face across the negotiating table who would cut my heart out professionally. We indulge in all kinds of social relationships in which he prides himself on reminding me of where he won little victories, and I do the same thing. We both forget all about it in the long run.

MR. WEINBERG: I would like to build on what Mr. Howe has said. It is refreshing to hear some of the practical experiences. Once you get your feet wet you discover the water is not that cold; in fact, you may enjoy the swim. I would like to go back to the matter of accountability. May we approach accountability from the administrative point of view?

If you have a grievance procedure under a contract it offers all sorts of benefits to both sides. The administrator of an institution (whether it is a university or a factory) can initiate change, and as long as it is within the framework of the agreement he has a tremendous range of opportunity. It is only when some injustice results from his initiative that his actions are subject to review. You do not bang heads over every little piddling issue that comes up. The grievance procedure is not a place where you try ideas; it is a vehicle for review of what has happened. It is an escape valve. This is one positive aspect that may come out of a bargaining relationship.

MR. AMBELLAN: On the accountability question, Mr. Lieberman remarked on the difference between being on a selection committee and being a chairman. I've just had long tenure, a year and one-half, as chairman of a selection committee. My God, it was triple-checked. It was checked not only by a watchdog kind of committee but also by the entire school and also by the administration. There was more accountability than you could really live through comfortably.

I don't think the chairman in serving his function goes at it as if he has to make good choices because these will be merit badges. I think that the same motivations operate in choosing an administrator as operate in choosing a faculty member.

I've been in universities where the senate has worked rather well and where you had a feeling that when it didn't work well there would be an effort to set up some bargaining procedures where you'd drive home the point. I know there are places where that doesn't work. I'd hate like hell, though, to see a single answer proposed that would prevent the kind of plural approaches we have in the situation I'm working in right now. I would not want deliberately to introduce a procedure that would build up more abrasions, an agency operation where one isn't needed, a mechanism that would cut down communication that is very valuable.

MR. HAYWARD: I'd like to repeat that the faculty association approach does not preclude the function of the senate. We can work and have worked and are working with the senates side by side. We went to the Board of Higher Education only with the salary portion of the proposal. This was the Salary Committee of the Association of New Jersey State College Faculties last year. We didn't get all we went after. We only got a 16 percent increase over the preceding year. And we did nothing in our negotiations that would weaken your position, Mr. Oberer, or your position, Mr. Hickman, or yours at Rutgers, Mr. Weinberg, because we were responsible for your 16 percent too.

MR. WEINBERG: We accept it graciously.

MR. HAYWARD: I just hope that all of you recognize that there is a way and there are very tangible compensations.

MR. MARMION: Mr. Blum, could I ask you about faculty involvement in the selection of presidents and department chairmen? Do you agree with Mr. Lieberman's answer?

MR. BLUM: Did he give an answer?

MR. MARMION: Yes. He didn't think it was appropriate for faculty to make selections.

MR. BLUM: I think that the faculty should have a voice. I tried to say that in my comments. I think we have paid far too much attention to it, because it's relatively irrelevant to the crux of what we're talking about, namely, representation for faculty as professionals and as employees. I think Mr. Lieberman suggested he was just giving us an example of the weaknesses of the senate.

MR. LIEBERMAN: I think you're resorting to what the philosophers call "picture language" when you say faculty "should have a voice." Such language doesn't mean anything to me. Should faculty have the power to veto a choice? Should the trustees be limited to choosing from a list submitted by the faculty? It's only when you translate a phrase like "a voice" into some specific policy that I can react to it. If you were to ask me, "Should the trustees be so limited?", I would say that such limitation would be very undesirable as a matter of public policy. You may be able to translate "having a voice" into some procedure that I'd accept. I don't know.

MR. MOSKOW: First of all, should the trustees ask the faculty for their opinion on who should be selected as department chairmen or a president?

MR. LIEBERMAN: I would not require such a policy if I were a trustee.

MR. MOSKOW: Then they shouldn't have a voice.

MR. LIEBERMAN: That's not true at all. They can say whatever they want. You have given "a voice" a very specific administrative interpretation. Others are possible.

MR. MOSKOW: But you don't think it's desirable.

MR. BLUM: That they shouldn't be officially asked is, I think, what Mr. Lieberman is saying.

MR. LIEBERMAN: I don't think it should be part of the required institutional procedure.

MR. MOSKOW: I disagree with that.

MR. HOLTZMAN: What do you do, Mr. Lieberman, with Mr. Moskow's claim that this is wasting crucial expertise? It seems to me you haven't really dealt with that question.

MR. LIEBERMAN: If the board of trustees can't pick a president without the recommendation of the faculty, then it's a pretty weak board of trustees.

MR. MOSKOW: How about the dean of a liberal arts school choosing a chairman when there are 15 departments in the college of liberal arts?

MR. LIEBERMAN: I think he could take faculty recommendations; he could ask for them.

MR. MOSKOW: Do you think that should be part of the institution's policy?

MR. LIEBERMAN: To me, asking an inbred department for its recommendation would really be nothing but a formality.

MR. MOSKOW: But he may know nothing about biochemistry or physics or whatever the particular subject is. As a dean of a school of business, which has a department of business law, of economics, accounting, management, information sciences—how can he possibly know enough about all these fields?

MR. LIEBERMAN: I don't think he has to.

MR. MINER: I think we have consistently overplayed the conflict idea involving negotiations and this whole idea of the adversary relationship. There were some of you who seemed a bit surprised by Mr. Howe's comments, based upon firsthand experience, to find that while there is conflict, it's not necessarily the instrument itself that creates the conflict. In fact, there are some reasons, I think, to look upon the professional negotiation process as being a continuing machinery for *solving* problems rather than necessarily creating conflict.

We have also assumed that what we are talking about here is instituting a kind of relationship which will for the first time institute conflict. The conflict exists already. It exists in those institutions in many cases where faculty senates have been well established for a long period of time. It's a foregone conclusion that at Cornell possibly a negotiations relationship would not be workable, and we've conceded that point for Harvard and other places as well. But there are, in fact, thousands of collegiate situations around this country where the senate has not served as a device to provide for the resolution of problems. So the senate in itself has created conflicts and has gone one step further: The conflict has been compounded by dissatisfaction and frustration on the part of a good many faculty members because it appears that the senate is simply not a device to make faculty impact felt.

Through a negotiations relationship proper machinery could be provided, and this is certainly not to say that the senate and the area of jurisdiction of senates would have to be wiped out. Mr. Howe has clearly indicated that the two can coexist. Mr. Hayward has developed some ideas on the basis of specific experience in New Jersey as well. So this is not necessarily an either-or kind of proposition. It's instituting a kind of process that in fact does have hope of solving many of the problems where there are no solutions right now on many campuses.

CHAIRMAN GERSHENFELD: We'll have a final comment now from Mr. Blum and Mr. Lieberman.

MR. BLUM: I do not think there is any university in America which could not benefit from collective negotiations of some sort. You have only to teach at one of the major Ivy League colleges and be an assistant professor to recognize that there are needs for some formalized procedures for determining promotions. The need may not exist in as crucial a form for some of the senior professors, but even then there may be needs.

Second, I think it is true that collective bargaining institutionalizes conflict. The conflict is there and always has been. The question is how damaging institutionalization may be. Most collective bargaining historically has been tough in the beginning, but once people get used to the process disputes that cause breakdowns, strikes, or boycotts diminish.

Third, I think we've unfortunately dealt with some of the wrong issues in this discussion—such as choice of presidents. There is a function for collective bargaining in the university. There is a function for discussions in a senate. They're not quite the same—they sometimes are—and how the negotiating relationship will develop will depend upon the college, the community, the leadership, the administration, the state. I don't see why we should expect a single answer in this situation. You don't get it any place else. Why in this field?

MR. LIEBERMAN: I won't try to summarize, but I'll say this. If we run a symposium like this again, we ought to have an anthropologist present. We're like an Indian tribe, uttering certain phrases like "industrial model" or "community of scholars." Everybody sees a long train of inferences from these phrases. To me, this approach is more theological than analytical.

I want to thank the people here, for I think a good critic is your best friend. I do appreciate the comments.

As to whether my comments have overstressed accountability, my defense is that I have never seen a critical analysis of accountability in faculty senates. Perhaps the reaction that it's overemphasized in my paper may be due to the fact that faculties have never really considered the matter seriously.

If faculties claim that they ought to have the authority to set broad educational policy, let's not forget that in a democratic society we reserve the right to change our policy-makers. Can we consistently argue for tenure and at the same time claim that faculties ought to have the right to set broad policy? Perhaps there is some inconsistency here or at least there is a problem that requires analysis.

Finally, there is one problem that has not been raised at all. One of the crucial problems will be what should be left to negotiation and what should be resolved by political action. The relationships between the negotiating and the political levels call for very close examination. I urge those of you who can to devote substantial resources to this matter.

ADJOURNMENT

CHAPTER THREE

MAN IN THE MIDDLE:
CONDITIONS OF WORK OF COLLEGE AND
UNIVERSITY FACULTY MEMBERS

JOHN W. GUSTAD

COORDINATOR
BOARD OF EDUCATION, STATE NORMAL SCHOOLS
STATE OF NEBRASKA

•

Several years ago, I summarized my views with respect to the working conditions of faculty members as follows: "The only thing that keeps faculty turnover . . . from getting completely out of hand is *the success many faculty members achieve in obfuscating established policies.*"[1] Now, almost a decade later, I am inclined to think that that assessment remains essentially correct. It is a sad commentary on a profession that devotes substantial time to telling others how to get and keep their houses in order.

Observable symptoms of the difficulties are hard to come by. There is, for instance, no evidence to suggest that unduly large or increasing numbers of faculty members are defecting to other callings. Indeed, there is some reason to believe that the number of prospective faculty members is increasing not only in absolute numbers but in proportion to other professions.

The continued high rate of mobility among institutions, a kind of ritualistic game of musical chairs, would seem to be one symptom of *malaise*. Some of this is normal and even desirable as individuals

---

[1]John W. Gustad, "An Ancient and Honorable Profession," *AAUP Bulletin*, Vol. 48, No. 3, 1962, pp. 261-65.

work out their career patterns. Yet one has but to look even casually at the patterns of such moves to see that lateral moves are almost as common as upward ones, and downward moves are not unusual.

A second indicator of difficulty is the increasing number of faculty members joining unions. Whether one is for or against unions, unionization is not characteristic of professions. Certainly, the implications of unionization for the academic profession are uncertain at best and, to many, disturbing. What it seems to suggest is that the traditional modes of affecting working conditions have proven to be ineffective, at least for significant numbers of faculty members.

This is particularly interesting, since faculty members have been operating in a seller's market for more than two decades. Salaries and fringe benefits have, it is true, been improving substantially and will probably continue to do so at least until the middle of the next decade when, if Alan Cartter[2] is correct, supply will catch up with demand. Teaching loads have also declined. Further, faculty participation in decision making has increased, and the scars of the (late Senator Joseph) McCarthy era have largely healed.

Part of the difficulty stems from tensions within the profession as it continues to undergo rapid changes. Riesman and Jencks assessed the situation correctly when they titled their recent book *The Revolution in American Higher Ecucation*.[3] There *is* a revolution taking place, and no one has yet been able to map its dimensions or directions. Faculty members, as much as students and administrators, are caught in the vortex of powerful and disturbing forces.

Part of the difficulty is essentially inherent in the profession itself. This sort of frustration is perhaps characteristic of all professions, for the reason that professionals are always aware of how great is the gap between aspiration and capability. If they were not, they would be technicians and not professionals.

A distinction needs to be made here between job satisfaction and morale. Job satisfaction is an individual matter; morale is a group matter. To build high group morale, it is necessary to establish acceptable goals and make sure that they are communicated to and understood by group members. Too few educational leaders are genuinely articulate, and too many who might be refrain from trying in deference to the widely held notion that administrators should be seen

---

[2]Alan Cartter and Robert Farrell, "Higher Education in the Last Third of the Century," *Education Record*, Vol. 46, No. 2, 1965, pp. 119-28.

[3]David Riesman and Christopher Jencks, *The Revolution in American Higher Education* (New York: Doubleday, 1968).

and not heard. Then, too, the communications problems in higher education, as elsewhere, are enormous.[4]

Very little work of a systematic nature has been done on conditions under which faculty members work. Stecklein[5] has summarized faculty workload research. Ruml and Tickton[6] have reported on trends in faculty salaries, and the AAUP annually produces a report on salaries. I have[7,8] analyzed the situation with respect to policies and practices of faculty evaluation. Stecklein and Eckert[9] and I[10] have studied the backgrounds of faculty members and the reasons for their deciding to enter the profession. McCall, Jamrich, Hereford, and Friedman[11] have reported on the problems of new faculty members, and I[12] have done some work on programs for orienting them to their jobs. Caplow and McGee[13] and Stecklein and Lathrop[14] have studied the academic marketplace and reasons for faculty turnover. These, however, are bits and pieces. From them, we can draw some inferences, but what we need is some comprehensive, broad-scale re-

[4]John W. Gustad, "Communications Problems in Higher Education," *Journal of Communications*, Vol. 12, No. 1, 1962, pp. 11-22.

[5]John E. Stecklein, *How To Measure Faculty Work Load* (Washington, D.C.: American Council on Education, 1961).

[6]Beardsley Ruml and Sidney G. Tickton, *Teaching Salaries Then and Now* (New York: The Fund for the Advancement of Education, 1955).

[7]John W. Gustad, "Policies and Practices in Faculty Evaluation," *Educational Record*, Vol. 42, No. 3, 1961, pp. 194-211.

[8]John W. Gustad, "Evaluation of Teaching Performance: Issues and Possibilities," in Calvin B. T. Lee (ed.), *Improving College Teaching* (Washington, D.C.: American Council on Education, 1967).

[9]John E. Stecklein and Ruth E. Eckert, *An Exploratory Study of Factors Influencing the Choice of College Teaching as a Career* (Minneapolis: University of Minnesota, 1958).

[10]John W. Gustad, *The Career Decisions of College Teachers* (Atlanta: Southern Regional Education Board, 1960).

[11]Harlan R. McCall, John X. Jamrich, Karl T. Hereford, and Burton D. Friedman, *Problems of New Faculty Members in Colleges and Universities* (East Lansing: Michigan State University, 1961).

[12]John W. Gustad, "Orientation and Faculty Development," *Educational Record*, 43, 1963, pp. 195-213.

[13]Theodore Caplow and Reece J. McGee, *The Academic Marketplace* (New York: Basic Books, 1958).

[14]John E. Stecklein and Robert L. Lathrop, *Faculty Attraction and Retention* (Minneapolis: University of Minnesota, 1960).

search on this topic, the working conditions of college and university faculty members.

One approach that might be taken with profit is that of the anthropologist. The tribes of academia have some wonderfully exotic rituals. Consider their puberty rites, for instance. These are administered by a shaman who is called the graduate dean. The rite consists of three ordeals. First, there is the ordeal of the written comprehensive. Here, the elders probe the neophyte to see whether he has mastered the arcane and esoteric lore of the tribe. Next, there is the preliminary oral where the elders continue the probing around a table, all the while sipping on a potent brew with great magical powers which the candidate is required by custom to provide. Finally, there is the ceremony of the final oral, accompanied again by the drinking of the magic potion provided by the candidate, during which the candidate's first creation is examined. The successful candidate is then allowed to don the paraphernalia of the tribe with whatever colors that particular tribe specifies. Following a solemn ceremony of investiture, he is then deemed to have passed puberty and is allowed to sit with the elders. He is even permitted, if he has done especially well, to have (intellectual) offspring and to bring them to the puberty rites.

Or consider the fertility rites. Annually, each tribe gathers its members from across the country or even the world (greater powers are associated with greater geographical spread) in what are called conventions. There, members display their fecundity in what are called paper-reading sessions. Tribal members who do not regularly display their fecundity in this fashion are driven from the councils of the elders and forced to teach undergraduates. Undergraduates are the raw material from which members of the tribe are drawn; if they cannot join a tribe, they are largely ignored and are forced to go into occupations deemed unworthy of Scholars.

Then, too, there are tribal wars. Most frequently, these wars are between a tribe called the Aaup's and one called the Administrators. Not frequently seen in the open but very deadly are the wars between the Administrators and a tribe called the Trustees. Usually the Administrators lose, in which case they find another encampment to join as Administrators, ask to be relieved of administrative responsibility to return to teaching (if their tribe will have them back), or are forced to wander in limbo as Visiting Professor of Higher Education.

Some day, I shall take my tape recorder, my Rorschach cards, and my interaction process analyzer and undertake an expedition among the tribes of acadmia again. My last one was fascinating.

One way to look at the conditions of work of faculty members is to consider their reward systems, the hierarchy of values to which they adhere. Admittedly, generalizations about faculty members are dangerous. Like other occupational groups, they are human beings first and faculty members second. However, there is a hierarchy of values, taken under average conditions of frustration and satiation, which can be helpful in understanding them.

First, there is freedom. This is essential if the dual responsibilities of scholarship and teaching are to be attained. Even Russia has learned this lesson, at least in the sciences. What we call academic freedom is a height which has been captured at great cost and which must be continuously defended. It has been said that a faculty member is one who thinks otherwise. Quite literally, he must *be* otherwise if he is to be effective.

The threats to freedom are many and unceasing. Some come from outside the profession and are therefore easier to detect and deal with. The public, legislators, administrators, and students have all at one time or another been guilty of trying to force faculty members to subscribe to certain ideas and to disavow others. Sometimes, they have had some temporary success. One can argue, of course, that this kind of pressure is a good thing in that it forces faculty members to be sure of their ground before espousing an idea and keeps them continuously reexamining their thinking. This argument has a certain amount of validity on the surface, but it neglects two essential facts: (1) the academic world has its own reasonably well developed devices for subjecting its members' ideas to critical scrutiny, and (2) it overlooks the fact that too much outside scrutiny can create an atmosphere of timidity and caution which is inimical to the development of those tender, tentative hypotheses which, in some cases, flower into the great ideas. At the time of the Scopes trial, the chancellor of Vanderbilt University was asked what his institution was going to do about the heresy of Darwinism. He replied that they were going to expand their research programs in biology.

For many years, faculty members and students have taken common cause against administrators, trustees, legislators, and others who would abrogate freedom. Now, oddly enough, it is the students who appear to be the greatest threat. They are charging faculties with having become too conservative, with having joined up with the "establishment." Their noisy stridency just may have some basis, and those faculties which react repressively will be guilty of doing exactly what they have on other occasions opposed—twice guilty, because they should know better.

Not only are there external threats to freedom, there are internal ones which are, therefore, more insidious. I refer here to the growing power of the professional societies themselves. Each discipline has more or less well developed canons against which it judges the worth and substance of members' ideas. As the societies become institutionalized, however, there is increasing danger of their determining what is respectable and what is not on grounds other than scholarly merit. Like trustees and administrators, these organizations must deal with a number of publics which have the power (usually based on the ability to give or withhold money) to express pleasure or displeasure with the ideas held by members.

Even individual faculties may on occasion become repressive. Their devices for dealing with those they consider to be mavericks are usually not as blatant as those of administrators, but they are nevertheless effective. Insofar as they are less overt, it is harder to document their sins, but anyone who has been around the academic world long knows of cases.

Next to freedom in the hierarchy of faculty values is independence. It is obviously related very closely to freedom but is somewhat different. What it boils down to is a desire on the part of faculty members to have a major if not determining voice in setting their own working conditions. Every registrar knows that 10 a.m. on Mondays, Wednesdays, and Fridays is the only possible time to teach (except 2 to 4 p.m. Wednesdays for seminars). Every comptroller knows that requisitions are bureaucratic folderol to be avoided like the plague. Every student knows that the schedule of office hours posted on the door is, at best, a very rough approximation.

Which is not to say that all of this is good. It is, however, traceable to strongly held feelings that faculty members have that they will be most effective if they can set their own pace. And there is some merit in this. It is ideas, after all, which are at the heart of the academic business, and ideas are very mercuric in their behavior. One noted mathematician used to ride street cars from one end of the line to the other through the night, since that was when he got his best ideas. It is difficult to convince legislators or the public that the faculty member who is at home puttering around may actually be working. Sometimes he is.

There is a never-ending tug-of-war between faculty members and others over such matters. There simply are not enough classrooms to permit everyone to teach at exactly the hours that please him. Students do need to see their advisors and instructors and cannot be expected to know that that hour might be the one when an idea is beginning to take shape. Business officers must have records to back up their purchases. One of the most important tasks of administrators is to mediate wisely and effectively in this cauldron of confusion.

Here, however, there is also a problem. Legislators, donors, and the public keep exerting pressures for colleges to become more efficient, to be run more like business or the military. The late Dr. E. R. Guthrie, a psychologist as well as an administrator, had the following to say about such proposals: "The relation of a college president to his faculty is less like the relation of a general to his subordinates than it is like the relation of a watchman on the end of a dock to the seagulls circling overhead."[15]

A third item in the hierarchy of faculty values is the opportunity to learn. Everybody in the academic world knows that the acquisition of the Ph.D. is merely a rite of passage. With the ubiquitous explosion of knowledge, keeping even reasonably close to the cutting edge of a discipline is an enormous task. There are faculty members at some institutions who are so far out of touch with their disciplines that their students are being badly shortchanged.

In this area, i.e., the opportunity to learn, working conditions are probably worse than in any other. Many colleges proclaim, for instance, that they are teaching institutions. On such grounds, they justify their niggardly appropriations for library purchases, laboratory equipment, faculty travel, and the like. No one can say for certain what an adequate library is, but surely 25,000 volumes, collected over many decades, would not be. Of course, I have heard Harvard faculty members complaining about their library, so no one should ever expect the faculty to be satisfied.

This notion that a teaching institution does not have to be concerned with learning is arrant nonsense. Colleges and universities are institutions of learning. The faculty has as much responsibility to continue learning as it does to help students to learn. In a properly conceived and operated institution, the relation between the faculty and the students should be that of colleagueship, the faculty simply being more advanced students. There is a long-standing and, I be-

---

[15]E. R. Guthrie, *The State University* (Seattle: University of Washington, 1959).

lieve, unproductive argument about which is the more important, scholarship or good teaching. For myself, if I were forced to make a choice, I would prefer to teach badly what is true than superbly what is false.

The difficulty is that higher education in America was built on the theory that faculty members did *not* need to go on learning. When they were hired, they already knew most of what relatively little there was to know, and new knowledge became available at a snail's pace. Libraries did not need to be large; laboratories were principally places for demonstrating well-known principles; professional societies were nonexistent. Beginning about a hundred years ago, however, that began to change.

It is anomalous that business and industry regularly budget substantial sums for research while even in many of the best universities faculty members have to bootleg research time and funds. It is in part in an attempt to gain research time that faculties have resorted to large lecture sections even in advanced courses.

Bernard Berelson has made a telling indictment of many colleges and universities by saying:

> The colleges have much to answer for. A large majority of liberal arts colleges in this country cannot provide poor library facilities, few research opportunities, heavy teaching loads, poorer students, restrictive intellectual atmosphere, low salaries—and then expect to get the better Ph.D.'s in substantial numbers. The graduate schools cannot and should not produce for that market.[16]

This has led to the situation described by Everett Hughes,[17] who said that, to remain accredited, colleges have to have a certain number of Ph.D.'s, "whether the holder of that honored degree be quite sane or not."

Next in the hierarchy of values is intellectual stimulation. This is obviously closely related to the previous one since it requires the presence of many learned (and learning) individuals to create the

---

[16]Bernard Berelson, "Theses on the Preparation of College Teachers," in John W. Gustad (ed.), *Faculty Preparation and Orientation* (Winchester, Mass.: New England Board of Higher Education, 1960).

[17]Everett C. Hughes, "The Issues in Summary and Perspective," in John W. Gustad (ed.), *Faculty Preparation and Orientation* (Winchester, Mass.: New England Board of Higher Education, 1960).

desired climate. Intellectual stimulation can come from students. If it did not, teaching would quickly become impossibly dull. However bright, though, students cannot provide the same kind of intellectual stimulation as faculty peers.

The vast majority of colleges and universities are woefully inadequate in this respect. If the opportunities for continued learning are inadequate, and they are, then it is impossible to have the kind of interplay of ideas that is to be found in the distinguished institutions. One has only to compare the kind of conversation one hears in the faculty club at Harvard with that at West Overshoe Tech to see the contrast. True, the talk at Harvard is not all "intellectual," in that batting averages, trout-fly tying, and beating to windward do come under discussion.

For most institutions having small faculties, the only solution would appear to be to give the faculty the opportunity to do research and scholarship on campus (or, alternatively, provide a liberal leave program) and to attend regularly and often meetings of relevant groups. The specialist in a two- or three-man department has, quite literally, no one to talk to.

Reference was made earlier to conversations in faculty clubs. Very few smaller institutions have them. Probably, they could not be self-supporting except on a few relatively large campuses. Still, if faculty interaction is a desirable goal, even the smaller ones should look into the possibility of having at least a comfortable lounge. Some fear that this will further separate the faculty from the students. Possibly so, but I would argue that, just as parents need to get away from children occasionally, so also the faculty needs a place of retreat. Intellectual stimulation, like good ideas, needs cultivation.

The last of the items in the reward value hierarchy that I propose to discuss is salary. I place it last because that is where the faculty places it. Faculty members are quite thoughtful, of course, in bringing to the attention of chairmen and deans competing offers from other institutions. No one would say that they are financially unmotivated. Far from it. What I am saying is that, given a decent salary level, other things are more important.

What is a decent salary? That depends. It depends on the faculty member's age and stage of development, on his family situation, on his needs and desires, even to some extent on his discipline. A 45-year-old professor of physics with children of college age who makes $12,000 a year is (probably) grossly underpaid. Stecklein and Lathrop[18]

---

[18]Stecklein and Lathrop, *loc. cit.*

have shown that attraction and retention are affected by many factors, only one of which is salary. There have been instances of men taking salary cuts to get to certain institutions or to get certain research opportunities.

Faculty salaries have, on the average, been rising rapidly, as Ruml and Tickton[19] have shown. Still, there is disagreement about how high they should be and go. Each year, the AAUP publishes its economic status of the profession report in which it rates salary levels. Since the number of institutions with A or AA rated salaries is small, it is obvious that the AAUP and the marketplace are in some disagreement.

Further, there is a matter of ratios involved. To a man earning $12,500 a year, another $2,500 might not be a significant enough increase to tempt him to move. To a man earning $7,500, however, the $2,500 increase could be very significant. No one has studied the problem yet with an eye to identifying the ratio that will be attractive. It is possible that no general ratio exists, that salary is so much just one of the factors involved in a move that it cannot be extricated from the matrix.

The subjects in my research placed salary where they did under average conditions of satiation and frustration. We psychologists have been studying motivation for a long time. It is sometimes possible to identify motivational hierarchies which say that, under certain conditions, motive A is stronger than B, which in turn is stronger than C, etc. However, these have a way of slipping around as the conditions change. Thus, if you find that an animal that is both hungry and thirsty goes consistently to the water when both food and water are available, you can say that thirst is the stronger motive. But after he has satisfied his thirst, he will go to the food.

So it is to some extent with faculty members. There are instances when the conditions of work are such that salary, normally not at the top, will become the dominant motive. Being human, however, and not rats, their motivational systems are more complex. It would be difficult to say, for instance, what it means to satiate the motives of freedom or of intellectual stimulation. It is easy to describe the conditions that frustrate them but not the reverse. Nor do we know much about what happens as the result of various levels of satiation and frustration. We do know that there are some institutions which experience a high turnover, and in many of these frustration is characteristic.

---

[19]Ruml and Tickton, *loc. cit.*

Before concluding, three other areas that have to do with the conditions of work need to be examined. One of these has to do with faculty evaluation. The second is the relationships of faculty members to other groups, primarily administrators and students. The last has to do with the role of the faculty in determining and implementing policy.

With regard to evaluation, someone once remarked that faculty members want not so much to be evaluated as to be understood. However, Logan Wilson[20] made the case for evaluation when he said, "Indeed, it is no exaggeration to say that the most critical problem confronted in the social organization of any university is the proper evaluation of faculty services and giving due recognition through the impartial assignment of status."

In my 1961 study of faculty evaluation,[21] every single college and university responding to the questionnaire said that classroom teaching was the most important thing considered in promotion and tenure decisions. Fine. Then, we went on to ask how they determined the quality of a man's teaching. The most frequently cited methods were: informal student opinion, formal student ratings, classroom visitation, opinions of colleagues, and opinions of chairmen and deans. The difficulties inherent in each of these are so obvious that they need not be considered further here. My article already referred to[22] goes into these in detail. The fact is, as I said earlier, that, "In general, to call what is typically collected or adduced to support evaluative decisions 'evidence' is to stretch the meaning of that honored word beyond reason."

Many universities and some colleges admit (privately) that they place publication at the top of the priority list when considering promotion and tenure. In this area, as Clark[23] has shown, we are on somewhat better ground. Even so, it is my impression that it is the number of pages in print rather than their quality which is determining in most instances.

Why should higher education continue to live with such patently inadequate means of evaluating its members so that fair and equitable decisions can be made? There are both good and bad reasons.

---

[20]Logan Wilson, *The Academic Man* (New York: Oxford, 1942).

[21]Gustad, "Policies and Practices in Faculty Evaluation," *loc. cit.*

[22]Gustad, "Evaluation of Teaching Performance," *loc. cit.*

[23]Kenneth E. Clark, "Studies of Faculty Evaluation," in *Studies of College Faculty* (Berkeley: Center for the Study of Higher Education; and Boulder, Colo.: Western Interstate Commission on Higher Education, 1961).

Those who are unsure of how they will fare obviously have reasons for wishing to conceal their deficiencies. As Dressel[24] put it, ". . . there are those professors who, knowing full well that they could do better, interpret academic freedom as being inclusive of the right to teach as badly as they wish. . . ."

However, the fact that much of the indifference or opposition to improving evaluative systems comes from some of our more distinguished academicians leads me to believe that something else is involved. I shall have more to say about this later, but what it boils down to, I think, is that there is a continuing power struggle going on between the disciplines and the institutions over the question of who is going to make the decisions. We usually think of evaluation as something which goes on on campus, something done by colleagues, chairmen, and deans. Formally and officially, of course, it is. The American Psychological Association does not pay my salary; the State of Nebraska does.

It does not take the prospective academician long to learn that the path to a professorship at a prestigious institution is lined with publications. The public to which the enterprising academician addresses himself is less his own institution than his scholarly colleagues across the nation. Then, if promotion and other benefits do not come quickly enough where he is, some other institution seeking to add stars to its crown will seek him out. At that point, his own institution can either promote him or lose him. This, of course, takes the effective decision power out of the hands of the chairman and the dean. They have been sand-bagged.

In such a situation, the quality of a man's teaching is, of course, of relatively little importance. Polite inquiries may be made about teaching ability, but as anyone who has read letters of recommendation knows, the range of teaching competence is from excellent to brilliant. Neither is service to the department or institution a variable carrying any significant weight.

Small wonder, then, that those who do not have the talent, the opportunity, or either to run the publications race should be frustrated. Having no way to acquire visibility off campus, their fates are decided by a set of procedures which are inadequate and in many cases unfair. Despite lip-service paid to teaching and service, they are keenly aware that the rewards go to those who publish. And since

---

[24]Paul E. Dressel, "The Current Status of Research on College and University Teaching," in W.J. McKeachie (ed.), *The Appraisal of Teaching in Large Universities* (Ann Arbor: University of Michigan, 1959).

the vast majority of publications are put out by tiny minorities in any discipline, this means that most academicians live in a constant state of insecurity and frustration. Small wonder that unions, with their tradition of promotion on the basis of seniority, should be finding increasing numbers of adherents.

Colleges and universities are made up of sometimes cooperating, frequently competing groups. These include the faculty, the students, the administrators, and the trustees. Views about the possible and proper relationships within and among these vary. Student disorders and faculty strikes are but symptoms of underlying difficulties which must be alleviated in the near future.

Millett[25] has suggested that consensus is the proper *modus operandi* for higher education. However, I have said[26] that, before consensus can hope to be attained, the fact that these groups are in actuality conglomerates of subgroups must be faced up to and dealt with.

The role that the faculty plays in determining and implementing policies varies enormously from institution to institution. The last hundred years can, in a sense, be characterized as a period during which faculties have struggled with varying degrees of success to attain what they regard to be their proper role in policy making. In some institutions, the faculty has achieved sufficient power to make administrators figureheads. In others, the administration still calls the shots. Most institutions are somewhere in between, and the struggle goes on.

It is interesting to note that it is precisely those institutions in which the faculty has attained considerable power that have also been the sites of the most virulent student protests. These faculties should realize if they have not already done so that, since the faculty has so much power, the demands for student power will almost surely mean an erosion of faculty power.

Except in times of crisis, it is not profitable to think of the faculty as a monolithic, united group any more than it is useful to think so of the administration or the students. Each group is made up of many smaller and frequently competing groups. Departments, for instance, compete with considerable enthusiasm among themselves. Even within departments there are subgroups competing for space, facilities, students, and funds. Getting a faculty to take common cause is difficult in the extreme and usually happens only in times of crisis.

25John D. Millett, *The Academic Community* (New York: McGraw-Hill, 1962).

26John W. Gustad, "Community, Consensus, and Conflict," *Educational Record*, Vol. 47, No. 4, 1966, pp. 439-51.

If relations with administrators have been changing, so have relations with students. Although these vary tremendously across the country, certain trends are discernible. What has been described as the "collegiate" culture is clearly on the decline. The hold which the Greeks once had on campus life, both social and political, has been much loosened. Some of the backward institutions still have strong Greek systems, but on the major and more advanced campuses this is not true.

No sooner in the late 1950's had we labeled students "the silent generation" than they became decidedly unsilent. There is reason to believe that the decibel level will continue to increase. Students are now demanding the right to make decisions about their own affairs, and they are discovering that it is not the dean of students nor the president with whom they must deal in the last analysis but faculty committees on student affairs. It has been a startling and troubling confrontation for both the students and the faculty. Since most faculty members are over 30, the generation gap promises to produce some interesting tensions until both groups learn how to communicate.

The difficulties will become acute when, as is now beginning to happen, students demand a voice in affairs now regarded by the faculty as sacrosanct such as the curriculum, instructional methods, faculty selection, and faculty evaluation. The students see quite correctly that, unless they can have a voice in such matters, the changes they believe must be made will continue to be made with the glacial speed typical of and traditional in higher education.

There is very little reason to believe that most faculty members see this as more than a hand-sized cloud on the distant horizon. With the steam apparently going out of the Vietnam issue, however, my guess is that the student activists will seek to effect an alliance between the black power and the student power groups. Several hundred colleges and universities are in the process of revising rules and regulations in the aftermath of demonstrations, but none of the reports I know of either had significant student representation in their preparation or got at the real issues.

What I am suggesting is that the avuncular authoritarianism which has characterized faculty-student relations in the past is rapidly disappearing. Berkeley, Columbia, and Wisconsin today, tomorrow Football A and M. This already is and will become increasingly a source of anger, anxiety, and frustration for faculties before a workable detente is achieved. I am one of the growing number of over-30's who would like to see a distinct change in the relationship between students and faculty members, but many faculty members are going to have to be cudgeled before they will concede to students some of the rights they have so painfully won.

Another conflict which is shaping up is between the faculty and the public at large. I am not as much worried about a major relapse into McCarthyism as some are. The point of issue is likely to be reached with officials who have statewide control, be they chancellors, co-ordinators, or directors. As public higher education continues to grow, legislators are going to insist on better and longer-range planning. This will include not only physical facilities and general budgets but also control over the right to install or expand new curricula. This power of the purse has already in some states come to be seen as an invasion of "outsiders" into realms which have traditionally been under the control of the faculty.

There is at present no effective response possible from faculties. Traditionally individualists, they have wrested substantial control from local administrators, but this new layer of administration is something else. I am not suggesting for a moment that statewide coordination of higher education is bad. It has its problems, but I am inclined to think it is both essential and inevitable. What I am saying is that faculty members are in the future going to become more aware than in the past of the wishes and needs of the general public. They will not have nearly as free a hand as they have had to shape their institutions. Whether devices like the statewide senate of California state colleges will prove to be effective or not remains to be seen.

This brings me to the last aspect of the topic about which I would like to comment: the role of the faculty in determining and implementing policy. Faculty members like to talk about an *Erewhon* in which there are no trustees, little if any administration, and complete control by the faculty. Aside from the fact that this impossible dream never existed and probably never will, it is by no means certain that it ever should.

As mentioned above, faculty members have fought for and won substantial authority in the conduct of the affairs of higher education. Power being what it is, no one ever feels that he has enough. Power also being what it is, others are forever seeking to erode it for their own advantage.

It is an axiom of administration that the person to whom responsibility is delegated must have corresponding power to meet that responsibility. To the faculty is delegated much (but by no means all) of the responsibility for student instruction. The question is: Do they have the corresponding power? An unequivocal answer is not possible, although most faculty members would say no. This is a constant source of frustration and a reason for the continuous clamor for more faculty power.

By tradition rather than under the provisions of a constitution, higher education lives with a system of checks and balances. Legally, power is vested with trustees who are representatives of the public. Necessarily, trustees delegate much of that power to the president, who in turn delegates it to others. In the better, more advanced institutions, matters having to do with admissions standards, faculty selection, promotion and tenure, degree requirements, and courses and curricula are very largely decided by the faculty. There is, however, the right of review retained by deans, the president, and the trustees. Recently, as indicated earlier, this review, at least in some areas has been extended to a statewide coordinator.

Tensions arise when this right of review is exercised. When a dean vetoes a departmental recommendation to grant tenure, he can expect considerable static. When the trustees do the same thing, it is viewed as an even greater threat. The system of checks and balances mentioned above normally operates to make such actions exceptions. From the point of view of the faculty, however, the system is imperfect in that it has no statutory status. It can exert a kind of moral pressure, but it has no official channel of appeal which could circumvent trustees. Further, when trustees start listening to faculty members who have gone around the president, they had better realize that before long they are going to be searching for a new president.

Because of the hierarchical organization of colleges and universities, the faculty commonly feels that its power to initiate is too limited. Again, there is little that can be done when a president decrees that a new degree program cannot be initiated (usually on financial grounds), because if he is unwilling to recommend to the trustees that additional funding be sought, they are unlikely to do so. The power of the purse is great.

Millett's thesis is that the four groups work together on the basis of consensus. As indicated, the fact that the groups are made up of frequently disagreeing subgroups makes this difficult. The relatively poor communications existing also places substantial obstacles in the path of this ideal.

Even where the faculty has substantial power, it is frequently said that the faculty shall make policy and the administration carry it out. This is not an entirely valid distinction, since those who carry out policy must necessarily have some discretion and flexibility. This means that what amounts to a body of common law, a collection of precedents, is built up. Since the same sort of thing occurs within the structure of the federal government, it is unlikely to be otherwise in higher education.

One possible solution to the difficulties I have outlined is for trustees to go on record spelling out the areas in which they are willing for the faculty to have final power of decision. Also needed is considerable attention to be paid to the communications among the several groups involved. This is, as I have said elsewhere,[26] likely to necessitate changes in the role of the president.

Thoreau said that "Most men lead lives of quiet desperation." Faculty members are, in this respect, no different from anyone else. One reason for their difficulty is that they are operating in substantial ignorance of how to do one of their major tasks—teaching. Mostly, they teach as they were taught and have very inadequate methods for finding out how well they are doing. There is growing interest in these matters, and research on teaching and learning has been developing very rapidly.

Some of the difficulty is shared by professionals in other settings who are also in a sense employees. Faculty members like to think that they are as much professionals as lawyers or physicians, but there is little or no chance to hang out a shingle and go into practice. To earn a living, they must be part of institutions. Yet, the academic profession by tradition has never dealt with this situation, has no effective devices for interacting with institutions.

Imperfect and full of frustration as colleges and universities are, they are, because faculty members are the kinds of individuals they are, the only wheel in town. Many who abandon professorships for higher-paying posts find themselves even more frustrated, and cases of men taking substantial salary cuts to return to teaching are by no means rare.

This is not to say that there are not many things that need to be done to improve the lot of professors. Some improvements have been made; some are under discussion. There remain, however, many sources of discontent which have not yet appeared on anyone's agenda. The academic profession itself has much to answer for and, unless it undertakes to do something, it may find itself faced with great difficulties. High on the agenda must be a realistic and imaginative

[26]*Ibid.*

reassessment of the relations between faculty members and students.

Nor should we forget that morale is not simply the sum of individual job satisfactions. It is, as was noted earlier, a group product. Since faculty members are men who think otherwise, trying to get widespread acceptance of reasonable goals will always be difficult. A faculty which knows where it wants to go is capable of generating a momentum which can overcome all sorts of obstacles. All of us who are a part of higher education have a lot to answer for. More important, we have a lot to do.

DISCUSSION OF MR. GUSTAD'S PAPER

MR. WALTER: Early in the paper Mr. Gustad mentioned a concept of policy, saying that universities function well due to the success of faculty members in obfuscating established policy. Presumably, with policies as they exist, if one were to take policy seriously and follow it, the whole organization might come to a halt.

If he wasn't completely serious, certainly there are people in our business who would take that view of policies. If you please, then, I'd like to take two positions relative to this.

In the first place, people who are apt to feel this way are talking not about policies but about what might better be termed rules or regulations. Secondly, only very rarely, in universities, does much which might be described as policy really exist.

Let me argue for the moment that policy ought to be established in order to achieve two purposes. First, it ought to articulate the goals and the purposes for which the organization exists. Articulating, in writing, communicates something not only to members of the organization but to the general public. It provides a guideline against which a number of things may be measured. Secondly, policy provides a boundary which limits executive discretion in an organization. Executive discretion clearly is going to be limited to the purposes of the organization. Furthermore, good policy ought to establish priorities. Not only does the organization feel that certain things need to be done, but through the explication of policy says, "We want this done, and up to this point we are willing to put resources of time and effort into doing it."

Policy, then, points directions and controls the means to be employed within the organization. Executive action does not necessarily refer only to the kind of action that the administrator takes, but is a function of the total organization. Everyone who is a part of the organization is constantly both making and implementing decisions. Consequently, everyone is engaged in a certain amount of policy action, and quite properly so.

When policy does not exist to say who may make what kinds of decisions and who has the authority to implement them, then the kind of border dispute that Mr. Gustad speaks of in his paper clearly is inevitable. There simply is no basis for determining who should do what, other than the existence of power relationships or perhaps vaguely understood tradition. Mr. Gustad speaks of a continuing power struggle. Manifestly, it is currently going on in a great many institutions.

This is a different premise from arguing that conflict is caused by stupid policy. In any circumstance where conscientious people are pulled by the requirements of their clientele (which in the case of those of us who are teachers would be our students) and at the same time by expectations of the organization to which they feel loyalty, a high potential for conflict simply does exist. One of Mr. Gustad's former colleagues—Professor Ronald Corwin of Ohio State—has written very effectively about this particular phenomenon.

Where clear-cut policies do exist in writing, the authority to make decisions or develop regulations is legitimatized; and the authority of administrators as well as all other members of the organization is both restrained and defined. This rule of law as distinct from the test of strength has served us well in other social organizations in our country.

It seems ironic that a university, which by its very nature should embody a confidence in the structured application of data and the use of reason, should be so hesitant to develop administrative practice based upon predetermined policy as a method of operation.

Mr. Gustad does, as a matter of fact, in the latter part of the paper suggest that one possible approach is for the trustees to spell out what power they will relinquish to the faculty. I suggest that a more promising approach might be to work toward a shared procedure for policy development as a means of clarifying, focusing, and limiting the use of power.

MR. GUSTAD: Although when I made that comment I had my tongue in cheek a little bit, I was still pretty serious about it. Someone has said that policy is what we write down after we have decided that what we're now doing is what we want to continue to do.

Though I'm not suggesting it is necessarily a good thing, to a certain extent institutions of higher learning seem to operate in the British muddle-through tradition.

Perhaps in my paper I used the word "policy" in too broad a sense. I was thinking not only of policy but procedures and rules and regulations.

My experience as an administrator at several levels in higher education tells me that every administrator who is effective has to operate to a certain extent from horseback. A lot of faculty members expect him to do that. I understand that one of the problems in the California state colleges now is that the whole policy structure and rules and regulations have been entirely too rigid.

MR. NASH: Mr. Gustad, you mentioned evaluation of faculty. This is something that has haunted every teacher ever since he first entered the classroom. Could we pursue that by drawing an analogy between the teacher and the minister, or the teacher and the doctor? How are our doctors and ministers evaluated?

MR. GUSTAD: I suggest that you read a splendid chapter on evaluation of faculty members in a book Calvin Lee edited last year. It reports on the 1966 American Council on Education meeting.[3] This is a problem to which I have addressed myself. It's in part a criterion problem. For example, take physicians. Do you evaluate them in terms of the amount of money they make? Not necessarily, because a very good man like Albert Schweitzer may make peanuts while some less able man might set up a practice on Park Avenue and do fine.

How about cure rate? That doesn't do very well either. It's a loaded criterion. The physicians at the Mayo Clinic, which is one of the better medical centers in the world, have a very poor cure rate, largely because when people get there they're in pretty bad shape to begin with.

At the moment I am inclined to think that the problem of the evaluation of teachers is going to have to go along several tracks. There are several reasons for evaluating teachers. One is the sheer administrative reason that you have to make decisions on whether to promote or not to promote. Secondly, you need to find out the effectiveness of instructional procedures. Thirdly, you need a criterion for research on the learning process itself.

I am inclined to think that in the present state of the art we may

---

[3]John W. Gustad, "Evaluation of Teaching Performance: Issues and Possibilities," in Calvin B. T. Lee (ed.), *Improving College Teaching* (Washington, D.C.: American Council on Education, 1967).

have to go along those three tracks, although I would expect some day that they would, if not completely converge, at least get a lot closer together.

When you look at what is now being done in higher education with respect to evaluation of teachers you find certain methods fairly commonly in use. The two most common bases for decisions are the recommendation of the chairman and the recommendation of the dean. On what basis do they make their recommendations? As a dean I used to get a fair amount of feedback. Students comment and faculty members comment and you form an impression. If you look at that with any degree of sophistication from the methodological point of view, you've got to tell yourself that the data on which you are basing your estimate are pretty shaky.

For a variety of reasons college faculty members don't like classroom visitations by their peers. When I was running a series of conferences in New England for the New England Board of Higher Education one faculty member indignantly said, "I would no more visit a college class than I would open the faculty member's mail." I know that there are problems with visitation, but I am inclined to think it is an important source of information that we should not rule out immediately.

There are student ratings. I have followed this literature for a number of years. Twenty years ago I was asked, with a couple of other faculty members, to set up a student rating system at Minnesota. I think the general problem with this source of information about faculty members is that we tend to ask the students the wrong questions. Why ask a freshman whether Professor X is competent in mathematics? How is he to know unless he happens to be one of the Quiz Kids? You can ask him what effect Professor X had on him, whether he made the course interesting for him, or whether he could understand it, and so on.

These are presumably legitimate questions, although they provide second-order kinds of information. The first-order kind of information about a faculty member is whether his students learn what the faculty member and other knowledgeable people think they should be learning. Ralph Tyler points out, of course, that students learn all kinds of things in college, some of which are not under our control and some of which we don't intend that they learn but they do anyhow. So we've got to find out what the teacher is trying to do and then the question is how well he succeeds.

This is not itself a simple matter, as you can imagine, and the more complex and the more advanced the subject matter, the more difficult it becomes—in part on statistical grounds because of variability.

I don't have an answer to the question of how to evaluate teaching effectively. I am not willing to accept the fact that it's an impossible task. I think if we will agree that it is an important task, that in the interest of equitable personnel administration we must turn our attention to it, then by a series of successive approximations we will in time develop some better techniques than we now have.

But I have no pat answers. I wish I did. Like any other administrator at any level, when you are forced to make decisions about colleagues and peers, if you have a conscience you also have some sleepless nights.

MR. LIEBERMAN: Did you say you felt no college in the country had an adequate system of faculty evaluation?

MR. GUSTAD: Back in 1961, when I was a member of the ACE Committee on College Teaching, I was asked to do an initial survey of evaluation procedures. Arthur S. Adams wrote to all members of the ACE and asked them to send their policy manuals, etc. We also developed a fairly extensive questionnaire. Reading all the accumulated material (and it was quite an accumulation), I couldn't find an institution which had a program I would consider even reasonably adequate.

MR. LIEBERMAN: This is a fairly serious criticism. How do you diagnose the failure to develop evaluation? Why should there be this tremendous gap?

MR. GUSTAD: I'm not sure. I've been troubled about this for a long time.

MR. LIEBERMAN: I was hoping you'd say the lack of accountability!

MR. GUSTAD: Actually, this may be part of it. But I think there are other aspects that I referred to earlier. There are some professors who interpret academic freedom as being inclusive of the right to teach as badly as they wish. It's those people who have reason to suspect that they wouldn't come out very well who are among those who oppose it. But the fact of the matter is that there are some very distinguished academicians, whose competence I at least wouldn't question on whatever imperfect grounds I may judge, who also oppose it for a variety of reasons. Some of them feel that any attempt to be more systematic is going to reduce the whole thing to a bunch of numbers.

I think the state of the art is now such that even if we can arrive at some relatively precise adjectives we'll be making progress. Although statistics is one of my areas of interest, I would hope that we don't start getting highly statistical about this. I'd settle for some fairly decent adjectives for a while.

One dean commented that as far as he knew there were no bad teachers on the faculty. If you read letters of recommendation you find that teaching competence ranges from excellent to brilliant. I've speculated a long time about why this is so. I think in part it's because administrators haven't either known or demanded that there be better evaluation, and this applies to administrators up and down the line. This is one of the things I object to most strongly in what I read and in what you put in your paper about the union attitude—no merit rating. I know that many principals and superintendents regard merit rating in any form as anathema. I don't quite understand this point of view, but nonetheless they have it.

I don't think colleges and universities can get away with that. Even in my relatively brief tenure in Nebraska I've had a number of questions from legislators and others; they want to know what we're doing with the money they're appropriating. How do you answer the question? In terms of the numbers of students that graduate? That's a very imperfect answer, and they're smart enough to know that it's not a very good one.

MR. MARMION: Mr. Gustad, as a result of increasing layers of external control, particularly in public education, do you see any change in the value system? For example, you said monetary rewards now rank about fifth, adding that if this factor rises to first you're in trouble. Do you think lack of identity with the policy-making level and possible lack of involvement will increase the faculty member's desire for monetary gains?

MR. GUSTAD: It could. At the level of control with which I'm involved now (and it's a relatively new level), nobody has really thought this problem through. To be perfectly blunt about it, I think in most of the places that have gone to statewide coordination the idea has been sold to legislators on the ground that they can cut out some offices and save some money. In fact, the reverse happens. It has happened in every single case.

This is one of the challenges I see facing me: how to keep this new layer of administration from producing exactly the kind of situation that you describe. Where it homogenizes institutions, where you have a master plan that says the institution will do A, B, C, and nothing more and you deprive the faculties of initiative, then I think this is a bad thing, and I would hope that sooner or later the faculties would revolt against it.

As you implied, if you frustrate faculty members, that is, deny them initiative to deal with educational matters as they want to deal with them, you start that reward value hierarchy slipping around. It's quite possible that faculty members will begin to see their relationship to "the system" as solely an economic one.

MR. SUMBERG: Mr. Gustad, I wonder if we might not turn our attention to the problem of the freshman faculty member. It seems to me that, increasingly, faculties are beginning programs of orientation for new faculty members. Yet these programs haven't had much visibility. How does an institution present itself to a new faculty member in terms of the values which it has *vis-à-vis* the values a new faculty member just entering the profession may have?

MR. GUSTAD: I would refer you to another article of mine in the *Educational Record* on this topic.[4]

There are all kinds and lengths and styles of so-called orientation programs for new faculty—either faculty members new to the institution or new to teaching as a career. I think these are somewhat different problems, of course.

As best I was able to tell, some of them on the surface look as if they might be useful beyond the level of giving you a key to your office and saying what hours you teach, which is the kind of orientation I had when I first taught.

I suggested—and I still believe this is the case—that we should not be talking so much about orientation as we do with students where we have an orientation week. We need more than an intensive beginning experience where we tell people about the nuts and bolts of the job, the things they have to know. Rather, I think that what we ought to be talking about is faculty development, which is a career-long business. A young man entering the profession has a different set of problems than one who is established. Yet, if you're not going to go dead above the neck you have a different set of problems throughout your entire career up to the point where you're spending your time worrying about whether to retire at 60 or 65, and so on.

I am inclined to think, then, that while some kind of a relatively brief nuts-and-bolts type of orientation probably is helpful (and I don't think the typical one-day or even a two-day faculty retreat is terribly useful), I would rather have institutions decide that faculty

[4]John W. Gustad, "Orientation and Faculty Development," *Educational Record*, No. 43, 1963, pp. 195-213.

development throughout the professor's career is something to which the institution and the faculty and everybody concerned ought to pay attention.

MR. EVANS: Mr. Lieberman's accent on accountability and the brief discussion here on evaluation cause me to speak out and offer some reasons for college professors' cop-out under the aegis of academic freedom and independence when it comes to the question of accountability. I suggest that we assume when we talk about policy and evaluation that stated goals are indeed goals of the organization, but if we were to sit down and identify the goals in higher education we might not want to make them public. I think this is a real problem and no one wants to face it.

Along with that, there are individual hierarchical goal perceptions, and we may find that universities somehow maintain themselves in spite of the fact that there is a great degree of goal conflict. But we don't look at this.

MR. GUSTAD: That's right. John Millett is insisting that what we have to do is get all these groups with different interests—students, faculty, administration, trustees, public—working harmoniously together. As I said a year or so ago, this assumes that these are relatively homogeneous groups which can agree among themselves.[5] But all you have to do is look at the competing internal and external demands made on the faculty to realize that a faculty is made up of all kinds of sometimes competing, sometimes cooperating, frequently conflicting groups. So are students and so are administrations. Therefore, I think Millett's notion, while it has a certain nice ring to it, probably is a long way from realization.

MR. STEVENSON: It may be unreasonable for a faculty to expect administration to evaluate their instruction effectively, as faculties have not really figured out an effective way to evaluate students. Once they do learn how to evaluate students effectively, perhaps we can generalize this to faculty.

MR. GUSTAD: This is one strand in the rope that I think needs to be woven. Having taught tests and measurements for a number of years, I am appalled at what passes for student evaluation; but if you raise this question you're accused of trying to pump "educationese" into faculty members. As you know, they resist that mightily. You have to sneak up on their blind sides.

MR. MONTANA: I did not notice the word "tenure" in your paper.

5John W. Gustad, "Community, Consensus, and Conflict," *Educational Record*, No. 47, 1966, pp. 439-51.

What are your comments on the effect of the attainment of tenure by a professor on his value system and working conditions?

MR. GUSTAD: Operationally, let me describe my feeling about tenure at least in one rather special case. When we were putting New College in Florida together, I hired the charter faculty. We gave them an initial three-year contract and said there would be no such thing as tenure but that we would write some very sturdy rules to protect the conditions of employment and academic freedom.

I suppose my general feeling is that tenure is probably the best of an imperfect set of alternatives at the most. I don't like some of the effects. All of us, I suspect, have had colleagues who start out like skyrockets and then after a while we hear that they've been promoted to associate professor and some months or years later we begin to think, "Gee, I haven't heard anything from so-and-so recently." This, too, is something, as some of you know, which is almost impossible to defend to the public. There *are* people who goof off.

On the other hand, in public I defend it on the ground that I know in most instances of no better device for protecting academic freedom (abused as that term and concept are).

MR. PEPPER: You hinted at but never quite touched earlier the comment that perhaps the student in a university may come to the point where he could expect contractual obligations on the part of the university to be fulfilled. For instance, since that catalogue itself is considered by the university as a prescription for the student, might not the time come when the student would also be able to expect that document to serve the same purpose for the faculty? If so, do you see this changing the role of the university both in the teaching aspect and from an administration point of view?

MR. GUSTAD: As I understand it, it is true that the implied contract reading of the catalogue *vis-à-vis* the student has been invalidated by the courts. Some of you who are attorneys can correct me if I'm wrong.

Having dealt with catalogues and with necessary changes and the vagaries of curriculum committees over a time, I am not at all sure that it will ever be possible to put together something about which you can say to a prospective freshman, "This is our mutual agreement about the kind of education we will provide and you will respond to." But it would be an intriguing idea.

Both faculty and students need a considerable amount of flexibility. Yet if we maintain the flexibility, I think we have to brace ourselves to live with some chaos and confusion. Which you choose I suppose depends on your preferred life style.

MR. HOLTZMAN: I've been puzzling over your value hierarchy, the fact that salary came not only fifth but last.

MR. GUSTAD: There were others, but I listed only the top five.

MR. HOLTZMAN: I have a question, but I won't wait for the answer. I'd like to hear that after I make some other remarks. I'd like to get some idea of what your method of determination was—whether it was simply asking people what was important to them and, if so, was it a matter of importance in picking among competing job offers.

I'd like to suggest some alternate interpretations to yours. It seems to me yours is that money is less important to faculty people than the other things that you ranked ahead of it. One rather reasonable alternative is that at least in the academic field you're not supposed to care about money, and therefore if you ask the question the wrong way money is likely to be put rather low, whether it really is or not.

A somewhat more complicated alternative, but one still worth considering, is that this kind of hierarchy really is a question of how much difference there is among the offerings, which is not the same as how important they are to you. Let me give you a kind of simple-minded analogy. Suppose the question comes up about how much attention we give to a car's ability to resist denting if someone runs into it in a city intersection and how much that would influence us in picking a car. To me it would be a rather important characteristic of a car, but it's one on which so far as I know Cadillacs and Chevies differ so little that it wouldn't be the basis for choosing. They're more different in other ways, and therefore the choice is going to be based on the larger differences rather than the smaller ones, even though the ability to resist denting might be more important to me than some of the variables on which I made the choice.

This opens a possibility that salaries, however different they may be, may be more alike than the other things that have come into this hierarchy. Schools may differ more in the amount of freedom they give their faculty members, for example, than in their salaries.

MR. GUSTAD: That is correct, and John Stecklein in his work at the University of Minnesota on faculty attraction and retention shows that it's exceedingly difficult to extricate any one of these factors reliably from the matrix in which it's imbedded. I concede that immediately.

Methodologically, these rankings were based on opportunity for rank ordering a whole variety of working conditions and values.

This ranking was based on mean, but there were differences among the means which led me to believe these are real differences. I will be the first to admit that, as I said, these were taken on a sample of faculty members—a pretty good-sized sample—under what you could call average conditions of frustration and satiation. In the process of depth-interviewing a sub-sample of these people, both presently employed and formerly employed faculty members, it became obvious that there were all kinds of permutations and combinations of these factors. My rankings are based on a set of averages. As you know, an average frequently conceals as much as it reveals, but when you're trying to typify a group, there you are.

MR. HOLTZMAN: But the basic point that each individual was asked to say where each of these factors fell in relation to others—is this a rank-ordering idea?

MR. GUSTAD: Yes.

MR. HOLTZMAN: What would you say, then, about the possibility of this hypocrisy being perhaps at large in our culture, but especially among academic people? Suppose you ask a cross-section of ministers' daughters how much they are influenced by the prospective wealth of their suitors in picking a husband. There are considerable forces that would keep them from saying they'd be influenced by that factor, but they might be influenced anyway.

MR. GUSTAD: The answer depends on the conditions under which you ask the question. If there is the condition of anonymity, where the social pressure doesn't enter into it—

MR. HOLTZMAN: Except that we're always part of our own audience, however secret it may be.

MR. GUSTAD: Of course, but we had ways of cross-checking our results, and the cross-checks came out reasonably well.

MR. ROSENTHAL: Can we pursue the question of tenure again? I wasn't quite satisfied with your answer. You said that at New College you wrote contracts for only three years—

MR. GUSTAD: And there was a promise that the faculty would participate in the writing of personnel policy.

MR. ROSENTHAL: But this was an attempt not to have tenure?

MR. GUSTAD: At the moment, there was no tenure.

MR. ROSENTHAL: And now you're suggesting that tenure is possibly the best guarantee of academic freedom. Without actually defining it (but at some time I would like a good definition of academic freedom), I wonder how you can maintain academic freedom without tenure? You need tenure to insure it. I wonder how many in this room feel there is tremendous safety after they've achieved tenure?

MR. GUSTAD: All I said was that this was a highly special situation. This was a brand new institution. We were hiring a rather unusual kind of faculty member, and we believed that we could avoid some of the problems of the more well-established institutions with their traditions.

I don't know whether they've changed their minds or not; I haven't been in touch with them closely. What I said was that, for most institutions, I don't have a better alternative than tenure at the moment, even though it's imperfect. There are all kinds of problems with it. It doesn't protect as it should. It does box in some incompetents.

MR. LIEBERMAN: I'd like to correct what I think is an error of fact in what you said and then maybe ask another question. I think you suggested that the union's position was against merit ratings for professors. Is that correct?

MR. GUSTAD: As I recall, your paper spelled out the $10,000-$30,000 salary range with automatic increments, and so on.

MR. LIEBERMAN: Wherever you got it, is it your position that the union opposes merit ratings?

MR. GUSTAD: That's my understanding.

MR. LIEBERMAN: I'm not sure you are accurate. I have here a copy of the Federation's proposed contract in New York for the State University. It has one proposal on merit promotion and another proposed clause that "decisions on merit promotions shall be made by the properly constituted and elected local faculty bodies at the department, division, and college level." It also includes many other clauses that indicate this particular union of professors accepts merit ratings under certain conditions.

If a faculty wants merit pay, its organization will support it, regardless of whether the organization is a union or an association or an AAUP chapter. The organization is going to adopt the faculty position regardless of the organizational label. If the faculty does not want merit rating, the organization won't support it. It is unrealistic to assume the organization will have a position different from its constituency on this issue.

I am not an AFT member or representative, but I do think it is somewhat inaccurate and unrealistic to assume that the union's position on this issue would be different from that of any other organization that had the same constituency.

Now I want to go on from there. One of the most important aspects of a collective approach is the tendency to treat all faculty alike when differences might well be justified. For instance, if you compare the input problem of the Latin professor and the professor of international relations, the latter needs more time than the former to keep up with the developments in his field. To treat them alike with respect to load would be a mistake.

MR. GUSTAD: Last year I was so indiscreet as to suggest this to the chairman of one of our departments!

MR. LIEBERMAN: Unfortunately, we are not making this kind of distinction in our faculty personnel policies. Perhaps the cost of higher education will force trustees and administrators to cease treating faculty as one undifferentiated mass for load purposes. We must stop treating the faculty as one vast industrial union, all of whom must have the same conditions of employment, and start making more practical distinctions among them in personnel policies.

MR. GUSTAD: I agree, but, as you know probably better than I do, the practical as well as the political realities of trying to get the classicist to admit that he doesn't have to spend as much time in preparing a course in Cicero as the international relations professor does for one of his classes are next to impossible.

MR. LIEBERMAN: That's why such decisions should not be left solely to the faculty. There is room for administrative decision, whether the faculty likes it or not.

MR. GUSTAD: That is one of the areas where I think a competent administrator does make some differential decisions.

ADJOURNMENT

CHAPTER FOUR

FACULTY PARTICIPATION IN ACADEMIC DECISION MAKING: AS TO WHAT ISSUES, BY WHAT FORMS, USING WHAT MEANS OF PERSUASION?

WALTER E. OBERER[*]

PROFESSOR OF LAW AND INDUSTRIAL AND LABOR RELATIONS
CORNELL UNIVERSITY

●

DEMOCRACY AND PROFESSIONALISM

In the wake of the "happenings" at Columbia and elsewhere, it is difficult to deny the force of arguments for greater faculty participation in academic decision making. Student involvement in the same process, a question of even hotter proportions, we may leave for another day. The democratization of the academy moves apace, for better or for worse.

Egalitarianism in higher education is a mixed blessing. The practices and procedures of democracy do not necessarily inspire a quest for excellence, without which the campus is a sterile place. Indeed, an inherent tendency of majoritarianism is to enshrine and protect mediocrity. There is, accordingly, a natural tension between democratization and professionalism. The latter exalts and rewards excellence, since the pursuit of excellence is the very meaning of professionalism. The former views the standards of excellence with a skeptical

---

[*]The author was a member of the Task Force on Faculty Representation and Academic Negotiations, Campus Governance Program, of the American Association for Higher Education, National Education Association, and has drawn upon the findings and report of that body, entitled "Faculty Participation in Academic Governance" (AAHE, 1967).

eye, as a threat to the interests of the majority. For professionalism is elitism.

It is important to keep in mind, therefore, as a qualifying prologue for what follows, that greater faculty participation in academic decision making, while desirable and, in any event, ordained by the trend of the times, is no panacea. It will improve the quality of higher education only insofar as the degree of professionalization of the particular faculty permits—no more.

The dilemma of the professor is that he is both a member of a profession and an employee. In the former capacity he must set his own standards, or at least share in their setting. This is so because of the two factors which create the societal need for and which define a "profession": (1) the grave importance of the calling to the public and the necessity therefore that it be held to higher standards than those generally applicable; and (2) the esoteric character of the calling and the consequent inability of nonmembers to set and enforce the necessary standards. In the other aspect of his dual capacity, that of employee, the professor's standards are set for him by his employer. The classical professions of law and medicine are not typically burdened with this ambivalence. Accordingly, the maintenance of the high standards which are the essence of professionalism is a uniquely difficult task in education, requiring a collectivized effort not merely in the promulgation and enforcement of the requisite professional standards, as in law and medicine, but also in the achievement of sufficient strength *vis-à-vis* the institutional employer to permit the autonomy essential to the promulgation and enforcement of such standards. Organized resistance from outside the profession is therefore implicit in the teaching profession's effort to formulate and enforce proper standards. What self-employed lawyers and doctors can do because they believe it to be professionally right, professors can do only after overcoming opposition from the administrators and trustees who hire and supervise them. The fact that the administrators are frequently "graduate" members of the profession of course mitigates the problem.

The purpose of this paper is to examine the environment of what may be called the "professor profession," so designated to distinguish it from the teaching profession at the elementary and secondary school levels, where the problems, though related, are sufficiently different to require separate analysis. In pursuing this purpose, the effort will be to delineate, first, the issues which properly concern members of the faculty in higher education; second, the organizational forms through which they may confront these issues; and, third, the measures they may take to effectuate their professional goals with reference to these issues.

THE SUBSTANTIVE ISSUES:
FACULTY REPRESENTATION AS TO WHAT AND VIS-À-VIS WHOM?

In considering the problems involved in faculty participation in academic decision making, at least three interacting factors must be taken into account: the nature of the issues which legitimately concern the faculty, the nature of the institution in which the issues arise, and the level at which the decision with respect to a particular issue is to be made. While these three factors are interrelated, clarity of analysis requires that they be separately examined.

The Nature of the Issues

Four broad categories of issues which legitimately concern the faculty can be identified. These categories, too, are interrelated. But, again, clarity of analysis is served by separation.

The first category involves the educational and administrative policies of the institution. The propriety of faculty concern over educational policy is obvious, and the close relationship of educational policy to administrative policy justifies also faculty concern over the latter, at least to the extent that administrative policy affects educational policy. Frequently the two are so closely geared as to be but separate phases of the same process: Administrative policies determine the process by which educational policies are to be worked out; conversely, decisions as to educational policy must be implemented administratively. For economy of discussion, the two may be jointly dealt with under the rubric "institutional policy."

Most basic to this institutional-policy category of issues are the procedures and agencies through which educational and administrative policies are to be determined. The fundamental question here is what the faculty's role should be in shaping the very structure and rules—the "constitutional law"—which govern the manner in which these policies are to be established. If the frequently repeated aphorism that "the university *is* the faculty" is an overstatement, it is nonetheless true that the single most vital element in higher education is the faculty. From this, the necessary conclusion is that the faculty should not only be consulted but have a major voice in establishing the "constitutional law" which governs the making of institutional policy. It should have a major voice, that is, in determining the extent of its own involvement and the procedures by which it participates in such decision making.

The only restrictions on faculty participation in the formulation of institutional policy, apart from those which are self-imposed, should be those which derive necessarily from the charter of the institution. And even these are not sacrosanct since charters themselves are not immutable. Moreover, quite apart from basic reformulation, the charter of any institution of higher education is apt to be a tangle of ambiguities, subject to a variety of emphases along a spectrum of reasonable alternatives. The points of emphasis determine the very mission of the institution. Since the members of a faculty are vitally concerned about these emphases and well qualified to share in the process by which they are determined, the wisdom of their involvement is self-evident. And since the implementation of the decisions made is frequently in their hands, the propriety of their involvement in the making of those decisions is even more manifest.

It follows that most questions of consequence in the area of educational and administrative policy should be subject, in one form or another, to faculty consideration, from the formulation of the basic rules and procedures for determining these policies to the content of the policies themselves—programs to be offered, admission standards, curriculum content, degree requirements, grading standards, standards for academic freedom, standards for student conduct and discipline, and procedures for the appointment of department chairmen, deans, and presidents. Although the resolution of these policy issues should reflect the interests of the institution as a whole, the faculty is clearly a vitally interested group.

A second category of issues in which the faculty has a legitimate interest consists of nonmonetary faculty personnel matters. Examples here are appointment, tenure, and promotion policies and decisions; course assignments; work loads; allocation of office space and secretarial help; and grievance procedures.

A third category of issues involves the economic interests of the faculty. There are four major interests here: The first concerns the total resources available to the institution for all purposes. In private institutions, this conceded "interest" of the faculty is not so much an "issue" as in public institutions, where competition between and among the various units in a statewide system can produce *issues* of the gravest sort. The second interest concerns the allocation of the total institutional resources to the various budgetary purposes involved. The sharpest concern here is likely to be as to the share to be allocated to faculty salaries and fringe benefits, such as sabbatical leaves, research grants, insurance and pension programs. The third interest concerns the allocation, in turn, to the various schools, departments, and ranks within the institution of that portion of the total resources set aside for salaries and fringe benefits. The fourth interest concerns the determination of the compensation, and other discretionary monetary benefits, to be awarded to particular individuals.

A fourth category of issues, less obvious than the first three but to which, nonetheless, faculties across the country have demonstrated their concern, consists of the institution's policies on "public" questions. An example is the question of the extent to which the institution should cooperate with Selective Service officials in providing data to be used in determining which students should receive draft deferments. Another example is the question of the extent to which the institution should accept grants from national defense agencies and become involved in research programs directed to a military goal. Another example has to do with the labor policy of the institution *vis-à-vis* nonacademic employees—the decision over whether to recognize and to bargain with unions of maintenance workers and other service employees. One of the most publicized of the issues in this "public" category was the one which, at least ostensibly, triggered the revolt at Columbia—the question of whether that university should build a gymnasium in Morningside Park, an area separating the campus from Harlem. The faculty interest in these and related questions derives in part from concern for the public image of the institution, which may be of critical importance to the faculty in terms of the generation of funds, of the recruitment and retention of faculty and students, and of general esteem.

The Nature of the Institution

In any consideration of the issues of concern to a faculty, the question arises as to what forms and procedures should be made available for faculty involvement. This question, in turn, requires analysis of the seat of power with which the faculty must deal concerning the particular issue. The locus of power is not the same with respect to all issues. Moreover, the locus may vary with variation in the type of institution involved.

Four broad varieties of institutions may be distinguished in this regard. First, there are the private universities and colleges. These differ profoundly from one to another—sectarian-nonsectarian, large-small, rich-poor, broad mission-narrow mission. The public institutions of higher education break down, in turn, into three categories: the junior colleges; the "emerging" four-year colleges and universities, a category which includes new colleges and universities as well as those which are undergoing the change of status from teachers colleges or junior colleges to institutions with a broader orientation; and "university centers" with heavy emphasis upon graduate training and professional schools.

The major ferment with respect to faculty representation in higher education across the country today is found in the first two categories of public institutions—the junior or "community" colleges and the "emerging" four-year institutions. This is hardly surprising, upon reflection, since these two have been the major centers of growth in higher education. Rapid growth entails unsettlement and ferment. Moreover, the traditional forms of faculty representation, so well developed in many of the older, stronger universities and colleges, are either shallowly rooted or nonexistent here. Similarly, the administrations in such institutions are frequently drawn from secondary school or teachers college backgrounds. A relatively authoritarian, superior-subordinate relation between administrators and faculty is therefore apt to exist, in contrast to the collegial relations present in the traditional university or college model.

The Levels of Decision Making

Further compounding the problem of faculty representation in institutions of higher education is the hierarchy of decision making. While this problem exists in all such institutions, public or private, the problem is peculiarly aggravated in the statewide public systems presently emerging because of the imposition of "super-boards" upon the preexisting framework. This development is the product of the effort to rationalize the allocation of resources in the state systems. However sensible the development, it poses difficult problems for the faculty in the effort to be heard in effective fashion as to matters of consequence to it upon which it has much to contribute.

The number of levels of decision making in higher education varies with the nature, size, and scheme of organization of the particular institution; whether it is public or private; and, if public, the organizational hierarchy within the particular state system. In any case, some or all of the following levels will be present: (1) the department chairman; (2) the dean of the school or college; (3) the campus administration—the president and his staff; (4) the board of trustees of the institution; (5) the higher board which in some state systems governs or coordinates all units of a particular variety (such as the board for all of the state colleges and the separate board for all of the state universities in California); (6) the super-board at the summit of the entire state system, including all state colleges and universities or university campuses; (7) the budgetary agency of the executive branch of the state government; (8) the governor of the state; (9) the state legislature. Nor do the foregoing exhaust the levels of decision making, since some of the higher boards have their own executive officers (presidents or chancellors) to whom authority is delegated.

A Case Study

The array of issues and of the various levels at which decisive action concerning them may be taken, particularly in the large state systems, underscores the problem posed for effective faculty representation. The latter must be echeloned to conform to the echelons of decision making. If analogy is sought in the collective bargaining system of private industry, the problem is one of unit determination: What is the appropriate unit for faculty representation? At the time of this writing, this question was before the Public Employment Relations Board of the State of New York with regard to the faculty of the State University. The pertinence of that litigation to the subject of this paper compels a statement of the facts and issues there involved.

The Public Employees' Fair Employment Act,[1] commonly known as the Taylor Act, went into effect in the State of New York on September 1, 1967. Applicable to all "public employees," defined as "persons holding a position by appointment or employment in the service of a public employer," the act covers, among others, the members of the faculty of the State University of New York—a discovery belatedly made by, and greatly dismaying, the central administration of SUNY. This means that the members of the faculty of SUNY, like all other public employees in New York, have the right under the Taylor Act to "negotiate collectively with their public em-

---

[1]New York Civil Service Law, Art. 14; N.Y. Judiciary Law §751, as amended 1967 (McKinney Supp., 1967).

ployers in the determination of their terms and conditions of employ-ment, and the administration of grievances arising thereunder."

SUNY is an incredibly complex conglomeration of upwards of 60 institutions—university centers, medical centers, colleges of arts and sciences, specialized colleges (e.g., forestry, home economics), agricul-tural and technical colleges (two-year), and community colleges (two-year)—literally spread all over the state. Its governing body is a 15-member board of trustees, its chief executive officer a chancellor. Still higher in the state scheme is the Board of Regents which presides in somewhat mystical fashion over the entire system of education in New York, both public and private, from kindergarten through graduate and professional schools. Lower in the state scheme is the array of local campus boards and chief executive officers, the latter designated presidents.

There is also a Faculty Senate of the State University of New York, consisting of from one to four senators elected from each of the cam-pus faculties (the number of senatorial representatives depending upon the size of the faculty at each campus), of two staff members of the State University appointed by the chancellor, and of the chancel-lor himself, who is the chairman and presiding officer of the Senate. (Effective July 1, 1969, the chairman and presiding officer of the Senate is to be elected by the Senate from among its elected members. Currently, a vice-chairman, who frequently presides, is elected by the Senate; this office is abolished as of July 1, 1969. The foregoing changes are the result of action by the Senate in July, 1968, which action was thereafter approved by the Board of Trustees.) The Senate serves as a forum for the interchange of ideas among the various faculties of the State University and between the faculties and the central administration.

Enters the Taylor Act. At five of the campuses, local affiliates of the American Federation of Teachers petitioned the New York Public Employment Relations Board for certification as the repre-sentatives of the faculty for purposes of collective negotiations as to terms and conditions of employment under the provisions of the Tay-lor Act. The claim of each of these petitions was that the local campus is the appropriate negotiating unit. The Faculty Senate intervened in these proceedings, as did the State University Council of the Ameri-can Association of University Professors, the Faculty Association of the State University of New York, and the Civil Service Employees Association. All four of the interveners contend, along with the em-ployer, that the appropriate unit for negotiations under the Taylor

Act is the statewide faculty. Each of the four interveners asserts also that *it* should be certified as the negotiating representative for that statewide unit.

Which unit configuration is appropriate for the purposes of such negotiations—the statewide unit or local-campus units? The Public Employment Relations Board had not yet answered this question at the time this was written. My answer is that *both* units are appropriate. My reasons are that some of the issues subsumed under the Taylor Act's "terms and conditions of employment" are statewide issues, while others are local-campus issues. Those issues which can be effectively dealt with only at the top of the pyramid—i.e., in Albany—will not yield to yakking at the local-campus level. Examples of such issues are the total amount of money to be allocated to the State University in the fiscal year; the manner in which this fund should be allocated, in turn, to the local campuses; retirement and pension programs; the determination of the educational mission of, and degrees to be offered at, each variety of campus in the state system; and the admission policies of those campuses. Similarly, issues which can be effectively dealt with only at the local-campus level will not yield to top-of-the-pyramid forensic efforts. Examples of such issues are the manner in which the money allocated in Albany to the local campus should be apportioned, in turn, to the various schools, departments, ranks, and individuals at the campus level; the implementation of personnel policies—appointment, tenure, promotion; the allocation of courses, office space, and secretarial services; and the handling of individual grievances.

If the answer to faculty participation in academic decision making is to be found in a collective bargaining framework, overlapping units for bargaining are the only viable answer. Faculty participation must be echeloned in accordance with the echeloning of executive discretion for resolving the questions at issue. Indeed, whatever the format for faculty participation, the problem of the echeloned levels of decision making remains constant. The forms for faculty representation must accommodate to this fact of academic life, much as the forms for employee representation in industrial bargaining have had to adjust to large corporate structures. The United Auto Workers Union bargains, for example, with the General Motors Corporation at the national level on national issues and at the local level on local issues. The product is a "master contract" covering the national and system-wide terms supplemented by local contracts at each appropriate local, or "plant," level.

PROCEDURAL ISSUES:
THE QUESTION OF FORMS OF REPRESENTATION

There are three avenues for faculty participation in academic decision making: (1) through the traditional *internal* institutions of academia—plenary faculty meetings, faculty senates, councils, committees; (2) through *external* faculty organizations operating informally or sporadically, such as the American Association of University Professors, the American Federation of Teachers, the National Education Association, the American Association for Higher Education, and other organizations appealing on a national or local basis for faculty support; (3) through an *external* faculty organization formally recognized as *collective bargaining representative* of the faculty. These three paths are not necessarily mutually exclusive, although the first will exclude the last if the first encompasses *all* issues; similarly, the last may exclude the first.

The ideal arrangement for faculty representation is clear, at least to me. It entails the utilization of a combination of the first two avenues. The primary dependence should be upon the traditional *internal* modes of bringing the faculty's viewpoint to bear upon academic decision making. The *external* organizations referred to above should play a supportive role. My reasons for this position are that the traditional forms for faculty representation can best accommodate the values of democracy and the values of professionalism. They can best accommodate, that is, the majoritarianism of democracy and the high standards and pursuit of excellence of professionalism. The traditional forms were developed, in fact, with this very purpose in mind. Faculty meetings, senates, councils, and committees of the traditional mode, entailing joint, non-conflict-oriented, faculty-administration decision making, afford the means for rendering democracy and professionalism complementary by countering the weaknesses of each with the strengths of the other—democracy's potential for softening standards is countered by professionalism's discipline for excellence; professionalism's potential for creating a tyranny of elitism is countered by the discipline of democratic procedures.

A key factor in achieving this happy blend of democracy and professionalism is the joint character of most of the traditional forms for faculty participation in academic decision making. The faculty meeting, for example, is typically chaired by the chairman of the department, the dean of the school or college, or the president of the institution, as the case may be. Each of these chairmen is, typically, both a member of the faculty and an administrator. As such, he is situated to bring an added dimension of knowledge and perspective to the common problems confronting the faculty and the administration—for example, those of recruitment, tenure, and promotion. In addition, his very presence changes the mood and mix of deliberations. Decisions made by a majority of those present at such a faculty meeting are not necessarily the same as would be the case were the meeting not joint, were the administrative head of the faculty unit not presiding.

To a large extent, the strength of decision making by such joint agencies is the product of the diffusion of power involved. The administrator holds a degree of power, both because of his leadership of the faculty and because of his presiding role at the meeting. The other members of the faculty also hold power because of their control of most of the votes. A mediocre faculty with a first-rate chairman or dean is less likely in such an environment to seek to protect itself from first-rate competition by softening standards for recruitment, tenure, and promotion. Conversely, a weak chairman or dean with a first-rate faculty (an unlikely situation, at least for any length of time) is qualified in the harm he can do by the countervailing faculty power. Moreover, the exercise of power by either of these two forces is less apt to entail destructive conflict. Power is more subtly exercised than in a collective bargaining environment. The resort is to reason; the power held by any one person in such a context is likely to bear a close relation to the degree of respect he has earned through superior performance as a teacher-scholar and/or as an administrator. Decisions reached through this process are more readily accepted by all involved.

Where the administration is stupid, arbitrary, or corrupt, the external faculty organizations "in the wings" can play a dynamic supportive role by rallying resources and pressures to bring to bear upon administrative officers and boards of trustees to preserve the values of this system of "democratic professionalism."

There are several problems inherent in the third or collective bargaining approach to faculty representation, which entails the importation and elevation of one of the external organizations as exclusive bargaining representative for the faculty. The first drawback to this variety of faculty representation is that it is premised upon—indeed, incites and institutionalizes—conflict between faculty and administration. Ideally, such conflict should be minimized; the common interests of faculty and administration should transcend them.

Collective bargaining maximizes conflict, with all of its trappings. The major trapping is reliance upon coercion as the technique for resolving disputes. When positions harden, as they inherently do in a collective bargaining context, there is no place else to turn. If strikes or related pressures on the employees' side and lockouts, firings, or other discriminatory practices on the employer's side are not to be indulged, the only alternatives are mediation, fact finding, and arbitration. But the latter are also power-oriented, acceptability by both sides being their key. The principles of professionalism, in which the public has a heavy interest, are likely to be among the first pawns sacrificed in this power struggle, for reasons which involve most basically a shift of power in the faculty from the professionally eminent to the politically able activists.

Collective bargaining as a form for faculty representation requires, as previously noted, the importation of a "foreign" bargaining agency into the campus mix. Not all faculty members will belong to the bargaining agency or participate in its affairs. Those eschewing it may include eminent members of the faculty who object for reasons of principle, lack of time, or both. Elements of the faculty, dissident from the traditional modes of faculty representation because of their own mediocrity and lack of advancement thereunder, may seize upon this alternative as an ersatz avenue to academic "success." And since the majority of any group, however elite, is necessarily less elite than the most elite in the group, there is apt to be resort by the less-qualified majority to the political power resulting from numbers to achieve the ascendency of "good fellowism," mediocrity, the less-demanding life, over high standards and excellence. The leadership of the faculty may shift from the most dedicated scholars and classroom performers to faculty politicians. The latter, to maintain their position as new leaders, must appeal to where the votes are, and in the "one-man, one-vote" context of democratic unionism the vote is not apt to be delivered by a program of incentives toward excellence, but by a program of immediate across-the-board benefits for the existing majority. The product of these forces might be expected to be a collective bargaining agreement containing standardized salaries, annual mandated increments, relaxed standards for tenure and promotion with primary reliance upon time-serving—in short, a surrender of the environment of excellence, of tough-minded application of high standards through the traditional joint agencies of faculty and administration.

This would not happen, of course, in the colleges and universities where the traditions of high standards and pride in excellence have taken deep enough root to have produced already an excellent faculty. Resort would not be had in such a school to collective bargaining; the latter would have no function in view of the *individual* bargaining power, the market value of the members of such a faculty, and the likely affluence of the institution which could recruit and hold them. Where resort might be had to collective bargaining, and most unhappily, is in weaker schools where a substantial segment of the existing faculty cannot really "cut the mustard," and where a sudden influx of new state money provides the potential for movement upward in quality. It is hard to imagine a more stultifying albatross for such an institution in the currently avid competition for outstanding faculty recruits than a system of faculty representation through collective bargaining, with all that this connotes to a young man with real horsepower, the urge to excel, to be rewarded for excellence, and to be surrounded by colleagues similarly motivated—to be party, that is, to a truly first-class operation.

In summary, a collective bargaining approach to faculty representation holds the danger of institutionalized conflict; of alienation of a part, perhaps the best part, of the faculty; of dampening of incentives toward excellence; and of a change for the worse, from the standpoint of standards, in the locus of faculty power.

Withal, it cannot be gainsaid that there are institutions of higher education where almost any change in faculty-administration relations would be an improvement, where a primitive administration, usually the product of a primitive board of trustees, precludes by its authoritarian manner any real potential for professionalism on the part of the faculty. Such administrations invite, indeed require, a power confrontation by the faculty. In such situations, collective bargaining may be the only realistic means by which the faculty can achieve sufficient control over its own environment to have a significant voice in the setting of the standards under which it works. When this voice is lacking, there is no profession at all, only employment. There is an old saw, the product of private enterprise employment relations, which is pertinent here: "An employer gets the kind of labor relations he deserves." If nothing but the power confrontation entailed in collective bargaining will emancipate a particular faculty from the toils of myopic administration, I am in favor of collective bargaining in that context. It may be that the use of such power is necessary in particular cases to achieve a salary level and basic conditions of employment affording the *material* wherewithal for effective instruction and scholarship. Where these rudiments are absent, it is fatuous to talk of loftier professional goals. A power confrontation in such circumstances is, by definition, a necessary first step along the professional path. I should hope, however, for all of the reasons previously outlined, that the mere incipience of such a confrontation would be sufficient to move the administration involved to provide the necessary environment for professionalism, including the development or vitalization, as the case may be, of the traditional forms for faculty representation.

Assuming the wisdom of the traditional internal forms for faculty representation in academic decision making, the question remains of how this approach can be implemented with respect to the various issues involved, in the face of the various levels of administration at which different issues are decided. Models, at the campus level, are available in any well-established, well-run college or university. There is a recognized faculty-administration forum with ample, well-recognized power at each level of decision making—department, school, or college, and campus-wide. The models vary, but their functions remain fairly constant. In the smaller units, regular and special meetings of the entire faculty, presided over by a department chairman or dean who is also a member of the faculty, are the agencies for joint resolution of important issues. Faculty committees supplement this process. In the larger units—at the campus level, for example—representative bodies such as senates and councils are frequently employed, made up of elected representatives of the faculty and of administrative officers serving by reason of their offices. Again, standing and special committees of the faculty, some elected, some appointed, are utilized.

There are, of course, difficult questions in determining the wisest structure and procedures for academic governance on any particular campus. What works well at one institution may work poorly at another because of the difference in size, relationships, traditions, resources, etc. The variety of potential forms is great, but they all have two things in common: (1) Their purpose is to provide for a joint faculty-administration consideration and determination of important issues. (2) They are all internal, "constitutional" structures and procedures, made part of the basic law of the institution. The principles that should be reflected in these forms for shared campus authority and the various structures and techniques for implementing these principles have been explicated elsewhere;[2] only one aspect requires further emphasis here.

The problem, in terms of available models, becomes acute with respect to the relatively new, statewide systems of higher public education. In these situations, means must be developed for effective faculty participation at every level of decision making. This requires a faculty senate, or its counterpart, i.e., an organ representative of the faculty, at each major level, including the statewide level or levels where super- and super-super-boards and administrations have been created in an effort to rationalize the allocation of resources to, and the governance of, entire state systems of higher education.

In conclusion, the structuring of academic government should be somewhat similar to the structuring of government generally. There should be a legislative body at each level of important decision making to establish policy. There should be a judicial body to apply that policy in particular cases. There should also be an executive at each level to carry out the decisions of the "legislature" and the "courts." The relationship between these bodies should be worked out in a fashion which facilitates their joint. goals. Since the goals are joint, gratuitous injection of conflict is out of order. The "legislatures" and, in many instances, the "courts" at each level should therefore be an amalgam of both faculty and administration—"mixed," as opposed to "pure." The lines for faculty-administration communication are thus more open, and the best blend of democratic process and professional standards is achievable. (The logic of my argument raises, of course, the question of *student* participation in academic governance. The organizers of this conference have chosen to leave that question for another day, and I am deeply obliged!)

PROFESSORIAL POWER: USES AND ABUSES

To the extent that power as to issues of concern to the faculty is accorded to the traditional organs for faculty representation in

[2]See, e.g., "Faculty Participation in Academic Governance," Report of the AAHE Task Force on Faculty Representation and Academic Negotiations (AAHE, NEA, 1967); "University Government in Canada," Report of a commission sponsored by the Canadian Association of University Teachers and the Association of Universities and Colleges of Canada (University of Toronto Press, 1966); "Statement on Government of Colleges and Universities," American Association of University Professors, American Council on Education, Association of Governing Boards of Universities and Colleges, *AAUP Bulletin*, Winter, 1966.

academic decision making, there is little need for the use of pressure tactics in establishing the faculty's point of view. The measures utilized are apt to be those of constitutional democracy generally— appeals to reason, the pressures of personal and political persuasion. This is the pattern in well-established, well-run colleges and universities.

But where internal agencies of the traditional mode do not exist or, if existent, are devoid of vitality, resort by the faculty to coercive efforts at achieving acceptance of its point of view are invited and therefore to be expected. Once appeals to reason have been exhausted, the faculty resort of first instance is likely to be to "professional sanctions"—a process culminating in a kind of professional blacklisting of the particular institution. This process entails several stages of involvement of one or more external faculty organizations: investigation to ascertain the facts; measurement of the facts against professional standards; a judgment of the extent to which the facts found are aberrant from the professional norms; efforts to subject the dispute to mediation or arbitration; if necessary, publication to the profession of any deficiencies found; and the imposition of professional taboos—in the extreme, blacklisting.

The taboos may entail cutting off recruitment of new members for the particular faculty. They may also reach to a challenging of the accreditation of the institution by the pertinent accrediting agency. In the case of public institutions, lobbying of various sorts may be employed. These failing, a strike or slowdown may be resorted to by the faculty.

The invocation of such professional taboos and employee pressures is the strongest evidence of the absence or breakdown of traditional collegial—which is to say, sensibly professional—relations within the particular school. The invocation of such taboos and pressures is right or wrong, good or bad, dependent upon the nature of the faculty grievance and the availability of some form of academic due process for dealing with it. The latter may be part of the institutionalized "rules of the game" or may be ad hoc procedures developed by agreement for resolving the particular dispute. In any event, resort to either professional taboos or employee strikes should be considered the ultimate weapon, to be used only after the fullest exploration and exhaustion of other less damaging means. The prior exhaustion of all tenable alternatives should be a condition precedent for reasons of both a philosophical and practical order. Philosophically, extreme and harmful measures are, by definition, measures of last resort among enlightened men; this is particularly true in the academy, the exemplar of reason and civility. On the practical side, the use of professional sanctions and strikes does serious injury to the institution and therefore to all who are associated with and dependent upon it. The harm may long outlast the dispute which produced it and heavily outweigh the benefits derived in any settlement of the dispute. Institutional prestige—so important in the recruitment of faculty and students and in fund-raising—is, like personal reputation, far easier to destroy than to develop.

SUMMARY AND CONCLUSIONS

The factor which most sharply distinguishes the "professor profession" from the classical professions of law and medicine is that the professor practices his profession as an employee. This means that he encounters difficulties in setting and maintaining the standards of his profession because of the intervention of an institutional employer (another standard-setter) between him and his "clients," those to whom he seeks to communicate his special knowledge. Two factors cause a society to designate certain callings "professions": (1) The calling is of such importance to the society that its practitioners must be held to higher standards than those of less vital callings, and (2) the calling is sufficiently esoteric, by reason of the degree of training required and the nature of the service rendered, that only practitioners of the calling have the understanding which is essential to formulate and enforce the necessary standards. Since, then, professors must establish and enforce their own professional standards, they must circumvent the standard-setting proclivity of the intermediary employer. This is increasingly difficult to do because of the increasing size and bureaucracy of colleges and universities, particularly those which are public and which have been incorporated into highly rationalized, highly complex statewide systems of higher education, with their super-boards, super-administrations, and super-budgetary systems.

In the effort to determine appropriate forms and procedures for faculty participation in the setting of the standards and policies which are of professional concern to the faculty, three interrelated questions are encountered: the nature of the issues which legitimately concern the faculty; the nature of the institution in which the issues arise; the levels of decision making with respect to the particular institution.

Issues which legitimately concern the faculty fall into four categories: (1) issues of educational and administrative policy, including the "constitutional law" by which the extent and the form of faculty participation are determined; (2) nonmonetary faculty personnel policies—appointment, tenure, promotion; (3) economic issues, such as the total amount of money to be available; the amount to be allocated to faculty salaries and fringe benefits; the amount to be allocated to each campus (within state systems), to each school or college, to each department, and to each rank; the compensation for individual members of the faculty; (4) "public" issues—those which involve the public image of the institution.

The levels at which these issues are effectively resolved at particular institutions include the following: department; school or college; campus; and, in statewide systems, the level of the one or more central administrations. For effective faculty participation in the determination of issues which legitimately concern it, the organs for faculty representation must be echeloned in the same fashion as the echeloning of decision making at the institution.

The three avenues by which faculty representation can be accomplished are: through the traditional *internal* organs of faculty representation — plenary meetings, senates, councils, and committees; through *external* faculty organizations, such as the AAUP, AFT, NEA, and AAHE; through an *external* organization acting as *collective bargaining representative*. The first of these, with supportive assistance from the second, is the preferred technique because it best accommodates the values of both democracy and professionalism. An internal organ of faculty representation should be provided at every level of effective decision making, preferably a "mixed" body, consisting of both faculty and (a lesser number of) administrators.

Collective bargaining as the mold for faculty representation should be avoided except where myopic and stiff-necked administration leaves no course of action for faculty participation in decision making other than through a power confrontation.

Where the traditional forms for faculty representation are available and viable, the means of persuasion used by the faculty are apt to be limited to those of constitutional government generally—appeals to reason, the pressures of personal and political persuasion. In cases of breakdown, these may be supplemented with professional sanctions. The latter, along with employee pressures—strikes and slowdowns—should be weapons of last resort, used only where all other means have been exhausted, because the damage inflicted on the institution may long outlast the dispute and outweigh the benefits achieved through its settlement.

To repeat, in closing, a note struck at the beginning of this paper, greater faculty participation in academic decision making, while desirable, will improve the quality of higher education only insofar as the degree of professionalization of the particular faculty permits. The tensions between the majority rule of democracy, with its standards-softening tendency, and the elitism of professionalism, with its accent on excellence, are classic.

DISCUSSION OF MR. OBERER'S PAPER

MR. FRANKIE: Mr. Oberer's paper has depth and scope. It is difficult to respond to a paper which comprises diverse levels of analysis. Mr. Oberer ranges from the broadest theoretical bases of democracy in governance to consideration of the practical and immediate issues of academic decision making. Lack of time will prevent discussion of some ideas that merit greater ventilation.

I feel we ought to start with Mr. Oberer's introductory remarks: "The practices and procedures of democracy do not necessarily inspire a quest for excellence, without which the campus is a sterile place. Indeed, an inherent tendency of majoritarianism is to enshrine and protect mediocrity." Then he added: "The former [democracy] views the standards of excellence with a skeptical eye, as a threat to the interests of the majority."

In this context I think we're forced to ask ourselves whether there is any significant, logical connection between the implications of democracy and the push to change the organization of decision making in institutions of higher education. Perhaps it is worthwhile to recall John Stuart Mill's great treatise on political philosophy entitled *Representative Government*. It was the first book to expound the modern theory of democracy. Mill wrote: "Democracy is the best form of government [because] it promotes, to a greater degree than any other form, the general mental advancement of the community," and it utilizes in better fashion than any other form "the moral, intellectual, and the active worth already existing" in the community. Mill's favorite theme was the superiority of an active character over a passive one. The best kind of person, according to Mill, is one who is not content merely to remain what he is, but who constantly tries to improve himself. He will not be satisfied with simply conforming to customs and prejudices of his community, but will blaze a new trail in a new direction. He will also be continually learning. He will be willing to embark on unusual paths of thought and action for the sake of discovery. Mill affirms that "this active type of character is greatly encouraged by self-government. Indeed, for many men participation in government may be the first step toward liberation from the chains of custom and conformity."

It would appear, then, that within the framework of John Stuart Mill's delineation of the functions of democracy there is room for considerable change in faculty involvement in academic decision making. If, as Mill suggested, the capacity to act responsibly grows with the opportunity for meaningful participation in the decision-making process, leaders of higher education need not fear, I would think, this enshrinement of mediocrity that Mr. Oberer referred to. In fact, in many institutions, my own notwithstanding, the expansion of participation by various units in decision making might indeed accelerate, as Mr. Oberer suggests, the pursuit of excellence.

Mr. Oberer goes on to state that there is a natural tension between democratization and professionalism. Is it necessarily true that this is a natural phenomenon? If professionalism refers to how a subject is taught or the quality of research or, as the author states, "the esoteric character of the calling," the democratic participation in academic decision making is not necessarily related. In fact, an administrative authoritarian approach can often bring about or promote professionalism as well as inhibit it. Participation can have the same effects. Democracy, I think, refers to governance and hence to policies. Professionalism, on the other hand, I think refers to competency, operations, and related concerns.

Having read the paper I would say, then, that faculty participation must occur from a position of *power*, and I am concerned with this aspect at my own institution, having come from Wayne State to The Ohio State University. Faculty, I think, have the power of their services being in demand elsewhere, as Mr. Gustad suggested, referring to "external audiences in other institutions."

For state-level bargaining or decision making to be effective there must be a united body *backing up* the faculty representatives. Judging from what Mr. Hayward and others have said, if you're going to move to the state level you have to have a strong organization at that level. If this kind of support is organized and available, then Mr. Oberer's concept of multi-level participation in decision making is soundly based.

The "linking pin" approach advocated by Rensis Likert and others can be a viable form. The emphasis on group participation or "System 4,"[6] as Likert designated it, will be particularly valuable, especially in view of the fact that an ever-increasing number of decisions are being made at the state and federal levels. However, I think we're moving here into the realm of theory. In this regard, Mr. Oberer has presented an excellent theoretical analysis of several areas of interest. However, the actual and primary concerns of the faculty, whatever they are, will determine, I think, what organizational structures they will seek. And, again, instead of getting into general situations, as you suggested this morning, we will have to deal with specifics.

I'm always interested that at the higher education conventions we have panels of presidents to talk about general administration. Each one always says, "My institution is unique." I heard President David Dodds Henry of Illinois and President William Rea Keast of Wayne State University, and each one said, "There are some basic principles, but I want to talk about how our institution is unique. This approach will work here, but it probably wouldn't work at X or Y University."

I concur that emphasis upon the nature of the institution or system and its context cannot be stressed too much. The issues will always be general unless situated within a specific framework. Mr. Oberer's case study of SUNY is useful in this regard to illustrate how tremendously complex our systems have become.

Interpretations of the Taylor Act in New York led me to suggest that of the forms of representation Mr. Oberer presented—internal (faculty senates), external faculty groups such as the AAUP, and then the recognized collective bargaining units—the second two avenues are the trend and probably will be the ones that predominate.

In fact, I want to question Mr. Oberer at this point. As I recall, you were one of the members of the AAHE-NEA Task Force that visited 34 separate institutions, and in your paper you say as a result of these visits that senates and external organizations can in fact *coexist*. You said that your preference would be the first one.

MR. OBERER: Let me interrupt. I think that's inaccurate because what I say is that the ideal arrangement as far as I'm concerned "entails the utilization of a combination of the first two avenues. The primary dependence should be upon the traditional internal modes. . . . The external organizations . . . should play a supportive role."

MR. FRANKIE: Perhaps we might have some discussion on that

---

[6]Rensis Likert, *The Human Organization* (New York: McGraw-Hill, 1967).

later. I thought this was the development. We may have had some changes.

My own view is that arrangements for internal governance of the university should be vigorously reviewed to provide maximum inter-action not only of the faculty and administrators, but also should include the students, as Mr. Oberer said. The degree of faculty participation will be dependent in part, however, on some of the following variables:

1. The degree of administrative coercion.
2. The degree of incongruence between faculty and administrative goals.
3. The availability of existing participatory structures or devices.
4. The local autonomy compared to state-level control.

The last is illustrated in an issue involving the Ohio Board of Regents. I recall that when I was a student at Michigan, Chancellor John Millett stated that the trimester was the best answer to higher education's calendar year. He took this position while president of Miami University (Ohio). Then, when he was appointed chancellor of the Board of Regents, he said that every institution in Ohio must go to the quarter system.

MR. GUSTAD: Actually, he said if state institutions wanted to get money from the state they must go to the quarter system.

MR. FRANKIE: The ratio of cosmopolitans to locals on the faculty is another variable to be considered.

Another major variable, I think, is the degree to which given issues evoke an activity need within a sufficient number of faculty members. As Herbert Simon stated, the zone of indifference within which faculty will accept leadership and direction is certainly critical.

Still another variable is the ratio of the desire to stay and (1) work for improvements and (2) leave things as they are, to the "ability to make an acceptable move elsewhere."

With these variables considered we can take heart from words written by Woodrow Wilson in his monumental 1887 work entitled *The Study of Administration*. Wilson wrote: "Trust is strength in all relations in life; and as it is the office of the administrative reformer to create conditions of trustfulness, so it is the office of the administrative organizer to fit administration with conditions of clear-cut responsibility which shall insure trustworthiness. And let me say that large powers and unhampered discretion seem to me the indispensable conditions of responsibility. There is no danger in power, if only it be not irresponsible."

With these words maybe we can go on and give Mr. Lieberman a chance to rebut.

MR. OBERER: I want to respond with just a couple of remarks. I don't feel defensive; therefore I'm not going to try to catalogue responses to all of the items mentioned.

First of all I want to say that I believe in democracy. I also think, however, that there are some areas of human endeavor which should not be democratized in the full sense that I at least mean when I use that term. Let me give an example. There is a movement afoot now to unionize professional athletes. I have in mind a satire which I plan to write sometime on the unionizing of professional football players. Which 11 will start a given game? Those with the most seniority, of course. And how do you get promoted to what you consider to be a better position on the team—quarterback, for example? You put your name on the promotion list. If you're a 270-pound tackle, when they get down to your name it's your turn to be quarterback.

Relating this to some of the egalitarian tendencies on the campus, the business of students objecting to being graded, not wanting to compete, not wanting to find out how good they are or how much they're really putting out—my union of football players will ultimately demand the doing away with the keeping of scores.

That's just to illustrate what I mean by the competition between the tendencies of democracy in some applications and the necessities for the pursuit of excellence.

MR. SUMBERG: May I ask how you would "tackle" the "impasse" problem?

MR. OBERER: A nice pun.

MR. MacRAE: Quite often you have said, Mr. Oberer, that democracy views excellence as a threat. How about this supposedly sacred tenet of democracy in its concern for individuals? Have you thrown that out?

MR. OBERER: No, I haven't thrown it out. I think that's a real problem in the academy—unduly due process, let me put it that way. One of the places where I gain experience and from which I draw the tentative inference you have just re-expressed, and which Mr. Frankie latched onto, is the bargaining table at sessions between public school teacher organizations and school boards. Let me be specific.

I was out in the Midwest two or three months ago mediating one of these impasses. One of the demands of the teacher organization (and I've encountered this elsewhere) was that in cases of denial of tenure the person denied tenure should have the right of appeal to an outside arbitrator.

What are the implications of that with regard to standards for the granting of tenure and the denying of tenure in the particular situation?

MR. CRONIN: Is that a question on the standards or on the process by which competence is determined?

MR. OBERER: I'm going to relate the two.

Put yourself in the position of one who is called upon to evaluate a colleague for the purpose of granting or denying tenure—a question which is frequently presented, I presume, to faculty members at any quality institution, one that is not authoritarian (and I don't in any way support authoritarianism). The question asked is whether the fellow should get tenure.

What do we do under these circumstances? Certainly we understand it's a terribly important question. We agonize over it and we take whatever position we take on the basis of the fullest kind of consideration. Let's take two cases. In case one we can adopt our position without this due process paraphernalia; I mean by that, without appeal by the person to some outside arbitrator. I use that as an example because that's the way it came up in the instance I mentioned. Case two: We know that our judgment is going to be second-guessed, that we're going to be subjected to cross-examination.

What I submit is that we as human beings would act differently in those two frames of reference, and I suggest that the standard would be diluted in the second. We would be apt to heave a sigh and approve somebody (let me assume hypothetically) whom we would not approve under the first scheme of things.

MR. CRONIN: Some professional individuals might try to find standards of competence.

MR. OBERER: But whatever the standards, I'm talking about the application of them. We all have our standards. In the final analysis, you in passing upon the question of tenure for anybody else apply the standards which have become part of you. Words may be given to you by somebody else, but you interpret those words and give them meaning in terms of your own experience and judgment. And I think as a human being you would act differently in those two cases.

The argument advanced for what I call unduly due process is that administrators are incompetent and in a sense corrupt—that is, willing to play favorites. While I concede that there are instances of favoritism and of incompetence on the part of those who evaluate others in education, I frankly consider those the exceptional cases. I don't think that standards should in all cases be diluted to take care of the exceptional cases.

MR. MacRAE: I suppose Mr. Lieberman would say that the second one is the better because there is accountability.

MR. OBERER: Yes.

MR. LIEBERMAN: Frankly, I don't understand this discussion of professionalism and democracy because I don't understand how you relate the discussion to an internal mechanism versus some other mechanism. I'm saying this very sincerely. I simply don't understand what your point is.

For example, should issues be decided by one person-one vote in a faculty senate? If they should, how is the outcome any different than if you have a bargaining agent on that particular issue?

Your paper suggests a vague identification of democracy with some external representational mechanism. Professionalism, whatever that may mean to you, is a sort of elitism. But I don't know how you come out with the conclusions that you do. I'm not even sure I know what the conclusions are.

For example, how does a faculty senate resolve your problem of democracy in a way that an external agent does not? Unless you don't believe in a one person-one vote procedure, there would be the same tendency to mass decision making in a senate as there would be in an external bargaining agent wherein each person had one vote.

This illustrates the difficulties I have with your position.

MR. OBERER: I really don't know how I can explain any better than I have in the latter part of my paper the whole business of the diffusion of power in the traditional scheme of faculty representation, the business of mixed legislative bodies—faculty and administration. These traditional forms for faculty representation didn't materialize overnight. They're not the product of blind chance. They're the distillation, in my judgment, of decades of experience and agonizing, consciously and unconsciously, with exactly the tension that I've tried to describe; the effort being to accommodate democracy to the pursuit of excellence.

Those of us who have had experience with collective bargaining in the private sector (and I take it this includes many at the table here) can hardly be blinded to some of the implications of the organization of a plant. For one thing, there can be a chilling of aspirations toward superior performance; the "rate buster," for example. That may be a rather poor analog for the faculty scene, but at least it establishes—

MR. MOSKOW: That's a very poor analog, Mr. Oberer, because we have individual bargaining in higher education and we can bargain for much higher salaries than what the standard might be.

MR. OBERER: That's true, and I'd answer in two fashions. First, I would say that where you have individual bargaining power you don't need collective bargaining. Collective bargaining is a device developed and calculated to equalize strength for bargaining purposes. Secondly, I would be afraid that under a collective bargaining scheme of things you and I would be deprived of our individual bargaining power.

MR. MOSKOW: I'd probably agree with your second point. From a personal standpoint I would resist collective bargaining because I might be hurt by it. However, as to the first point you made, we've seen other cases where we've had individual bargaining and collective bargaining combined. It was the Webbs'* original idea that the minimum wage be negotiated and that people can negotiate over it. We have individual bargaining in the performing arts in this country, for instance, and we're going to have it in professional sports. Individual and collective bargaining are not incompatible.

MR. OBERER: Let me give another example from the same Midwestern contract impasse experience. One of the provisions actually put into the contract was that the school board could not recruit anybody from outside the system into the system and pay that person more than that person's experience in terms of years of teaching would permit under the schedule which had been agreed upon. There's a ceiling on individual bargaining power.

MR. LOWENBERG: That's the way that particular situation was developed. I really believe that the performing arts illustration might be more applicable if you're talking about professional standards; you still haven't seen the chorus girl taking over the lead role just because she has seniority.

MR. MOSKOW: May I comment in regard to the democratization that you talked about before? You spoke of the satire you would write on professional sports. I think it would be very humorous and would probably sell, but I don't think the analogy holds. Again, look at the performing arts. We have organizations at the Metropolitan Opera, the San Francisco Ballet, the League of New York Theater. All of these groups have collective bargaining. The Metropolitan Opera

---

*Sidney and Beatrice Webb, *Industrial Democracy* (London: Seaham Divisional Labor Party, 1902).

bargains with 13 different unions, and yet no one suggests that the arrangement hampers the quality of performance at all. We have soloists who receive $2,000 for one performance and we have people in the chorus who are paid $200 a week. Performance is not affected.

There is a "democratization" of certain parts of the working environment there, but not of all parts.

MR. HOWE: I would suggest that there are some built-in potential contradictions in Mr. Oberer's position. I learn a great deal from having a fourth-grade daughter. Our conversation at a recent breakfast was typically fourth-grade—very big on riddles. The riddle I'm reminded of was: "Daddy, what do you get when you cross a tiger with a canary?" Playing the role of straight man I said, "Amanda, I don't know. What *do* you get when you cross a tiger with a canary?" The answer is: "I don't know either, but when it sings you better listen."

The creation of a balance of power, which is the intent of collective bargaining legislation, promotes the probability of persuasion. When I walk to the bargaining table I am not afraid, but I am reasonable.

A second contradiction has to do with facts that Corwin put forward. He found that an increase in professionalization promotes and correlates with an increase in militancy; the most militant personalities he detected were by and large the most professional people. It seems to me that in your emphasis on persuasion and "professionalization" you open yourself at least to some question in this regard. What you say doesn't contradict the desirability of the collective bargaining arrangement.

MR. LIEBERMAN: Undesirable clauses in collective agreements are irrelevant. The school board that accepted the clause, not the procedure, should be criticized. Let's not assume that in the absence of a collective agreement there never was a bad personnel policy.

Is there anybody in this room now who can tell me how Mr. Oberer concludes that an internal mechanism would avoid the majority threat to elitism, while an external agent would not?

MR. OBERER: Mr. Oberer will if you'll give him a chance!

MR. LIEBERMAN: Try me again then. Explain it a different way. But I have a hunch that the rest of the participants don't understand your argument either.

MR. OBERER: Here is my fear. My fear is that the leadership of the faculty will not be the same under a collective bargaining approach as it is under the standards approach. I remember what Mr. Howe said yesterday to the effect that the constituency of the collective bargaining representative at his school was precisely the same as the constituency of the faculty senate. In that situation I would ask this question: Why dichotomize? Why not deal with all the issues at one table with one representative? In that situation I can see where there wouldn't be the kind of conflict that Mr. McHugh was worried about yesterday in trying to, as Mr. Blum suggested might be done, cull out the terms and conditions of employment for dealing in the collective bargaining environment and leave the rest of it for faculty senate dealing.

What I anticipate would happen—I'm sure it would happen in my faculty and I think it's typically what would happen—is that some professors would choose not to play the game if it were a collective bargaining game, whether out of principle, whether out of blindness, asininity, or what have you. Some might choose not to play because they don't want to get involved in a time-consuming business and the politicking. As a consequence you would have a different kind of leadership (this is my fear anyway) in a particular faculty. Some members of the faculty who were politically activist anyway and maybe some who are disgruntled by the current scheme of things might well gain the ascendancy. It would just be a different environment.

Beyond that, let me add this point, Mr. Lieberman. You keep asking what the difference is between collective bargaining and the more traditional scheme of things. I would answer you most basically in this fashion: Collective bargaining is a power confrontation, and that's something we haven't kept in mind enough in these proceedings. There is no reason for collective bargaining except the power leverage which will produce for the ones engaged in collective bargaining something they feel they couldn't get otherwise.

MR. BLUM: Because you referred to your own institution and I spent one year there, let me say that I remember the faculty meetings. The leading political activist was a person who didn't publish a thing, had tenure a long time, and was the most actively oriented toward going to faculty meetings, while some of the others who wanted to write books or articles didn't show up. The political activist could be active in the senate while the rest wouldn't be.

I agree with everything you say in terms of elitism in the university, but what bothers me is the approach. I find myself arguing with you concerning the approach this morning, while yesterday I might have argued with Mr. Lieberman. It's your whole attitude, which is reflected in your paper where you refer to a "foreign element" in collective bargaining. You speak of a foreign bargaining agency and say that "not all faculty members will belong." All faculty members may belong to the senate, but that doesn't mean they show up at the senate or participate in its affairs. Some prominent faculty people won't participate in the union; they also frequently don't show up at faculty or senate meetings. The one person at my university who is most active—and he happens to be a reasonably good scholar—is always there talking; people don't even listen to him any longer because he's always making a speech.

And then there is the phrasing of your argument. Judge George Baer could have written some of this about the union movement. He has the same attitude toward "foreign elements" of an external organism.

MR. OBERER: I say "foreign" only in the sense that it's external, not part of the institutional—

MR. BLUM: It's using words, I know. It's why I said "either-or" yesterday. Mr. Lieberman emphasizes "either" and only in a few words talks about the "or," and you emphasize "or" and say only a few words about the "either." Everybody then gets protected.

MR. OBERER: Let me respond to your first point first. You say that faculty people don't always go to faculty meetings. That's true, but I remember that when I was executive director of the Public Review Board of the United Auto Workers a problem arose in a local of the UAW at a Ford Motor Company plant. The plant had 4,000 workers. There was a union shop and a regular union meeting every month. It took us two months to get a quorum of those workers present. Do you know what the quorum was? One percent. It took us two months to get 40 people at a union meeting. This is collective bargaining, and—

MR. BLUM: I don't say there is more participation in unions. Don't misunderstand. I'm just saying both may have no participation.

MR. WEINBERG: How many people show up at contract ratification time? That is the key.

MR. OBERER: The same thing is true at faculty meetings. When we had the issue at Cornell of whether or not the university should give data to the Selective Service for draft purposes, there was a hell of a turnout.

MR. BLUM: This is why we really ought to be thinking (and this is what bothers me) about what are the things that are important in the university in terms of what either an external or internal group can deal with best. What we're going to end up with is what is presently happening in the public school system, if indeed Mr. Lieberman is in the vanguard. I'm afraid of what that vanguard would bring. It will bring things that I'm opposed to and that you're attacking. By labeling these things we're not going to resolve anything. We're just going to let it happen without, I think, controlling it as it is happening. And this is what disturbs me about his whole meeting. We've been labeling, rather than looking at, some of the fundamental issues that perhaps ought not to be negotiable by any group coming in from the outside, or even operating on the inside.

MR. WEINBERG: The difference between the senate and the collective bargaining unit is not a difference in the power concept. There is power in the senate. It is a different application of power. If the senate does well it is not because of its persuasive ability; there are all sorts of things unsaid in parentheses. If a university has a faculty with a tremendous amount of academic status, a raise of the eyebrow is an indication of power. It may cast an anathema on the university. Berkeley has a problem of recruitment because some faculty members are disenchanted.

There is little difference between the use of polite power in the senate and a dirty, open use of power in a bargaining situation. It is still power, except that in one case they are not talking strike. They are talking about other pressures which are a little more polite and perhaps more effective. At times a powerful university faculty may raise an eyebrow and have more power than a junior college faculty strike.

MR. OBERER: I would respond to you in this fashion. I think you have to analyze power. You can't just generalize about power. It isn't like gold bullion piled up on somebody's desk. It's different things for different purposes. It means different things in different hands. And what I'm suggesting is that through the faculty senate approach the power is situated in different places than it is likely to be situated in a collective bargaining approach.

MR. WEINBERG: But it is still use of power.

MR. OBERER: I don't decry power. As a matter of fact, when I talked about persuasion in my paper, I talked about the personal and political power of individuals on the faculty. It's true in our faculty meetings that when some people talk we tune them out, and when other people talk we listen. This is because we have learned over a period of time that the second person is somebody whose judgment is to be valued, and he draws water. He draws water because of his performance in all respects on the faculty—as a classroom teacher, as a scholar, because of the soundness of his judgment, his articulateness.

I think power earned in that fashion is power properly used. I don't see any potential for abuse there, that is, in an academic scheme of things.

MR. WEINBERG: I am not so sure it may be on the merits. There may be some implied threats of action short of a strike; for example, an important professor may threaten to leave a department. It may be viewed as a display of power, and it may be irrational, unstructured power.

MR. MacRAE: How about this cliquism that we sometimes have in faculties, where if a person in the majority clique makes a motion it's seconded at once, and if somebody else outside the clique makes a motion the clique freezes up with respect to that? What happens to this sort of thing with different organizational forms?

MR. OBERER: Faculties are made up of human beings and you're going to have cliquism, as you call it, whenever you have human beings involved in group endeavors.

MR. EVANS: We're right down to the nitty-gritty here. I see that this discussion isn't over the relative merits of the effectiveness of internal and external representative groups. Really what it boils down to is that you, Mr. Oberer, pose a certain value system that says that certain kinds of people will be the power base in one kind of representative group and other kinds of people in the other. Then someone comes out and says that the wrong kind of people are the power base in the current type of internal organization. This is what the discussion is really about.

MR. OBERER: I would agree that that is an important part of what we are talking about.

MR. ROSENTHAL: Mr. Oberer, you mention in your paper that the leaders of this symposium have wisely chosen to omit the question of student participation in academic governance.

MR. OBERER: I didn't say "wisely." I just said, in effect, "Thank God."

MR. ROSENTHAL: It implies relief and I share that relief because I think it makes our discussion here a lot easier. But I also think it makes our discussion to a large extent irrelevant. In talking about power I think we have to recognize that the students have the power to paralyze a university. In fact, they're the ones likely to be most inclined to use that power, as we've seen. I think they want to be involved, and I don't think it's enough to say that the questions they're concerned with are questions which we're not concerned with here. While we may view some of the issues as purely economic so far as the faculty is concerned, to the students they're academic in the best sense of the word.

Take issues like contract hours and tenure. Students are going to want to be involved in those issues, and they're going to argue that the education they receive is involved. We're going to argue that it has to do only with our economic position and that only we should be concerned.

I think students are going to assault questions like tenure soon, and I don't see an answer here yet on how we involve students in the process. If we bring them into the faculty meetings, they outnumber the faculty. Franconia College tried this; I'm not sure what the results were.

UNIDENTIFIED PARTICIPANT: The president left.

MR. ROSENTHAL: I'm not so sure that was because they involved the students and the janitors and the secretaries as part of the community. But I know they tried.

Israel is very much afraid that if they let the Arabs come in they're going to be overrun by Arabs, and I wonder if the students aren't our Arabs.

The question may be easier to solve in a small rural institution, but it may be more important that we think of it in the context of a large urban institution. I wonder if you have some answer to that, Mr. Oberer?

MR. OBERER: You have raised important questions. Within the last two weeks I had a delegation of students in my office at Cornell. Their purpose was to start the ball rolling with respect to, number one, student involvement in tenure decisions and, number two, student involvement in recruitment decisions. The pitch made was an understandable one: that nobody has a deeper interest in and concern for the quality of the faculty at the Cornell Law School than the students who have to sit in the classrooms and put up with it.

MR. MARMION: Why do you think collective negotiations are the vanguard of the future? As a lawyer, what do you see as the main reason for this?

MR. OBERER: I can't answer the question, but if you like I'll extemporize with regard to it. I have never felt as much of a malaise in my now 47 years as I have felt in the last year, and it really deepened to its nadir some time shortly after the Tet offensive. Those of us on campuses have been infected by the mood of the students, and I think the mood of the students at Cornell changed for the worse some time around then.

I've lived through the depression. I was old enough to understand it. I was brought up in Detroit. I had friends and relatives who were out of work. We had breadlines. I spent three and a half years in the service in World War II. I lived through the McCarthy era. I practiced law in Detroit and I experienced all of the pressures. But I still say that the current period is the one that most concerns me. I'm talking now not only about Cornell or the academy but about our free society.

It most concerns me because I can't understand it. I understood the depression and I thought we would come out of it. I understood World War II and I thought we would win. I understood the McCarthy era. I understood the forces aligned aginst me and I thought ultimately we would prevail. But I don't understand the situation now.

I was on a university commission at Cornell last spring, a commission engendered in this fashion: The Students for a Democratic Society locked in the Board of Trustees at one of its regular meetings and extracted as ransom for their release an agreement on the part of President Perkins to constitute a university commission. To deal with what? To deal with university investments. Investments in what? In four New York banks which were members of a 10- or 11-bank consortium, which consortium was extending credit to South Africa.

There were two faculty members on the commission; I was one. There were two students, one of whom was a member of SDS. There were two Board of Trustee members and two administrators. The SDS student, interestingly, was in my freshman class in contracts at the Law School and I had gotten to know him; and in the process of the commission's deliberations and in walking with him back to the Law School I had the opportunity to explore his thinking at great length and depth. I have high regard for this student. He's a very bright, upright sort of fellow. Indeed, I've been reading avidly everything I can get my hands on with regard to the New Left, the SDS, and the other groups.

I come out of that still not understanding anything. What I am forced to do is to psychoanalyze. I think to myself that the current generation of young people has never known any condition other than affluence; that's one thing. And they've been deprived of something that I experienced. During the depression my father was in the garage business and ran a gas station. I used to work in the summer for him 50 hours a week, and I wouldn't take more than 50 cents, a penny an hour, because I understood our family's problems and I felt that I was contributing to the family's well-being; and it was a wonderful thing for me. I think the current crop of young people have been deprived of that opportunity.

We can all speculate beyond that. I just don't know. In part it's the easy life. The students are rebelling against the demands of high standards, and grades are the way these demands are brought to bear upon them.

MR. CRONIN: There's a rival hypothesis. It is that the students are railing against injustice. I'm not going to explain the civil rights movement, or that South Africa is essentially a racist society, or that students who perhaps have been deprived of personal discomfort or family loss of income are now affluent enough to worry about what is happening in Southeast Asia. Perhaps there are some very healthful aspects of this malaise that perhaps *we* were deprived of. Certainly my generation, the silent generation of the 1950's, was completely irrelevant to most of the fundamental world problems which were festering during those golden years of affluence.

It is difficult to understand social forces and social movements, but you've got to look at the fact that although there are a few dozen privileged universities which are able to make the decision not to grow (Harvard is one of those and Cornell is another), there are also a large number of colleges and universities which have to grow in order to accommodate the great numbers who want to pursue higher education. Here the very nice position of individual bargaining just seems to be breaking down in a large number of these places.

The community college, which, of course, is caught between several social movements, including the movement of high school education up, is just an extreme example. But I think looking five and 10 years ahead we've got to see that the fact that there are 5,000 assistant professors in a state system, all of whom cannot negotiate individually with deans and presidents and the like, is breeding a request for a new system. It's breeding a desire to know what the ground rules are for promotion.

You talk about the need to write a satire on the unionization of professional football. I'd like to suggest that the satire on academic hiring, retention, and promotion practices has already been written. It's called *The Academic Marketplace* and it was written as a serious sociological tract. There are some flaws in that particular document, but I'd like to suggest that there is a linkage between the Lieberman-Oberer papers and Mr. Gustad's paper which, if you strip away the very amusing comments, is a very serious indictment of promotion practices because it suggests the extent to which excellence in teaching has to be ignored because of the Byzantine system that we have right now. There is a three- or four-page indictment in there which is very much in the tradition of Caplow and McGee, and it is this that younger faculty members certainly are going to be fighting for in the next decade.

If the AAUP procedures and methods are deemed not sufficient—and I'm one who believes that the AAUP has fought some very important battles and won some very important victories in the past—but if these are not sufficient to handle the problem of size and of bureaucracy, then this I submit is the reason why there is going to be a movement toward collective negotiations as an additional way to get reasonable procedures.

Again I remind you that *The Academic Marketplace* was not intended as a spoof. It just comes out that way when you see the effects of cliques and of favoritism and of hiring a member of a department because he fits into the baroque music group and can play the recorder. It comes out that way when you see all the other factors irrelevant to excellence in any classic sense that come into so many of these decisions today. I think that elitism and oligarchy do not necessarily breed excellence. They may in a few places where there are other social forces that are perpetuating excellence. Certainly the curriculum and the grading system at the Harvard Law School were not indicative of excellence and were in need of rather fundamental reform. It can show that an elite perpetuating itself can simply perpetuate the nineteenth-century approach to the study of law, which isn't particularly relevant to the problems of the 1960's. Thank heavens, things are changing there rather rapidly in a wholesome way.

I want to side with Mr. Frankie, I think, in suggesting that there are a variety of kinds of methods of using democratic machinery. Although I have to concede that negotiations in so much of the industrial sector are a device for exercising raw power, it need not be so. Negotiations can be a device where a great deal of persuasion and a great deal of rationality are introduced into a system which is now riddled with irrational procedures and policies.

MR. MARMION: I'm aware of decisions at Harvard, at Yale, at Tufts, where excellence in teaching, which presumably is an important factor, was seemingly ignored. I wouldn't have known about it except for the fact that the students brought it to the attention of the rest of the university and to the mass media. Under public scrutiny universities were forced to behave either in a more rational way or in a way which made their criteria more explicit.

I don't think it's very healthy to have these things aired in public. There is a need for confidentiality, but there's an even greater need for rationality.

MR. OBERER: Let me add this footnote, then, to what we've been saying. I agree with you that performance in the classroom is terribly important. As far as I'm concerned, that's the number one obligation of a member of any faculty.

I am of the opinion further that you can't teach in the same building with a colleague for any length of time without in one fashion or another getting a pretty good idea of how he is performing in the classroom. I broached this thought before an NEA-affiliated organization at a bargaining session when the school board was caucusing. Tenure procedures and the like were being considered. I said, "Now, isn't this true in a grade school or a high school where there is any degree of stability of the teaching staff?" They agreed. They said they had a pretty good idea who among them were cutting the mustard in the classroom and who weren't.

MR. CRONIN: How?

MR. OBERER: In the same ways that I find out, I presume, at law school. I go to cocktail parties and the students start talking, their tongues loosened by a drink or two. They engage in give-and-take. You know the students. You know the good ones, the fair ones, the poor ones. You put all this together. You hear subsequently of their other experiences, and they either fit together or they don't; and over a period of time you learn.

MR. CRONIN: Is this a rational system?

MR. OBERER: It's not irrational. It's a system which operates because, as Mr. Gustad pointed out, there is no other way.

In law school we visit the classroom too. We sit in on the classes and ascertain for ourselves this part of the jigsaw puzzle; but the other pieces are important.

MR. CRONIN: I will concede this. A number of American law schools have about the only system of visitation of fellow teachers that I'm aware of.

MR. GUSTAD: Medical schools do, too.

MR. CRONIN: That kind of evaluation I think is very defensible, and I simply say that negotiations might serve as one vehicle to spread this quite possibly desirable method of peer evaluation or evaluation by superiors.

MR. OBERER: Let me relate this to something Mr. Lieberman said yesterday. At this same bargaining session I mentioned, the representatives of the NEA affiliate had told me they had a good idea of who was not performing well in the classroom in their particular school. I said to them, "Then why doesn't that find expression with regard to tenure?" They said that it was the function of administration to grant this. Then I said, "It seems to me terribly important, then, that you have something to say with regard to who the administrators are. I assume you, as I, want to be party to a first-class operation, which means you don't want to recruit people into your school system who are not good people. You want to keep good people, but you don't have to keep people who don't contribute to the reputation, the status, the quality of performance of your particular school."

They agreed with all of that, but they said they had no voice at all in the selection of the principal, superintendent, and other administrators; but they would like to have. And indeed as a result of the discussion that followed a committee was constituted, a joint committee of administrators and teachers, which was going to look into the manner in which supervisors were chosen to see to what extent faculty involvement could be obtained.

MR. ZWINGLE: I don't know whether I'm the only one here whose decades of administrative experience put him somewhat outside this fraternity. I recognize in comments made here many of the problems I've had to deal with and the imperfections of the methods of dealing with them; so I want to suggest, as a readdress to a problem that we all feel, and a problem which does not come into focus very well, that there are four points (as an oversimplification) with which we are dealing:

One is judgment about productivity—how to judge. We haven't made a great deal of progress on this point because this is a problem that cannot be reduced to a simple formula. At best you come out with a partially subjective judgment. The confusion about writing versus teaching is basic. I don't think we're any further along on that problem than we were at the beginning of my chain of experience (I won't say my career).

MR. GUSTAD: Socrates didn't publish.

MR. MacRAE: He perished, too!

MR. ZWINGLE: This is a very neat lead-in to the second point I want to make. It bears precisely on Socrates. Great difficulties of judgment arise when we must take personal idiosyncrasies into account. Here you have a problem with the range of (1) acceptable and (2) unacceptable idiosyncrasies. The idiosyncrasies of Socrates were fatal.

Tenure has been granted to a number of persons under my own observation, and indeed with my own participation, when the institution decided that it could live with this particular hair shirt. So we come to something even more complex: how you can assess the standards to be used objectively, and subjectively, within the society comprising an institution. This becomes even more complicated by the new problems of mass. It is difficult enough in a stable institution undergirded by "tradition" (usually an accumulation of habit, good or bad).

The final point: We have a problem of self-criticism. I don't believe that it can be properly said that any social institution is self-correcting. Such corrections as are made most likely result from external circumstances. Sometimes they come from internal leadership, but not often.

The puzzle here is this: Given the circumstances of life today—the new mass, new elements we confront, the relationship between institutional standards and judgment about productivity, the lack of judgment about institutional goals, the confusion about the degree of personal idiosyncrasy that an institution finds tolerable or intolerable, the absence of any rational mode of self-criticism in an institution—I am led to share Mr. Oberer's deep concern. When you talk about national educational organizations and their possible services, this leads to an even greater sense of futility.

It seems to me that for the next little while, while the power play takes its own course, the problem before us is to see whether we can ask the right questions frequently enough in the right places, whether we can stimulate the kind of conversation required in the scope of higher education.

Let me sign off with this remark. It has been my particular experience to have lived through some extremely critical situations. For example, I found myself quite unprepared to be the fulcrum in a threatened race riot in 1943 in a Southern town. It was sheer good luck that I managed to survive this experience and help avert a crisis.

This experience has been repeated time after time in the academic setting with less drama. All this experience has made me believe there could be a vertical scheme of systematic conversation extending from students to trustees to alumni. Back in the days when this was a novelty, we went through the business of admitting Negroes to a self-contained residential college; the results were a little hard to assess at the time, but the only way we got through that one was by keeping the conversation alive.

Those of you who are professionals in negotiations know what is involved in the timing and in the direction of such conversations. But I fear that the capacity for meaningful conversation among the power groups in higher education is diminishing. If so, we're in for pretty hard times.

MR. LIEBERMAN: At your institution I assume you have some internal mechanism for evaluating faculty. Is the person being evaluated entitled as a matter of right to know the specific recommendation and the basis of it for each person who performs the evaluation?

MR. OBERER: The answer is no.

MR. LIEBERMAN: How is that different from McCarthyism? The person being evaluated could be evaluated most unfairly, yet he would not know the basis of it.

MR. OBERER: My answer is that it's different in that my colleagues and I are not Joe McCarthy.

Let me add something else. We do have questionnaires for student evaluation of teachers at Cornell, too, and indeed one of the best measures you can get on a colleague's quality of performance in the classroom comes from a third-year student who had him in the first year and who has been around long enough now to appreciate what the fellow was trying to do and how much of it he got done. And even better than that is the student who has been out a year or two or three and then comes back and gives his testimony.

MR. HIXSON: I must say to Mr. Oberer that I share to some degree the same kind of *Welschmerz* because of the traumatic experiences of the past year, but I wonder if I might quote briefly from Ed Schwartz, former president of the National Student Association. I think he has something relevant to our discussion today. And I have the feeling that it applies to the new instructors who will, I think, form the nucleus of the vanguard of the future.

Schwartz said recently in Colorado: "When leaders of the society and of the university resist the kinds of changes which students propose, the students then demand institutional power so they may enact changes themselves. Bob Dylan's exhortation that fathers and mothers should get out of the way if they can't lend a hand is as clear and vibrant an expression of this feeling as any which has been offered. The student demand for power further tests the university's humaneness. A university which is decent to its students will grant student power as an expression of trust and as an indication that it sympathizes with the student concerns.

"When the university administration or faculty rejects the student cries for power, often by using arguments which skirt the real issues and insult the students' integrity, the young's image of the corruption of the old order is reinforced. Yet the young will no longer accept corruption without a fight. Those who miss this sense of urgency do so at their own risk. What young people lack in argumentative skill and political experience they make up for in growing tactical sophistication and a willingness to apply it. They are determined to win points, and judging from the pace of events they probably will. The question is no longer whether, but how; no longer how far, but how fast. And these depend essentially upon the ability of an old order to move, to change, and to grow."

MR. OBERER: I'd like to respond to that in this fashion: I agree wholeheartedly that there is need for student participation in university governance, and indeed we have done a good deal of that sort of thing at Cornell. This is one of the reasons (only one) why we haven't had the Columbia or the Berkeley type of confrontation yet. But part of my malaise comes from the fact that the issues which the really radical students seize upon are issues of opportunity. If you satisfy them on one score then there's another one, a new confrontation. Indeed one of the ways we get surcease is by taking care of one of these issues of opportunity, and then there is a period during which these students have to lie fallow; they've got to regenerate their energies before they come back with another issue.

The whole strategy of the administration of Cornell is this: to deny to the really radical student leadership the support of the less radical but potential followers; and we can deny the support of the more moderate students to the, in percentage terms, really infinitesimal number of radical ones if we do the sort of thing that I think Ed Schwartz was talking about there.

For example, the questions of student discipline at Cornell are now determined by a trial board, chaired by a student, on which the students are in the majority.

MR. HIXSON: It seems that students have essentially grasped the philosophy of the union, and I think you know what that is, having been with the UAW. When the union leaders were asked, "Now what do you want?," the classic answer was "More." And that's dangerous, of course.

MR. OBERER: This is particularly troublesome in the academy for this reason: We just happen to be caught in between the students and their alienation on the one hand, and the establishment on the other. We're convenient. That's frustrating. How do you deal with them? An SDS student was telling me it's a sick society and he was saying this in all sincerity. And I asked him, "Compared to what?" He didn't know compared to what.

MR. WEINBERG: I have two questions. Mr. Oberer, would you explain what you mean by a "judicial body" in a university structure?

MR. OBERER: Once you have developed legislatively whatever rules, regulations, and policies are going to be in effect, there are repeated occasions to apply those rules and those policies in particular cases.

MR. WEINBERG: A judicial body does not apply rules. I am confused now because I thought there was agreement between you and Mr. Lieberman—and was appalled by your possible agreement. I thought you meant some type of appeals procedure.

MR. OBERER: Of course, there is that in the standard internal traditional forms of faculty representation. There are grievance committees. Mr. McHugh can perhaps tell us about the appeals systems within the New York State university system. His faculty senate some years back adopted a policy to the effect that there should be grievance committees on each campus and then the appeal could be from the decision of that grievance committee to a similar grievance committee at the faculty senate level. Is that correct?

MR. McHUGH: With possible ultimate determination by the chancellor. Concerning dismissal for cause, this starts at the campus level. When it finally reaches the statewide level it is before a statewide committee of faculty.

MR. OBERER: Let me add this on your remark concerning Mr. Lieberman and me. We're together in this sense: I don't disagree that there should be rules, policies; and usually the more clearly stated they are, the better they are. He contends that such policies should only be generated out of a collective bargaining contract.

MR. LIEBERMAN: I have argued that academic senates are contrary to public policy for a number of reasons, but you attributed to me the notion that collective negotiation is the only moral representational system. My criticism of academic senates does not lead to the conclusion that you have attributed to me; at least, I don't hold it. My belief is that any representational system that avoids those objections and doesn't create some new ones that are more objectionable would be perfectly consistent with public policy.

MR. OBERER: In any event, I'm in agreement that policies ought to be reduced to some understandable form, and frequently that entails writing them down.

MR. LIEBERMAN: Wouldn't you agree that negotiations does have that effect?

MR. OBERER: It's one way of producing that result, certainly.

MR. WEINBERG: Going back to tenure, it is conceivable that a judicial process may be added to tenure that would have an appeals procedure. It need not depend on the fact that you and your colleagues may not be McCarthy-like. But some of us have come across some unfortunate situations where a person may not be McCarthy, but may not be Oberer either.

MR. OBERER: I agree.

MR. ROSENTHAL: I submit it is probably worse than McCarthy-like to have you people administer an imposed process, because I think that with McCarthy when an accusation was made you assumed that the person McCarthy was accusing was in the right. When a distinguished group of professors makes a charge, the assumption may be that they're right.

Let me put it another way. Even to get away from your individual considerations, the education process demands that a person who perhaps survives your process ought to be informed of some of the criticism against him so that he may improve his teaching.

MR. OBERER: He would be informed.

MR. ROSENTHAL: At your discretion.

MR. OBERER: Well, Mr. Lieberman asked me whether he had access to the positions of every individual who had passed judgment upon him. My answer to that was no. But the dean, or somebody in a comparable position, would certainly get together with him and explain as best he could—

MR. ROSENTHAL: But that's only a distillation, so I think it's probably better to let him see everything.

MR. AMBELLAN: I too am beginning to get a bias which is somewhere around 50 percent toward Mr. Oberer and 50 percent toward Mr. Lieberman. There is a problem that to too great an extent we talk as if universities need to be dragged, clawing and kicking, into the twentieth century, or maybe the nineteenth century, in this whole matter. Also, there is the thought of jumping from one too-narrow platform to another.

As far as the old situation is concerned, sure enough, senates can be effective. They can be a real forum for progress and for intercommunication. And just as true, they can be a kind of company union, a kind of manipulative arm for authoritarian administration. They can be places that just get people involved in nonsensical busywork. So much for the old system.

This new system, surely because it's different and because it works, is something that we look at. It offers a new joy—confrontation. There are the new politics and the new politicos and power brokers that come into it as well, and they might be either tremendous statesmen or opportunists. We have to look at it that way. Unfortunately, the new system can exclude some of the good contributing citizens and the professorial leaders in institutions.

I'd like to comment on another notion mentioned here, the "What do you want next?"—"More" syndrome. A lot of the confrontations tend to be for the sake of more progressive confrontations, which can lead to a sort of patchwork fabric. We can't predict that it will be a complete garment.

The more I've listened to yesterday's and today's thinking, the more I feel that we have to beware of the either-or, that we have to watch the changeover—and we're sure as hell at a position of changeover. We need to recognize that not only are tough days here, but that tougher days are coming; and we need to see transitional stages in this instead of jumping from the one platform to another.

CHAIRMAN WALTER: Gentlemen, I'd like to give Mr. Holtzman an opportunity to speak.

MR. HOLTZMAN: We've shot past the right point for what I have to say, but earlier we talked about elitism, democratic values versus the quest for excellence. It seems to me that Mr. Oberer's way of contrasting excellence and democracy conceives of administrators as excelling at whatever it is that their faculties do. In other words, somehow you sift out from faculty members for, say, scholarship purposes people who excel in this and then they become the administrators.

I've been around several institutions and I've been in both seats. In fact, I'm a chairman now and I strongly suspect that the reason I'm the chairman is that I don't excel particularly at things that my colleagues in this department do. They wanted somebody to mind the store while they could go ahead and do these other things. I don't consider that particularly inappropriate, but I think it's a mistake to build our model on the supposition that the leaders are out front there because they excel at just the same things that the peons are presumably working on.

MR. OBERER: Where in my paper do you find me taking the position you have just ascribed to me? I don't take that position. I take the position that there ought to be joint involvement, and I comment expressly upon the fact that you can have a weak dean and a strong faculty, a strong dean and a weak faculty. I talk about the diffusion of power which is present in a traditional model.

MR. HOLTZMAN: You missed my point. My question is not whether the administrator is strong or weak, but whether his strengths, whatever they are, are in the same things that the faculty has been selected for. What I'm really getting at is the question of whether administration is simply a higher level of the same thing that, say, teaching is all about. My answer to that is no, but it seems to me your paper rests on the supposition that it's yes.

MR. OBERER: This gets back to what we talked about yesterday: whether or not the faculty should participate in the process of selection of their deans and presidents. I strongly assert that they should. The faculties that I've been party to have, and as a consequence we've had good leadership. Deans of law schools continue to teach; they just teach a lesser load. And they continue to write, although not as much, because of administrative demands.

MR. McHUGH: Two thoughts occur to me on the need for tenure review. Take for example a campus that increases its faculty by 20 or 30 percent in a two-year period. With such rapid growth it's not uncommon to have a substantial number of tenure review situations coming up under pressure. In some cases a department may expand from four to 15 in two years. It may be that there isn't the time nor the stability within the institution to make the kinds of evaluations Mr. Oberer's talking about and which are so effective in an established and stabilized institution. I think Mr. Lieberman may have a point in these situations. Perhaps there is a greater need for specific procedures and more formalized checks in the tenure review system.

Second, there is some pressure from some faculty unions to have similar kinds of formal procedures for nonrenewal of contracts wholly apart from the tenure situation. I'd like to get Mr. Lieberman's and Mr. Oberer's reaction to that. When a contract is not renewed, aside from the tenure question, is the person entitled to learn the reason why his contract is not renewed; must such nonrenewal be justified or "accounted for"?

MR. OBERER: Let me first of all respond to your first point, Mr. McHugh. The task force of the AAHE of which Addison Hickman and I were members concluded, among other things, that one of the prime reasons for the unrest among faculties now is the rapid growth of institutions such as you have just described. And, of course, in the ferment of growth and rapid expansion there is room for more aggravation than would be present under more serene circumstances.

MR. MONTANA: No one has mentioned faculty interest in academic decision making. In my experience faculty members tend to avoid plenary meetings, senates, and council meetings whenever possible. Unless they are pressed, there has to be leadership among the faculty to obtain desired action. Generally I do not see this happening and I question whether democracy will succeed under traditional channels.

MR. SUMBERG: I'm not sure we are looking at a vanguard of collective negotiations in the future if we're talking about traditional collective negotiations. As I said yesterday, I think we need some very creative thinking as to what collective negotiations in higher education will be if there is going to be any at all. Certainly the faculties of the junior colleges and the new community colleges are primarily concerned with professionalism and faculty senates, if our mail and our campus visits are any indication of what their interest is.

I think we ought to take a very close look at all the forms—faculty senates, the internal organizations, and the supportive agencies. I don't feel a sense of futility about the ability of the supportive agencies to communicate with one another. Rather, I think they're at a point in their own transition where they can provide some very wise counsel to the whole academic community.

MR. McHUGH: Early in your paper, Mr. Oberer, there is a slight error in fact about the New York situation. You say: "The claim of each of these petitions is that the local campus is the appropriate negotiating unit." That is not correct. There is only one petition that takes that position and that is the petition of SUFT (State University Federation of Teachers). The Civil Service Employees Association, the AAUP, the Faculty Senate of the State University of New York, and the Faculty Association of the State University—all four organizations take the position that the appropriate unit should be university-wide. And, parenthetically, so does the university.

The AAUP excludes from the bargaining unit people who do not hold academic rank. The CSEA, the State University of New York, FASUNY, and the Faculty Senate put everybody in the professional service in one unit on a statewide basis. The "Professional Service" is a term of art under New York law and includes professional support staff not holding academic rank, such as certain student personnel and admission people.

That essentially is what the various contentions are in that proceeding.

MR. CRONIN: I'd like to try to increase the complexity of the discussion of the issues because I think occasionally we flail away at straw men, one of the most recurrent being that there is such a thing as a traditional form of collective bargaining. I would agree that there are some characteristics that are shared among those who engage in collective bargaining, but the one thing that I've learned from arguments with some of the labor economists at Harvard (notably Dunlop) is that there are as many different types of collective bargaining and styles and modes as there are industries or crafts or public service professions; and that we have to a great extent, either in public employment or in education generally, a lot of options and a lot of room for experimentation.

Among these, for example—and I've seen this happen in elementary and secondary education—is the use of negotiations to create the functional equivalent of a faculty senate in situations where none exists right now. In many, many public school systems, for example, superintendents have not had, nor have they initiated, any kind of periodic conversations over policy issues, curriculum, personnel procedures, etc. But in some situations the bargaining or negotiated contract has called for periodic meetings to discuss professional issues, thereby providing the kind of dual system that was mentioned yesterday by Mr. Blum.

This is a quite reasonable and perhaps desirable outcome whereby one can have negotiations on a relatively limited set of topics, such as the minimum wage structure or certain controversial personnel policies, but also provide a forum for professional issues. That we can have it a number of ways is really the burden of my message. We needn't employ the model of steel or the garment workers or any other particular model. I have learned that collective bargaining is a relatively loose shirt that can be used in a variety of ways. Furthermore, I've learned that it can be an instrument for professional reform and has been in a number of situations.

I want to recognize the fact that it's open to abuses and in some heavily labor-oriented communities seniority has cropped up in places in teacher contracts where I certainly would disapprove, governing transfer and even the assignment of classrooms. There have been some ridiculous excesses which we want to be very, very sensitive to. But it's not as monolithic a device as we may think.

MR. GERSHENFELD: Let me try to de-escalate the complexities by pointing out that despite the myriad structural forms available and utilized, there is an aphorism heard in labor relations which is the epitome of accuracy in describing them, namely: "The parties deserve each other."

I think that says a lot about what you can expect in the way of future relationships. Where the parties are miserable and backbite, bad relationships will come about. Where the parties live in an atmosphere such as apparently exists at Cornell, a totally different kind of relationship will come about.

MR. HOLTZMAN: That sounds like a counsel of despair: that nothing can be done—if it's bad, they deserve each other and that's that.

MR. GERSHENFELD: No. The important point is that you will in time, if you persevere, bring about change in your opposite number.

MR. OBERER: The way I've heard it put in the private sector is this way: The employer gets the kind of union he deserves.

MR. BLUM: But the purpose of this meeting, I thought, was to help the world be one infinitesimal bit better as a result of such meetings. Theoretically, we are supposed to be in this business because we believe we are capable of improving society through education and through learning; otherwise it's a waste of time.

I agree that particularly in the professional, white-collar fields people usually don't go into unions unless management forces them. But also, it seems to me, there are varieties and forms, as Mr. Cronin just suggested, and we ought to be trying to evaluate them and learn something. I sit back here and wonder who determines allocation of funds in a university. I as a faculty member have nothing to do about it. Is the decision made in most senates? I doubt it.

Someone has been making these decisions which determine academic programs and salaries. We must think about how faculty members can be involved, for I hope we don't get what we deserve!

MR. OBERER: I want to direct attention before we close to one aspect of my paper that has escaped discussion thus far and which I think is terribly important, whatever the form of representation of the faculty. Let's take the State University of New York as an example. What is the appropriate bargaining unit, if you want to talk in terms of collective bargaining? If you want to talk in terms of some other form of faculty representation, you've still got the same problem. In what ball park are we playing? What are the issues?

Let me tell you what transpired at a state college in the State University of New York scheme of things. Two years ago I went to this state college to investigate the relations between the faculty and the administration. The you-know-what had hit the fan just before I got there, and it hit in this fashion: At the top of the pyramid in Albany the decision had been made, after consultation with the faculty senate and the chancellor and the director of the budget and the governor and the legislature, finally, that there would be an eight percent salary increase for the faculty of the State University. The decision was further made that three percent of that would be across-the-board and the other five percent would be left to the local campus president to play with.

So down to this particular state college comes this eight percent additional amount of money over what they had had the previous year, and the then president there allocated the five percent which he controlled in a fashion that meant some of the people got little, if anything, above the mandated three percent across-the-board. One other person got as much as 32 percent—and he happened to be someone that many members of the faculty didn't have very high regard for. He was looked upon as a favorite of the president.

A short time before this an AFT "cell" was organized there. It had, as I recall, six or seven members and an ambitious president. He seized upon this incident. He either went or wrote to Albany and availed himself of public records there—the names and numbers of all players. This is a state university I'm talking about, and therefore if you try hard enough you can find out about salaries, etc.

He got the names and numbers of all the players, Xeroxed or mimeographed all this, and distributed it around the campus. It was explosive enough that immediately membership of the AFT increased to something like 25 or 26.

This is the most concrete example I can think of to demonstrate how you can't, at the top of the pyramid in Albany, with the faculty senate or the AFT or the CSEA or FASUNY or anything else, deal with all the problems entailing terms and conditions of employment of the faculty. This problem was one that could only be dealt with at the local campus level.

If you'll think about the problem of the overlapping character of this necessary scheme of representation and then get back to something we talked about in connection with Mr. Marmion's paper—the problem of who is going to be representing the faculty at these different levels—you begin to see the complexity, whatever the forms of representation, of the representation problem in higher education, at least in the state university systems.

MR. McHUGH: There is an interesting sequel to that story. The first reprisal case under the Taylor Law came when the AFT president's contract was not renewed by the local president. I had the dubious distinction of losing the first such case under the Taylor Law in New York.

MR. SUMBERG: A further sequel is that we have a new president at that particular state college.

MR. McHUGH: Not yet.

MR. SUMBERG: An acting president.

MR. GERSHENFELD: There's a sanguine note to your comment, though. We're not likely to witness industry-wide bargaining.

MR. OBERER: It all depends. President Perkins recently predicted that by 1980, 50 percent or more of the funds of universities such as Cornell would come from the federal government; and this gets back to something Pat Carlton said yesterday, raising the question of who is the employer. Indeed, the more money the federal government puts in, the better the case can be made for the federal government being the employer.

MR. SUMBERG: How close are we to the line where we may very well come under the jurisdiction of the NLRB?

MR. OBERER: There is an express exemption of state governments and state employees from coverage by the National Labor Relations Act.

MR. SUMBERG: By legislative mandate.

CHAIRMAN WALTER: Mr. Oberer has been doing his best to get us de-escalated and de-sanguined and to have a little sweet reason. Before it all blows up again I'll adjourn this meeting.

ADJOURNMENT

•

CHAPTER FIVE

FACULTY ORGANIZATIONS AS AN AID TO EMPLOYMENT RELATIONS IN JUNIOR COLLEGES

MAURICE R. DUPERRE

CHAIRMAN, DIVISION OF TEACHER EDUCATION
LITTLE ROCK UNIVERSITY

•

It would seem that every popular magazine and learned journal and every educational conference catalogues with morbid fascination the latest outbreaks in the struggle for dominance by various groups. Thus, in discussing junior college faculty-administrative relationships it may well be superfluous to proclaim the gravity of the situation by providing an up-to-date box score of collective bargaining elections, group contracts agreed upon, strikes under whatever euphemistic lables, and state legislation on public employee negotiations. In fact, it may be impossible to compose an up-to-date list, given the accelerating rate of occurrence of such events.

Now, let us not assume that because some radical changes are taking place in education (or for that matter anywhere else), such changes are necessarily damaging in whole or in part. Such change may or may not be beneficial or, as is more likely, may consist of elements both helpful and harmful. It shall be my intent to report here an analysis of several actual situations, with the expressed purpose of ascertaining the pitfalls and pratfalls, agreements and arguments, and especially the new bonds and subsequent strengths which a few groups of teachers and junior college administrators experienced together.

I should like to emphasize the constructive attitude which I attempted to maintain during the course of this research. The title of the dissertation[1] which in large part is being reported on here is *Junior College Faculty Organizations as a Conflict Reducing Mechanism*. The emphasis is justified, I think, since several people on hearing the title have commented upon their assumption that faculty organizations usually seemed to produce conflict rather than reduce it.

Before embarking on a report of the study proper, we need to take two brief but essential side trips. The first of these will explore the nature of conflict, that word we use so often and so glibly. The other will acquaint us with the chief concerns of junior college teachers.

A number of writers,[2] have pointed out that some degree of conflict is healthy. We need both strong faculties and vigorous administrations to emulate the healthy pluralism of democracies. The conflict with which this study is concerned is that which exceeds healthy pluralism and approaches harmful disruptiveness. But such a statement implies a defined point beyond which conflict is disruptive. In addition to the difficulty in determining when that point on the continuum is reached, political philosophers would differ in the assignment of that point. Georg Simmel,[3] and others after him, held the extreme view that all conflict was beneficial. The present author heard an expert on collective bargaining[4] in education imply that the bargaining process in school situations could be a positive good. We have heard him argue that case again in our meetings here.

Goldman,[5] an early thinker in this field, gave conflict the following definition:

> CONFLICT SITUATION: A social relationship between two or more parties (persons, groups, or empirically distinguishable entities) in which at least one of the parties perceives

[1]Maurice R. Duperre, *Junior College Faculty Organizations as a Conflict Reducing Mechanism* (Unpublished doctoral dissertation, University of Texas, 1968).

[2]Mary Parker Follett, "Constructive Conflict," in Henry C. Metcalf and L. Urick (eds.), *Dynamic Administration* (New York: Harper, 1940); and Burton R. Clark, "The Role of Faculty in College Administration," in *Studies of College Faculty* (Boulder, Colo.: Western Interstate Commission for Higher Education, 1961).

[3]Georg Simmel, *Conflict and the Web of Group-Affiliations,* translated by Kurt H. Wolff and Reinhard Bendix (Glenco, Ill.: Free Press, 1955).

[4]Myron Lieberman, Address given at 48th Annual Convention of the American Association of Junior Colleges, Boston, February 29, 1968. Selected papers in press.

[5]Ralph M. Goldman, "Conflict Processes and Organizational offices," *Journal of Conflict Resolution,* Vol. 10, September, 1966, pp. 328-43.

the other as an adversary engaging in behaviors designed to destroy, injure, thwart, or gain scarce resources at the expense of the perceiver.

The adversary relationship which was included in this definition pointed up the nonintegrative nature of conflict. Conflict would seem to be harmful when the adversaries channel very much of their effort into resisting the perceived threat rather than into constructive criticism. Coleman[6] also touched upon this idea when noting that conflict often deteriorates from issues to personal attacks.

Goldman's definition added to the thinking of earlier writers the idea of perception. According to him, perception of conflict by just one of the parties would suffice to result in a conflict situation. Goldman accepted the necessity of resource scarcity, however, and while such a concept is still accepted for some resources, modern sociological theorizing on zero-sum games has questioned the universality of the concept.

The paragraphs just preceding this one have attempted to grapple with several abstract concepts by bandying about a number of polysyllables. This procedure may have been more soothing than enlightening. Perhaps an example might lend life to the discussion. The subject of merit pay has caused vociferous debate in the groves of academe as well as on the production line. When this topic is broached (usually by an employer), some, perhaps many, of the people who would be affected by adoption of such a plan see it as an attack on them. They question the motives: Are there some pet people to be paid off? Are they trying to sow dissension in our ranks? Shouldn't the money be shared by all of us? They question the implementation: What are the criteria of "merit"? How effectively can they judge us? This questioning does not go on very long before the originators of this bright idea react to the criticism. Why are they trying to thwart this? They really are afraid because they don't have much merit to evaluate.

Very soon we have a "them-'ns and us-'ns" relationship with charges being hurled back and forth, and the clients of the system suffering, as well as many members of the system too, until somehow the situation is resolved. Now perhaps such a conflict as this could prove beneficial in the long run, as some theorists would argue. It does seem, though, and here we lapse again into the vernacular, that the process

---

[6]James S. Coleman, *Community Conflict* (Glencoe, Ill.: Free Press, 1957).

just described is nonintegrative; that is, the struggle involved contributes little if anything toward achievement of the institution's goals. Indeed, a great deal of time and effort by all parties may be consumed in the process and, regardless of the outcome, vestiges of enmity may remain toward those with whom we should be working closely. In this political year we have heard the phrase often, but it seems to me that we *can* do better.

The subject of merit pay was chosen just as an example. It may have served as an illustration of a potential conflict situation, but what areas are most apt to provoke conflict? It seems to me that those areas of most concern to teachers have the most potential for conflict. Individual goals not met by the organization will result in dissatisfaction which, when acute enough, demands alleviation.[7] Conversely, if the preeminent concerns of teachers are satisfactorily resolved, conflict can be minimized.

The chief concerns of junior college teachers were learned by means of a checklist distributed at public community colleges in four states.[8] A rank order listing resulted in competitive salary at the head of the list, followed by academic freedom, small class size, chance for further study, sabbatical leave, a voice in curriculum policy, and tenure.

At this point we know some of the chief concerns of junior college teachers and want to know how best to meet them, if for no other motive than our desire to avoid conflict. This is, of course, not the sort of problem that lends itself to experimentation. Several methods of investigation were open to me, all of them examining somehow the relative success which actual organizations were experiencing in these areas of potential conflict.

Burton Clark has written of the merits of the case study method:

> To assess the nature of an organization systematically and in detail an intensive case analysis is necessary. The research on which this report is based took the form of a case study. A number of interrelated activities needed to be seen in connection with one another. This could hardly have been done by surveying a large number of organizations on a few selected characteristics or, for that matter, by using a single technique for gathering information.[9]

---

[7] James G. March and Herbert A. Simon, *Organizations* (New York: Wiley, 1958).
[8] Maurice R. Duperre, "The Concerns of Junior College Teachers" (Unpublished paper).
[9] Burton R. Clark, *The Open Door College* (New York: McGraw-Hill, 1960).

I decided to prepare case studies of five public community colleges with varying systems of faculty organization. The actual schools were selected in various ways. I became acquainted with some of them when they were mentioned in passing in journal accounts of faculty developments. One was chosen because of personal familiarity with the school and its system of faculty representation. Others were contacted at the suggestion of people familiar with a particular type of organization. The chief administrative officer at three of the five colleges tentatively selected agreed almost immediately to cooperate in the study. Another man asked to know more about the study, but then agreed after a telephone conversation. The last to agree did so after correspondence and personal conversations over a period of several months.

The decision to carry out a study of such varied organizations meant a geographical distribution of the cases. I was unaware of any one region of the country where all of these types of organizations could be found in proximity to each other. There was, moreover, an even better reason for this distribution; junior colleges are becoming ubiquitous, and their study should not be contained by state or regional lines. There are regional differences in junior colleges,[10] and regional representation was therefore recommended for studies of general trends. Unfortunately, there seemed to be a dearth of cross-sectional studies in the junior college field. For all of these reasons, the cases in this study were drawn from five different sections of the country.

The study was conducted for a week at each of the colleges, during which time some 30 people were interviewed for approximately three-quarters of an hour each. Interviews were with two or three top administrators and sometimes with a board member, with officers of the faculty organizations, and with a cross-section of the faculty selected at random except for an attempt to include a variety of teachers.

The interviews were semi-structured and designed to determine in what manner each of the seven chief concerns of teachers was handled. Care was taken to insure that respondents were not led by the phrasing or sequence of questions to identify a faculty organization as a major influence in any of these areas. If the respondent did not himself mention a faculty organization in the course of the interview, then he was asked about it at the end of the session. This topic was usually handled in two parts, first asking the respondent what he would

[10]James M. Richards, Jr., *et al.* "Regional Differences in Junior Colleges," *Personnel and Guidance Journal*, Vol. 45, June, 1967, pp. 987-92.

like to see an ideal faculty organization doing, and then asking him how well any organization at his school measured up to this ideal. Respondents were also asked their reaction to collective negotiations in education, particularly at the junior college level and, if they were less than enthusiastic, as it turned out most of them were, what alternatives to collective negotiations they could suggest.

At each of these schools also, an extensive review of pertinent documents was made. Board minutes and minutes of faculty meetings, constitutions of various organizations, correspondence files, mimeographed handouts, newspaper reports—all were examined with an eye toward supplementing and verifying the information gleaned in interviews. Whenever possible I sat in on a meeting of the faculty organization.

Let me summarize my findings beginning with each of the areas of concern we have noted. Teacher load was the first concern discussed with the interviewees at these colleges. It seemed to be an important concern at all of the colleges; three of the five faculties evinced some dissatisfaction with the present loads during interviews, and a fourth had submitted several letters to its faculty organization asking for attention to be given to load. At each of the schools, there were a number of teachers whose load was regulated by some outside agency or by the number of laboratory spaces available. Some teachers wanted fewer students, but others would be willing to teach the same number in fewer sections, and still others would like to innovate some teaching methods with variable class sizes. Flexibility would seem to be the key, considering these different comments. Judging from their actions and from their expressed desires, faculties would in large part prefer to work through the various departments or other administrative channels to achieve the necessary flexibility of teacher assignments. A substantial minority could see a faculty organization playing a role in this matter, especially at the college which had a union local, but also at colleges where recommended standards of national groups were cited. This choice may have been dictated by the attitude of a college's administration. For instance, one of these presidents had increased load and hours for most of his teachers. A member of an *ad hoc* faculty committee, which was studying the problem of load at that school, expressed little hope that loads would be lightened unless they could come up with an economic justification of such a proposal.

Load was certainly an economic issue. At one of the colleges, nearly all of the teachers supplemented their salaries with extra-contractual earnings. The role of the faculty organization in connection with the salary scale at each of the schools should be analyzed. All five of the faculties were involved in this matter to some degree. But at none of them had the faculty influenced any aspect of the scale to any extent. At one school, the faculty organization was not very satisfied with the result of a year's work, although the administration and the board were pleased. At another school, the group was involved in preparation of a scale, but was very sensitive to what it regarded as the president's wishes on the matter. Even in communities which had experienced strikes, either at the college itself or in the public schools, respondents were nearly unanimous in denying that such organized protest had any significant effect on salaries. About the only organizational influence detected was in the frequent references to AAUP or NEA studies of salaries which were heard during interviews. One factor which may have had a bearing on the findings in the area of faculty salaries was that, through chance, each of the five colleges visited boasted an excellent salary scale for its geographical region.

Chance selection, in the form of the large segment of older interviewees at one of the five schools, also may have resulted in further study not being valued highly there. It was valued at the other four schools. Two principal facets of this topic emerged, sabbaticals and attendance at professional meetings. At the college where state law forbade sabbatical leave, the faculty organization wanted to attack the problem but was uncertain as to its effectiveness or even as to how to approach it. The college with a state-affiliated group was attempting to influence legislators in discussion of sabbatical and other leave. A local group was given an administrative plan for sabbaticals for its suggestions.

There was some feeling by the teachers everywhere, but particularly at one college, that the junior colleges were not enthusiastic about further study for their teachers; teachers with a master's degree, no more and no less, were what was desired. On the other hand, there was some indication that the teachers themselves at four of the colleges visited were not dedicated to the lofty concepts of sabbatical leave; where it was available, the quota was rarely filled, and there was criticism that the half-pay provisions were not generous enough. The faculty with a union had asked for better sabbaticals, but stressed more a generous travel budget, which would benefit the many rather than the few. Another faculty group sought a democratic basis for selection of travel fund recipients; its recommendation had been rejected, but it was still pushing for acceptance.

All in all, there did seem to be a role for faculty organizations in facilitating policies and procedures regarding further study for teachers. This role would probably vary, though, depending on the particular needs of a faculty and the locus of decision making for these matters.

At least a part of a college's curriculum policies and procedures would also appear to be a likely area for faculty involvement through an organization. Which part seems to depend again on the needs of a particular faculty. For instance, some of the colleges investigated here left the individual and the department a great deal of leeway in selection of texts and preparation of course outlines. These faculties either had or wanted some voice in determining college-wide curriculum. There was a minority opinion that such policy determination was largely out of the hands of the college anyway, and so faculty involvement would be fruitless. There was also a desire on the part of at least one faculty for a greater voice in policy on selection of texts. Even though the expressed desire of the faculty in this matter ran counter to the opinion of the president, there was hope for a compromise through the mediation of the faculty organization. In fact, in several of these colleges the faculty had had some influence in curriculum matters through its organization.

The next topic of discussion with teachers was tenure. Tenure policy was, or until recently had been, a state-level matter. In one college, a state agency formulated a tenure regulation shortly after my visit to the school. In another college it was still covered by state law. In the other three, recent changes in the status of the junior college meant that the state law no longer applied to them. In the four colleges not presently covered by state regulation, the faculty organization had a substantive voice in the development of tenure policy. An interesting, and to me surprising, sidelight on tenure at these colleges was the substantial disinterest in tenure discovered in the course of these interviews. This finding would seem to contradict the earlier indication of the faculty checklist.

This contradiction may have resulted from the fact that few, if any, violations of academic freedom were recalled by the respondents. Their nonchalant attitude toward tenure may be questioned, too, when a number of them distinguished between tenured and non-tenured teachers after a hypothetical infringement of academic freedom was posed. Most respondents felt that a faculty member might speak out on a public issue with impunity, although many added that he might be urged in private to refrain from such activity. One of the faculty organizations was probably going to work up a statement on academic freedom shortly after the time of these interviews. One of the colleges with an AAUP chapter had adopted the 1940 Statement on Academic Freedom of that organization; another college organization had rejected that statement in favor of preparing one of its own which would be more suitable for its particular institution. When pressed for an avenue of recourse if a faculty member should be convinced his academic freedom was endangered, many teachers suggested the AAUP. There were other suggestions too, including the state organization which supplied California teachers with lawyers when needed, the Florida Education Association, and the local teachers' union, if available. The teachers' union at one of these colleges had included a clause on academic freedom in its contract with the school board. One AAUP member there noted sadly that academic freedom now seemed to be a negotiable item.

The respondents in this study were asked about unionization and collective negotiations in junior colleges and were also asked to describe their conception of an ideal faculty organization. Not very many of the teachers who were interviewed in this study championed unionism and its concomitant militancy. On the other hand, very few would balk at striking if all other avenues had been exhausted. Suggested alternatives were numerous. Teachers sometimes cited prototype organizations which they visualized as feasible alternatives; other teachers described the functions of their ideal organization.

The ideals cited fell into three main categories. First was an organization to facilitate communication both ways between the faculty and the administration. Ideas on composition of the group varied. Some respondents wanted administrators included in the group, while others would restrict membership to teachers. There was general agreement that the group should be advisory only, but with their advice heeded whenever possible. Some people would also provide for some sort of appeal process to the governing board if the organization should deem this desirable.

The second main category of ideal organization was one which would go a step further. This group would recommend policy, reflecting the best thinking of the faculty, at whatever level was necessary. It would influence legislation, work with similar groups at other colleges, and probably have some sort of state-level affiliation.

The third category was one which would satisfy the professional aspirations of junior college teachers. The organization would be one which would upgrade the profession through improvement of its members and would also strive to improve the status of its members. Teachers cited the American Medical Association and the AAUP as similar types of organizations. There was substantial feeling, however, that the AAUP was not a completely satisfactory organization for this purpose, even though there was a chapter of AAUP at three of the five colleges. Objections to this organization ranged from the unarguable fact that junior college teachers were not university professors and did not share all the concerns of professors to the accusation that the AAUP was "out of step with the times." Part of the reaction may be attributed to the fact that at each of the three colleges with AAUP chapters there were also newer faculty organizations which may have been in competition with the older groups for the allegiance of teachers. From time to time, teacher comments implied that unionization would increase to the extent that AAUP was seen as not really representing teachers in the junior colleges.

The union was rarely cited as an ideal type. This was stressed even by the faculty which was represented by a union. The teachers there backed their union and the idea of collective negotiation, some of them vociferously and others reluctantly, but almost unanimously. They added, though, that this was their only practical way to keep a voice in the administration of their professional affairs, given the structure with which they had to deal. Those few teachers who were opposed to unions were undergoing a trying experience. Practically all of the faculty there saw an ideal organization as one which would cooperate in forming policies concerning academic affairs. Not even economic issues, while admittedly important, were of more concern to them.

In the dilemma of the reluctant union members can be seen one key to the effectiveness of a faculty organization. This key is the personality of the administrators or board members with whom the organization must deal. In the first case study of this report an earlier president had squelched attempts to form a modest faculty organization. The incumbent president, on the other hand, not only encouraged formation of such a group but encouraged, assisted, and heeded the group in its early months. The second case study revealed a president who balked at the main recommendations of his organizations, attempted to block their communication with the governing board, and generally clung to every vestige of the decision-making process. Another study described a conservative governing board which fought every inch of the way with the teacher union and which tried to enlist the most effective leaders of the teachers on the side of administration. Still another college boasted an effective, well-liked president who solicited recommendations from one of the faculty organizations at his college and actively encouraged the formation of another to meet a different set of needs of the college. The final study involved an intense, hard-working president motivated on the one hand to use a faculty organization in the operation of the college, but at the same time unable to delegate even minute aspects of the operation to such a group on its own.

A second key to the effectiveness of these organizations was the attitude of the other body each organization dealt with, the faculty at each college. In the sense that, as contrasted with power, authority can be conferred only by the people involved,[11] an organization would be ineffectual without the willingness of the faculty to bring its concerns to the organization and to accept the decisions of the group on its behalf. The feedback process in each case played an important part in this obtaining of faculty support. At one college the lack of communication was noticeable. An organization accomplishment there was negated through noncooperation of the faculty, and interviews revealed a lack of knowledge of other organization activities. At the second college the faculty was informed through meetings, news releases, and referendums, and supported the organization in the face of administrative discouragement of the group. The third college and its organization had ample coverage of its strikes in the public press as well as in bulletins and other releases of the union local. It was interesting to note that activities of the other two organizations at the college were known only through the mimeographed minutes of their meetings. Another organization released the minutes of the frequent meetings at its college; support of the organization had been diluted since the original optimistic attitude of the faculty. Still another college had an excellent organization publication, and knowledge and support of that group was high. Another organization there used dittoed bulletins, and the lower level of support by the faculty may have been due in part to the difference in publicity.

The previous paragraphs have hinted at differences in the effectiveness of various organizations on a single campus as well as on different campuses. The competition and cooperation of different

---

[11]Peter M. Blau and W. Richard Scott, *Formal Organizations* (San Francisco: Chandler Publishing, 1962).

organizations at the colleges emerged during these case studies. It would seem that initially at least, existing faculty organizations suffer when a new group springs up. A reason for this may be that teachers are not able to subscribe wholeheartedly to more than one primary group of the same general type; allegiance may be indivisible. Of course, it is quite possible that the newer groups came into being when the older organizations had lost, for whatever reason, the ability to represent the faculty in a meaningful way.

In any case, it was encouraging to note signs that in some instances an accommodation of different organizations may be reached. At one of these colleges, two organizations appeared to have divided responsibilities satisfactorily. Some officers of each group even sat as *ex officio* members with the other group to improve intergroup communication. At another college, the senate has become something of a resurgent force with the encouragement of the union, although the role of the AAUP chapter there did not emerge very clearly during the study. At two other schools, the AAUP chapter has encouraged and cooperated with the organization which in each case was more involved with the multiple concerns of the faculty.

Some of my fellow panelists have addressed themselves to recent developments in the area of faculty organizations. I was pleased to hear them also prognosticate. As for myself, I see faculty organizations in junior colleges and probably throughout higher education as here to stay. Until we learn more about the ways in which they can be best utilized, the frictions will be inevitable.

But in time and with experience we will learn. The frictions will not be exacerbated, as they so often are in these initial years of faculty organization emergence, but will remain within manageable limits. In time we will all be pulling in the same direction rather than in divergent directions. When that day arrives we will have set out upon a new era in higher education, the extent of which cannot yet be calculated, and we shall look back upon these trying days with nostalgia and perhaps with pride that we were all a part of that great development, the growth of faculty organizations.

DISCUSSION OF MR. DUPERRE'S PAPER

MR. McHUGH: Given the trend toward multi-campus state systems like those in Illinois, New York, Massachusetts, Connecticut, New Jersey, and California, and given further the concurrent trend of states adopting public employee relations acts, it is fair to say that a substantial amount of collective bargaining activity is going to take place in publicly supported institutions, especially state systems.

New York is really the first state that I know of which applies a comprehensive public labor relations act (Taylor Law)[1] to a university system. I have already referred to the fact that there is a formal representation proceeding now in progress. Accordingly, my reference to the State University of New York is not born of provincialism but of the conviction that the New York collective bargaining experience and the resolution of its problems will most assuredly have a profound effect upon public higher education throughout the country.

Let me turn briefly now to Mr. Duperre's paper as it concerns the idea of conflict. Heretofore we have been talking principally of conflict between the faculty and its administration. We should also think of the adversary relationship involving both the executive and legislative branches of government. Tension rises because the educational enterprise needs substantial funding and funds are not unlimited. The executive and legislature must assign priorities among many competing branches of government and allocate all state resources. Under the rubric of "public service," government sees the educational institution not only as providing instruction and research but as serving as an instrumentality of social change. Thus there are great pressures to undertake programs for the disadvantaged, continuing education for industrial interests, and the like. With all of this will come the pressure for accountability.

Thus there is no question in my mind that conflict will exist in the future—substantial conflict giving rise to a felt need on the part of faculties for collective action to advance and protect their interests. For in this era of rapid change there will be genuine disagreement as to what the mission of a state-supported institution is or should be—what academic, public service, or social programs should be supported. In the decades ahead there are going to be some hard decisions. These decisions will affect the assignment of priorities, the allocation of public resources, and the professional and economic interests of faculty. One of the principal means by which many of these conflicts will be resolved or compromised will be by collective bargaining.

Let me turn now to the "interests of faculties," which really touches

---

[1] New York Civil Service Law §§ 200 et seq. (McKinney Supp . , 1968); Governor's Committee on Public Employee Relations Final Report, State of New York (March 31, 1966). Write the governor's office; William F. McHugh, New York's Experiment in Public Employee Relations: The Public Employee's Fair Employment Act, 32 Albany L. Rev. 58 (1967).

on the concept of scope of negotiation in higher education. Mr. Duperre mentioned salary, academic freedom, class size, sabbatical leave, tenure, curriculum. Let me reel off a few more based on the positions of the various contending employee organizations in the representation proceeding in New York. All of the faculty organizations consider as potentially negotiable such items as salaries, tenure, grievance systems, property rights in educational TV tapes and correspondence courses, admissions policies, faculty-student ratios, extra compensation, recruitment, athletic policy, parking, budgets, the nature and character of involvement by faculty in budget formulation, participation in planning of capital construction, and selection of administrators, deans, and department chairmen. One can expect that the faculty concept of what is bargainable will be all of these matters and then some. The rationale is rooted in the "shared authority" notion: that faculty should have a part in the governance of the institution.

"Management" had better start thinking about what the scope of negotiation should be and what constitutes management's prerogatives. What is outside a contract is just as important as what is in the contract.

Let me raise a number of problems for your consideration. First, on the unit question, should professional support staff be in the same unit as faculty? That is, do student personnel staff, admissions staff, librarians, instructional resource professionals (computer education, etc.), and directors of disadvantaged programs and specialized institutes share a community of interest with faculty? Should we place part-time faculty in one unit and full-time faculty in another, as the New York Public Employment Relations Board did in the case of the City University of New York?[2] The latter may be a problem peculiar only to a large university in a large metropolitan area.

Further on the unit question involving a state operated system of higher education, should the unit be established on a campus-to-campus basis or on a statewide basis? That is, should all employees be in one unit? If separate elections are held at each campus and it becomes necessary to negotiate with 26 different state-operated campuses, there is a loose confederation and whip-sawing in the extreme. A one-unit determination does not preclude negotiation on the campus level by "locals" of the statewide professional union. I agree with Mr.

---

[2]*In the Matter of the Board of Higher Education of the City of New York v. The Legislative Conference of the City University of New York* (Petitioner) *and United Federation of College Teachers, AFL-CIO* (Intervenor), 1 PERB 3; see also, Director of Representation Decision, same title, 1 PERB, pp. 1-407.

Oberer when he says there will be local issues and there will be state-wide issues, but the distinction between university-wide issues and local issues is not clear. There is a whole range of issues that require *joint* university-wide and local participation. Take the nitty-gritty of parking. Are you going to have a building or just a plain old asphalt or dirt parking lot, and are you going to charge faculty to park? If you have a capital construction program that is conducted on a university-wide basis and you're planning your buildings on a university-wide basis, you have to establish priorities to determine what goes up first. Do you put up a parking building at the downstate medical center to help the doctors get somewhere near the hospital in Brooklyn, or do you build an extra wing on the teaching hospital?

Even the simple matter of parking, then, at one of the urban university centers has a tremendous impact on the total university-wide capital construction program and the amount of resources available affecting buildings on other campuses. And indeed the critical problem of parking in an urban university can be just that—critical. It may not be so critical up in rural Fredonia, New York.

It seems to me that you lend stability to your negotiations if you have one statewide professional union, which, by the very nature of its components and the complexity of a university system, will have to delegate within its own structure substantial authority to the local campus chapter. This is preferable to individual professional unions developing at a campus level and then forming joint councils to negotiate on statewide issues.

Under a single unit determination in a state-operated university system, I think one of the first problems for negotiations will be determining what is local and what is statewide. What are the gray areas that require joint involvement? What are the terms and procedures by which such joint involvement will proceed?

These are some of the problems that are beginning to come up. Unquestionably, when you apply collective bargaining to education one of the critical issues to be faced is determination of the appropriate employee unit.

One of the topics that hasn't been discussed here is the need to recognize the uniqueness of education in the public employment statute itself. To what extent can those states which may be considering new laws learn from our experience in New York, Michigan, and soon in New Jersey? To what extent should there be a recognition of the uniqueness of higher education in those laws? What form should that recognition take? Should special procedures be provided in the

Public Employee Relations Act relating only to education and insuring that the agency administering those procedures is educationally oriented? I understand that Connecticut recognized the uniqueness of education in its statutes. I think some thought should be given, particularly by national associations, to developing model statutes.

Who is the public employer? With whom does the professional union deal? Who will represent management at the bargaining table? Take again a multi-campus situation. How and when should the state budget office be involved in negotiations? Will other representatives from the executive branch of government be involved? Indeed, will some member of a working fiscal committee of the legislature be involved? How and when do you key in the various echelons of "public employers or management" in the negotiating process? Which issues are solely within the province of the educators and which require joint participation with state officials?

What are the pitfalls of binding arbitration? Are there any pitfalls? What are the implications of putting into the hands of third parties outside the academic community questions concerning recruitment and tenure or disagreements over contract provisions that relate to recruitment and tenure?

What are the interrelationships between the professional and the nonprofessional? One of the things that the AFT says it wants to negotiate is the number of secretaries per faculty member, and yet the secretaries are represented in a statewide unit represented by another union. The other union may have to be factored in if this is going to be a subject of negotiation. The hours that professors expect their secretaries to work may be entirely different from the hours a secretary is expected to work in other governmental agencies. Holidays may be different.

I understand from a paper given before the National Association of College and University Attorneys in June, 1968, that we can expect certain faculty members to honor picket lines or strikes by nonprofessional unions.[3] The point is simply that collective bargaining may offer in the future the prospect of a closer alliance between the professional and nonprofessional.

There is a great need for direction in this field, in what the character of collective bargaining will be, how it should be conducted. There is a tremendous need for developing expertise, for having informative

---

[3] *The College Counsel*, Vol. 3, No. II, 1968, p. 95. (Sympathetic strike by academics not mentioned in paper but mentioned orally.)

programs (like this one) within the academic community itself to begin to familiarize faculty and others with the implications of collective bargaining. It's essential that the faculty grasp the implications of collective bargaining and provide the kind of responsible leadership that will be sorely needed.

What about bargaining as a tool for reform by those charged with the responsibility of the educational enterprise? To what extent will this be a device to reopen and reexamine the whole question of tenure, class size, and computer and TV instruction?

What about the store of information needed in the bargaining process—comparative wages and all the other statistical information upon which to make judgments and agreements? Who provides this from what sources? It is remarkable how little we in education know about our own institutions.

What will be the impact of collective bargaining on state systems which place emphasis on local institutions with local governing boards? Assume that one union succeeds in organizing most of the individual local faculties, leading to uniform or similar bargaining styles and contract demands pursuant to statewide union "policy." Albeit the colleges' governance mechanisms are structured locally, can one expect that such statewide unionism will trigger comparable statewide management associations with countervailing policy and styles? Will collective bargaining under such circumstances tend to depluralize the colleges into a uniform de facto system by shifting the decision-making apparatus toward a statewide level?

These are some of the thoughts and questions I have had since becoming involved in the prospect of collective bargaining in New York.

MR. DUPERRE: I don't think this need for statewide planning or statewide coordination of faculty organization efforts holds true in most states, not for the junior colleges at least. It perhaps would be a lot more convenient for the people at the State University of New York to be able to handle it this way, but even in his own state, when Mr. McHugh talks about the local community colleges, it seems to me that most issues can best be handled at the local level with the local board and administrators through a local organization.

MR. MARMION: Mr. Duperre, in your paper you say that the question of number of class hours taught is an economic issue, at least in the colleges that you are discussing; and you talked about overload and extra compensation. Isn't load more usually associated with working conditions, or is it usually an economic issue?

MR. DUPERRE: You can argue that any issue in a college is an economic issue because a service is involved which has to be paid for. Or you can argue that any issue is an academic issue because it involves the college. In my thinking, load is very closely related to salaries, in junior colleges at least, because your instructional budget goes further if you have fewer teachers. When you have fewer teachers you have heavier loads. That's why I say it's very much an economic issue, very closely tied to salaries.

MR. HOWE: This is a very critical problem in the initiation of bargaining. There are two very distinct views as to what represents an economic issue. From the administrative-board point of view it has to be whatever requires the expenditure of money. From the point of view of faculty, however, it tends to be whatever enhances the income of the faculty member. When you receive demands that are classified as economic and noneconomic you frequently find that the cost implications of the noneconomic greatly exceed the cost implications of the so-called economic, and the educational process that has to take place at the table is perhaps the most painful aspect of the whole deliberation process.

MR. HIXSON: I remember how many times we have started off negotiating sessions with management saying, "First we'd like to discuss the noneconomic issues."

MR. HOWE: May I interpolate that I've said that myself. There certainly is role playing in all of this.

MR. HIXSON: I'd like to comment on Mr. Duperre's remark and an item in the paper having to do with the popularity of the AFT on the community college campus. If there were a popularity contest in which the AFT were entered, whether at the K-12 level, the community-college level, or the four-year college level, inevitably the AFT would lose. Certainly it would lose at the four-year college level. Popularity, while a factor, is not necessarily an important one, and I'm speaking now strictly from an organizing standpoint.

As to the AFT local creating conflict, let me explain that when we go to a community college we go there by invitation only. And I think there are some real problems in these colleges because without exception I have always had to meet secretly with a cell—in fact, I have created a cell. When we establish a local of the AFT on the community-college level (and I think this is true of the NFA, too—they're no more popular than we are, I've discovered, because they are also an external organization) we look at several stages. The first one is the establishment stage, in which we actually create the cell. The second stage is the survival stage, in which we surface and do a lot of praying, among other things. The third stage (and these overlap) is the membership growth stage. The last stage would be the collective bargaining stage.

We do not create the conflict on campus. That conflict already exists. What we do, of course, is identify the conflict and exploit it, from an organization standpoint.

I would say that while salary is a factor on the community-college level, almost without exception a more critical factor, one realized at least by the cell, is the question of academic freedom. The kinds of intimidation of teachers used by administration on these campuses is unbelievable. Techniques range from threats to family security to outright dismissal and to blackmail. Academic freedom is really one of the most important factors.

MR. WALTER: Taking that analysis just a step further may cast some light on our earlier discussion as to what difference it makes whether the organization representing the faculty is internal or external. The external organization first enters the situation as a result of conflict.

I think we also need to keep in mind that any organization has two dimensions of responsibility. One is to get its job done and the other is to maintain itself as a functioning organization.

On our hypothetical campus let's assume your organization comes aboard and solves a particular rasping problem. Let's assume also that no further problems arise. It would seem to me your organization would then face the same question we talked about earlier: The members begin to say, "What have you done for me lately? I want something more done." Which almost builds in, I should think, a pressure to create additional issues that then will justify the existence of the organization and the collection of dues.

If the traditional faculty senate, on the other hand, begins to wither on the vine for the lack of anyone needing its services, there is no problem of organizational security. No one's self-interest is threatened. This is a distinction.

MR. HIXSON: One of our young faculty leaders who was instrumental in forming a local said when he surfaced, "I hope that we've solved the problem and then, like the state, the AFT can wither away." But that doesn't happen.

MR. MINER: I think Mr. Hixson will agree with me, since we have both observed a great many community colleges over the past year, that they have very serious problems. In fact, I sometimes believe that the most serious faculty problems of all exist today within the community college, and for a variety of reasons, among which is their explosive development as a completely new and rather unique kind of institution.

Generally speaking, I do not argue that there is no role for a faculty senate on a community college campus. I do argue, however, that as the only instrument for faculty representation on a community college campus, the senate simply cannot resolve the kinds of conflicts that we find there.

I agree completely that in many respects the senate has been used in the community colleges (and I limit myself right now to the community colleges) as an instrument to delude the faculties into believing that in fact they really do have a voice in determining policy. Generally speaking, I would say, in most of the community colleges where we have been called in, the conflict is there. The senate has already failed to serve as an instrument for resolving this conflict, and our role has pretty largely been to extend a device to the faculty by which hopefully their voice can be felt in policymaking and shared decision making. We give them an instrument by which they can hope to solve rather than create conflict.

Without any question, there is substance in Mr. Walter's observation that an organization does have the problem of maintaining itself. On the other hand, with the organization of community college people that I represent—and this is true with Mr. Hixson's organization as well—I don't think the international of AFT or the national body of the National Faculty Association goes in and creates new problems to maintain that organization. Heaven knows, we've got enough to pray over without doing that kind of thing right now.

Most of the issues which will have a tendency to maintain that organization are going to be local issues that are instigated and formulated and activated by the local organization.

MR. SUMBERG: I want to say a few words along this same line because I'm always running into Mr. Hixson or Mr. Miner of the junior colleges. Since we are the largest membership organization in the junior colleges we feel very strongly that the problem there is essentially one of a search for professional status or professionalism. Frequently our chapters are established at community colleges as quickly as possible because they want to identify with higher education, so I'm a little bit concerned with what Mr. Hixson just said, because I'm not sure he really means it (if he does I'd be shocked)—namely, that when his organization spots conflict it goes in and exploits it. Maybe he is right. Avenues of resolution of conflict are frequently lacking, and we're called upon quite frequently to provide them. But why exploit conflict and confrontation? Why howl over the demise of a faculty senate? Why not go in and assist it and give it some meaning at the same time that your own organization and other organizations are playing supportive roles?

Is that what you really meant, Mr. Hixson—to exploit conflict?

MR. HIXSON: I said that from the frame of reference of an organizer, so I meant exactly what I said. That does not preclude a solution, because even from the frame of reference of an organizer the problem has to be solved. Otherwise the organization is lost, the goals you hope to accomplish will never be achieved, and you're done. But certainly if the conflict exists there, from an organizing aspect it most certainly has to be exploited. Otherwise that sore will fester.

MR. SUMBERG: Well, wouldn't you go in and offer them consultive service?

MR. HIXSON: Absolutely.

MR. ZWINGLE: I'm glad the issue of academic freedom has come up, because our organization plans to examine the boundaries of academic freedom in the light of current circumstances. I wonder if anybody here can give us any informal word on the progress of the task force organized to reexamine the 1940 AAUP statement on academic freedom, and whether the 1940 statement or its successor is likely to be of any effect in the junior college field.

MR. SUMBERG: I'll be glad to answer that. First of all, we are involved in meetings with the AAC over the reexamination. We have too many sponsoring agencies to completely throw it out and start all over again. There are many refinements necessary in the 1940 statement, and this is what we've been working on in terms of interpretations as well as refinements.

The 1940 statement has always been applied to the junior and community colleges.

MR. ZWINGLE: But I gather that it really hasn't taken hold. This is a fundamental document among the established institutions.

MR. SUMBERG: We're getting quite a bit of interest now. Over the past five years we've noted that community college boards adopt the 1940 statement at the same time they establish the tenure system. The best example is Northampton Community College in Bethlehem, Pennsylvania. Before the board even opened the doors they adopted the 1940 statement and the 1958 statement—all the AAUP statements. The report and censure of Lorraine County Community College last year stimulated a number of boards into adopting the 1940 statement very quickly.

MR. HOLTZMAN: Isn't that an example of exploiting a difficulty?

MR. SUMBERG: Not on our part.

MR. HOWE: As recently as March of 1968 the current president of the AAUP, speaking to the American Association of Junior Colleges, declared that his research had revealed but one attempt—he characterized it generously, but I will characterize it as a feeble attempt—to deal with the question of the applicability of academic freedom to the community college. I characterize it as feeble because it was mine. But academic freedom in the community colleges has been a sadly neglected area.

The application in Lorraine, in my opinion, falls short of dealing with the classic questions of academic freedom.

MR. SUMBERG: However, we've always worked on academic freedom in community colleges. The cases we've resolved don't get visibility.

MR. HOWE: I agree with that. I do, however, paraphrase your president.

MR. MINER: I want to comment on and perhaps make more concrete what Mr. Sumberg said about the role of an external organization. He said, I believe, that it should consult with the faculty on the kinds of conflicts and dissatisfactions and frustrations that may prevail on a campus in order to shore up and support the faculty senate.

One experience that I have had within the last two weeks leads me to believe that this is going to be a growing function. A college group recently called us to come in; with no membership strings attached, we responded to their call. We took a look at the situation and realized that their minds were already made up. They said, "We have problems here that cannot be solved by patching up and modifying the faculty senate. We have already decided what to do." What they intend is to pull that senate out from under the college machinery entirely and incorporate it as a separate external organization for the purpose of entering into negotiations.

Had we gone into that situation and tried to consult with that faculty and shore up the faculty senate we would have looked pretty stupid. I have seen much of this same kind of feeling among faculties around the country. It may be a trend. They're looking for an instrument removed from the college machinery by which their problems can be solved.

MR. LIEBERMAN: I think people here should know that Mr. Miner was the executive secretary of the National Faculty Association, which is an organization of junior and community college peo-ple, although that is not his present position.

I want to ask the speaker this: There are three organizations that are competing for members—the NEA and NFA, the AFT, and the AAUP. Who do you think is going to win the allegiance of junior college teachers and why?

MR. DUPERRE: I don't know that I can answer that, nor that anyone else can at this stage of the game. I can only guess on the basis of my familiarity with various junior colleges I have visited. But I doubt that the NFA, an NEA affiliate, will make much prog-ress unless it has already adopted a different approach from the one it started with.

MR. LIEBERMAN: Would you explain that? I don't know what you mean.

MR. DUPERRE: I can see Mr. Miner bristling back there already.

MR. MINER: I'm not bristling. I just think you're completely wrong.

MR. DUPERRE: I will agree with you on one point, Mr. Miner: You said that the community college is where most of the activity involving organizations will be. I think this is where it is and where it will be, in the foreseeable future. But I talked with a member of NFA at a large public community college. This is a college which has some definite problems, and lots of dissatisfaction among the faculty. This man was trying to enroll members in NFA and wasn't making any headway whatsoever, because the faculty senate at that school was taking substantive steps to resolve the faculty's difficulties. If I'm not mistaken, out of over 200 faculty members he was the only one who belonged to NFA.

The reason I don't think the NFA is going to get very far in com-munity colleges is twofold. In the college I cited as an example some other organization beat them to it. Faculty people looked around and said, "Why do we need an additional organization? Many of those faculty members also belong to AAUP and to the state organization. I might as well point out that this was in California and the state or-ganization was the California Junior College Faculty Association.

The other reason I don't think the NFA will get very far is the pres-tige factor. The NFA is, after all, a part of the NEA, and the NEA is considered to be primarily concerned with elementary and secondary education. "We're college teachers. We're not going to join that high school group," is the attitude one finds.

This is my thinking. As to the AFT, I don't feel they will get very far except in the crisis situations; and, Lord knows, there are a lot of them. This is really where the AFT has got the jump on other organizations.

What is the total AFT membership in junior colleges now?

MR. HIXSON: I'd say about 60 community-college locals out of 800 community colleges.

MR. DUPERRE: And the colleges are growing in this country at the rate of 50 or 60 new ones a year.

MR. SUMBERG: I think the total now is 924.

MR. DUPERRE: The AFT is doing a service in the places where it's needed, but in the big picture it's not pervasive.

The AAUP, I think, will make some great strides, partly for the same reason that I said the NFA would not—the prestige factor. Community college people would like to be associated with university professors. But the AAUP has one problem they have to resolve for themselves: What do you do with the vocational and technical instructors who aren't really university professors by their own count or by the count of the present membership of AAUP?

That's why I say that the picture right now is indeterminate.

MR. MINER: I had identified the college you were talking about as probably being in California. I don't think the community college system nationwide revolves around that particular college. There are states all across the nation where the opportunities for organization of National Faculty Association chapters are really very exciting at this point.

In the entire state of Michigan, for example, the NFA is linked with the Michigan Association for Higher Education. In almost every case these colleges have entered into negotiations. The union has a local at Henry Ford Community College and I guess at a couple of others. But the idea of negotiations is without any question catching on. There is no doubt in my mind, although I know there are some who will take strong issue with me, that academic or professional negotiation is going to be a rapidly growing concept within the community colleges. There are those today who are beginning to look at professional negotiation as a less desirable answer than they might prefer, but they have been pragmatic enough to recognize the values of a negotiated agreement.

As the program of the National Faculty Association develops (I grant this is an extremely biased point of view), the NEA and the NFA are in good position to gain a majority membership of community- and junior-college people. I have to disagree with you, Mr. Duperre. A year ago I would have had much the same outlook that you have.

The great desire of the community college people to identify with university professors does exist, but we have also found another rather interesting development; and I dare say that Mr. Hixson and Mr. Howe would confirm this. We are dealing with a very pragmatic, realistic group in the community colleges, and it is naive to assume that they are always going to labor under this rather vague desire to associate only with university colleagues. You find too many elements involved in the community colleges which differ from the four-year institution.

Today I can find whole state systems of community college faculties, in fact, who are looking for an instrument that will solve their problems; and that becomes more important to them than the image of identifying with and living in the shadow of the university.

I have talked with Mr. MacRae about this. I believe that the gap is going to begin to widen between the community college people and the four-year college people as the former begin to recognize the unique character of their institutions and faculties.

MR. GERSTL: I have a strong suspicion that we can't get accurate predictions here, because of vested interests. However, I think there is general agreement that the one place in higher education where professional negotiations are likely to come out most strongly will be at the junior-college level. However, I think it's necessary to consider just why this is the case.

MR. DUPERRE: Explanations have been advanced. One is the fact that the faculties and administrators of community colleges have been, at least up to this point, largely drawn from public school systems. In fact, although there is a trend away from it now, there are still many states where the community colleges are part of the public school system.

MR. LIEBERMAN: Do the junior college faculties that join the AAUP get adequate recognition as junior college teachers, or do they feel overshadowed by the professors from Harvard, Chicago, and so on? I'm interested in their outlook when they get in the AAUP. Do they feel they're always going to be a secondary concern in an organization dominated by people from prestige institutions, or do they not?

MR. DUPERRE: I don't know, but I'll give you my opinion. I don't believe they feel like orphans at all. I think most AAUP chapters in community colleges are quiet groups which look a little bemusedly at the other organizations which are vying for their attention at the community college level. They don't give too much thought to being overshadowed or dominated by those gray eminences at the four-year institutions.

MR. GERSTL: And yet you find they're chiefly concerned with money. Isn't the opinion you have just advanced inconsistent with your finding that income is the number one concern of the community college faculty?

MR. DUPERRE: I don't think there is necessarily a link between the two.

MR. FRANKIE: You will recall that Mr. Gustad discussed his study of seven or eight years ago indicating that salary was fifth or lower in his hierarchy of concerns among college faculties. Your study showed that salaries were number one and academic freedom was number two. The AAJC has just published two studies of 20 institutions by Roger H. Garrison covering 1966, 1967, and 1968. I read them thoroughly and found not one mention of academic freedom as a problem.[4]

Now Garrison has another publication out and there is no mention of the area of salary as a problem.

MR. DUPERRE: Garrison's two studies were not conducted on a formal basis with validated instruments. He merely talked with community college faculty members and got some impressions. He himself said that the first study you cited was very impressionistic. In that study the chief problem cited by teachers was a lack of time.

MR. FRANKIE: His sample, though, was 650 to 700 faculty people. How many did you talk to?

MR. DUPERRE: First of all, I have cited two studies. In the checklist study about concerns of teachers I have 278 responses. The checklist provided 32 choices and some blank spaces; chief concerns were ranked. I found out that academic freedom was very hot on the heels of competitive salary, by the way, and I can cite as substantiating evidence an NEA survey by William Graybeal.[5]

MR. FRANKIE: That's another thing I'd like to ask about. Did you find in your discussion that the community college faculty people thought academic freedom was a privilege or a right or a responsibility?

MR. DUPERRE: I didn't ask.

MR. FRANKIE: Did they discuss those kinds of elements? I think

---

[4] Roger H. Garrison, *Junior College Faculty: Issues and Problems* (Washington, D.C.: American Association of Junior Colleges, 1967); and *Teaching in a Junior College* (Washington, D.C.: The Association, 1968).

[5] William S. Graybeal, "What the College Faculty Thinks," *NEA Journal*, April, 1966, pp. 48-49.

someone said yesterday that academic freedom could be a negotiable item.

You said it was the second highest priority item?

MR. DUPERRE: In the first study, yes, but no discussion was involved in my study. A checklist was sent to four public community colleges in different states. I got responses, compiled them, and weighted them. I had respondents pick six items and rank-order them. The question was phrased like this: "Which of the following items are of concern to you?"

I tried to make clear that I wasn't asking whether at the moment a particular concern was salient. You might have a fine salary at the moment, but that's irrelevant. "Which is of most concern to you?" is what was asked.

MR. WALTER: Did you define academic freedom for them?

MR. DUPERRE: No. I gave a lot of thought to this, and you have perhaps put your finger on a weakness of the study, Mr. Walter. Academic freedom is one of our labels, like apple pie. It's hard to vote against academic freedom. I thought and schemed and tried to figure out how else I could say it, but there is no other way to say it and make clear what you're talking about. I did find that the results were constant through the four colleges, though.

MR. HIXSON: When I said academic freedom was very important I meant that, but this is the heart of the matter. You can go into one of these situations and say, "How's your academic freedom today?" And they'll say, "It's fine. We can teach evolution, and so on; anything we want to do in the classroom we can do." Then I can say, "If you've got academic freedom all you have to do is sign the charter here with your 10 people and say you're members of the AFT." And they'll say, "Are you out of your mind?"

So the real problem is that their concept of academic freedom is very, very narrow.

MR. DUPERRE: I'll go along with you, Mr. Hixson, and I tried to emphasize in this questionnaire that is doesn't matter whether you've got it at the present or not. With this clarification I think that many faculty people, especially when they reply to an anonymous questionnaire, will say, "Yes, we don't really have a lot of academic freedom here."

The *NEA Journal* published a survey two or three years ago which, among other things, showed that a surprisingly large proportion of junior college teachers felt they had either a critical or serious lack of academic freedom at their institutions.

MR. SMITH: That was the 1964-65 national study.

MR. STALLER: I'd like to go back and ask this: If the AAUP is going to take the lead in junior college negotiations, won't the organization have to change its position on collective negotiations?

MR. SUMBERG: Today up in Middletown, New York, there is a hearing going on in which representatives of the National Faculty Association and representatives of the AAUP are inolved as a result of an application for certification by the NFA. Our chapter is vying with that group for certification.

I don't see where we have to change our position. Our position is that they have a right to do this.

MR. STALLER: It seems that the group that is going to need the most in the way of collective bargaining in the future is this junior-college level, and it seems to me you're a little unclear on what your position really is.

MR. SUMBERG: It's not unclear at all.

MR. LIEBERMAN: You're clearly against it.

MR. SUMBERG: Why should we be at this hearing? A chapter has applied for certification and has asked for national assistance.

MR. CRONIN: Would the AAUP be for the repeal of the Taylor Law or at least those provisions which deal with community colleges?

MR. SUMBERG: Not at all.

MR. BLUM: Would the AAUP go into a junior college situation where there was a problem and exploit it so that it can be developed into a collective bargaining situation?

MR. SUMBERG: No. First we would try to resolve it.

MR. BLUM: Everybody would try to resolve it.

MR. SUMBERG: I'm not so sure about that.

MR. LIEBERMAN: The NEA had a policy against strikes, but when some of its locals went out on strike the NEA went in there and supported them. Why? Because when it came down to a specific situation, the NEA couldn't hold its membership unless it supported its affiliates in an action that was inconsistent with its nationally stated policy.

I think that's exactly what the AAUP is facing and will face more and more in the future. If the Association does not continually support locals that want to bargain, even though that is inconsistent with AAUP recommendations that they rely on internal mechanisms, you're going to lose them; in the meantime, you are going to act inconsistently until you are finally forced to come out in favor of negotiations.

MR. HIXSON: The AFT is not as altruistic in its attitude toward tottering faculty senates as the AAUP is.

MR. SUMBERG: Look what you did at Johnston and Wales. Look what you're doing to Onondaga Community College right now. You've exploited a situation at Onondaga, but you've done nothing to resolve it except that you've got a collective bargaining agreement which is atrocious and the faculty is in dire straits. The administration is no better off and there is a serious academic freedom issue there.

MR. McHUGH: What was the problem they exploited at Onondaga? I'm curious.

MR. SUMBERG: They've got a $12,000 debt.

MR. HIXSON: You have to remember that our locals are autonomous. As far as Johnston and Wales are concerned, it wasn't until that strike had gone on for some time that we were notified. I think had we been notified in time we would have advised against it. There was certainly some poor planning involved there, and the only thing I can say is that we lost the strike.

MR. SUMBERG: You not only lost the strike, but you did serious damage to the academic community.

MR. HIXSON: That was a hell of an academic community at Johnston and Wales.

MR. SUMBERG: I'll be glad to tell you the story, because we were asked by your officers to mediate that strike, and half an hour later we were told that the state AFT told the AAUP it was none of its business. When we set up a mediation panel the AFT never responded. Now, is that how you exploit a conflict?

MR. HIXSON: No, not at all. That's how not to exploit a conflict.

MR. McHUGH: Mr. Sumberg, are you saying that the national AFT was irresponsible at Onondaga? What did they exploit at Onondaga?

MR. SUMBERG: They exploited a very poor administration-faculty relationship at the very outset.

MR. McHUGH: What specifically in that relationship?

MR. SUMBERG: I don't know the issues, but it was a complete breakdown of communication—a president who doesn't talk to his faculty. The result is that we end up with a collective bargaining agreement, but that faculty and administration are still not talking.

MR. McHUGH: What should the national AFT do? What is the area of their irresponsibility? What should they have done there?

MR. SUMBERG: They have an academic freedom case there, and what they've said is that they won't touch it.

MR. McHUGH: What is the academic freedom case?

MR. SUMBERG: Dismissal of a professor who spoke up at a faculty meeting against administration policy.

MR. McHUGH: And the AFT said they wouldn't get involved? Is this right?

MR. HIXSON: No case has been brought to the AFT. That's a case for the Empire State Federation of Teachers, the local.

MR. McHUGH: Suppose the Empire State Federation of Teachers does not get involved. Do you feel there is a responsibility in the national AFT?

MR. HIXSON: We have a review structure.

MR. McHUGH: Has the case been brought to you?

MR. HIXSON: No, it hasn't. Out West we had a case where a teacher wouldn't salute the flag and they kicked him out of the local. Did we not, Mr. Howe, at that time revoke their charter?

MR. HOWE: Yes indeed.

MR. MINER: I'm interested, Mr. Sumberg, in the point that Mr. Lieberman brought up on the national policy of AAUP in terms of representation systems, because it appears to me that, in fact, as I read that position, it indicates that the AAUP would prefer to use means other than professional negotiation and they would prefer a senate arrangement to, say, having a representation election and establishing external means for resolving problems.

What that really comes down to, as I see it, is this: In fact, the AAUP has said that "if everything else fails and you really decide then that you're going to have a representation election, as a matter of expediency for the national office we hope that you will adopt us as the representation organization."

MR. SUMBERG: May I correct you on one point? Expediency for the national office? No. Expediency for the faculty of that college—what is best for the faculty of that college.

MR. MINER: Okay. Tell me how, then, you would look upon this situation as being best for the faculty at that college if, in fact, AAUP has a national position which opposes collective negotiations and therefore has not developed the machinery, the background, the experience to provide the kinds of services that could make a collective negotiation situation effective. It looks to me as though you're really setting yourselves up for the same kind of dilemma that you accuse the AFT of—going into a college when negotiations are entered into or it is decided that you're going to have negotiations; and then you are suffering from paralysis preventing you from going in and effectively aiding that faculty.

MR. SUMBERG: I can't agree with your whole premise. I don't think we're paralyzed. I think our policy is clear.

MR. MINER: What machinery do you have from the national office or at the state level that, in fact, could be of aid to a faculty entering a negotiations situation?

MR. SUMBERG: We have a wide variety of legal machinery available.

MR. HIXSON: As Stalin said, how many organizers has the AAUP?

MR. SUMBERG: What Stalin asked was how many troops the Pope had. But we don't put ourselves in that position.

Organizers? The faculty is its own organizer. Mr. Hixson, I think part of the problem in higher education is that you cannot impose upon a faculty what you think it should have. Essentially you have to go in and find out what a faculty wants.

MR. HIXSON: I'd like to say one thing about some of the strikes that we've had. Unfortunately, I think one of the most common phrases our organizers have used when they get called after the strike is probably in its first or second day is, "You did what?" And then, of course, we have to go into a situation. At that point you're beyond exploitation. Your job there is to save the troops and get them back alive. That, of course, we weren't able to do at Johnston and Wales. It was too late. I went there, and by then it was a heartbreaking situation.

MR. SMITH: I wonder if we could have an example of what would be a good case of exploitation.

MR. HIXSON: I can think of a certain community college in which the teachers were very much intimidated by the president, and were fearful of acting because they'd be run out of the system. I met with a nucleus of about 15 people in secret and asked what they felt should be done. I made some suggestions. They agreed to one of the suggestions. I went back to my office and mailed an open letter to the entire faculty of the community college spelling out the situation, with a simultaneous press release which forced the president (who was very foolish) to deny it in the open. That was exploitation. Eventually the president left the college, a new president came in, and there was improvement in faculty-administration relationships.

We have not as of this point achieved collective bargaining there, but we did achieve establishment, survival, and growth. So we're in the third stage.

That's what I mean by exploitation.

MR. LIEBERMAN: We have a lot of junior colleges that are parts of public school systems; they're the equivalent of grades 13 and 14. Haven't there been some cases where the junior college teachers tried to get out of the K-14 unit that was in effect? My understanding is that they were not successful in the cases I know about. Are there cases in both directions? Is my assumption correct?

MR. HIXSON: I think Henry Ford Community College in Dearborn, Michigan, is one of those locals which succeeded in splitting itself off from the K-12 system. I can't recall any others offhand.

MR. SUMBERG: Belleville Junior College in Illinois.

MR. McHUGH: One of the problems in the community colleges in New York State is that in some of the local jurisdictions, which under the Taylor Law can in certain circumstances make unit determinations, they will group the professional staff at the community college in with all of the county employees. This, it seems to me, raises some very serious questions.

MR. SUMBERG: You mean under a local civil service law?

MR. McHUGH: Yes. They'll take all of the county employees as one unit and they'll include presumably the janitorial service people and the local public works people, and so on.

MR. SUMBERG: What about the section of the law that says that professional staff do not have to belong to the same unit unless they have so decided?

MR. McHUGH: That's not in the Taylor Law.

MR. OBERER: That's in the National Labor Relations Act.

MR. McHUGH: The unit determination can take place at the local level, under Section 212 of the Taylor Law, where the local jurisdiction decides to establish a little PERB to handle the local public employee relations problems at the local level. When I say local I mean local government level. In some cases all the employees are grouped in one unit, including the community college professional people. I think that makes for a very difficult situation, to say the least.

I have a feeling this will ultimately work itself out, but these are the problems in certain areas of the state.

MR. LIEBERMAN: I'd like to pursue my previous question. I wondered whether the AFT and the NFA have the same position on this: Do you support as a matter of principle the right of the junior college teachers in this unitary system of K-14 to be a separate unit? Or do you decide that question on the basis of whether you'll lose those people if they break up?

MR. MINER: Our NFA position would be that there are enough differences so that they should be contained within a separate unit. We probably have an additional problem that the other organizations will not have. We have also recognized in certain states today where the Classroom Teachers Association is very strong (and I guess this supports your point, Mr. Duperre) that organizationally, aside from the legal position of how you're going to negotiate, there is a great necessity for us to form independent chapters for the junior college in the negotiation process rather than attach them to an already existing though maybe powerful local association.

This decision has really already been made and has cleared one of the roadblocks to organization in some of the states.

I don't think there is any question about it, Mr. Lieberman. That would have to be our position. However, on that basis the problem may resolve itself in some states. I don't know about that can of worms in New York, but in Michigan, for example, Mr. Howe, I guess the Henry Ford Community College and one at Grand Rapids are the only two junior colleges that still remain a part of the K-12 system.

MR. HOWE: There are five.

MR. MINER: There is a strong tendency away from this kind of thing. Washington has already taken that position and there is only one remaining in California. I think those problems will be solved. However, it's a different kind of·snarl that Mr. McHugh is talking about in New York.

MR. HIXSON: Mr. Lieberman, in some of our K-14 systems, if you spin off a junior college local I believe you have to clear it with the local itself, that is, the K-14 local. There are some community college teachers in a K-14 situation who don't want to spin off because they feel they're stronger running all the way through.

MR. LIEBERMAN: My concern was where you have a majority of one organization at K-14, but a different majority at the junior-college level.

MR. HIXSON: I don't think there's any policy on that.

MR. LIEBERMAN: I just wondered if in those cases you wind up following your organizational benefit rather than the principle of whether the junior college teachers should be separate or not.

MR. MINER: I'd like to throw this in, Mr. Lieberman, as something additional to chew on. One of the problems that any external organization is going to have to face involving a negotiations relationship is the present variety of systems of governance of community colleges. We've just been involved in discussing one of them. There is just no end to the numbers of various forms of governance that exist today in junior colleges, and they're constantly changing. You have things ranging all the way from local boards of trustees to completely state-controlled systems such as the one in Virginia. You have state co-ordination with local boards. You have state control with advisory boards at the local level. You have some remaining today as part of a K-12 system.

Then you have an interesting one in Maryland, where members of a K-12 board of education simply remove their hats, put on other hats, and become a board of trustees governing the junior college. Now that model is changing to centralize more control in the state system.

It would appear to me that any organization which intends to be effective in representing faculties—whatever that turns out to be—is going to have to be flexible enough to negotiate at the state level. It must have some strength, power, and resources at that level. It must also be able to function at the local level. And, frankly, I don't think we're far enough down the road at this point to understand all of the rather complicated factors that could be involved in this.

MR. FRANKIE: In Georgia the junior colleges are both run by the university.

MR. MINER: New Mexico's system is very interesting. Most of the two-year colleges are simply outgrowths or extensions of the four-year universities and are governed as such. As I understand it, a state law says that if a district wants a junior college it may establish one but will be immediately cut off from state funds.

MR. MacRAE: There has been no mention during this whole conference about a new development that has come on the horizon, and this is Mr. Smith's new status at the American Association for Higher Education. I wonder what's going to happen there. Now that the AAHE is practically independent, is the organization going to go out for members and compete with the AAUP and NEA? What is going to happen there?

MR. SMITH: I just hope you have your crystal ball out because I honestly don't know. We are not yet an independent organization. Let me say for the benefit of those who are not familiar with it that the AAHE includes both faculty and administrators. The NEA set up a choice of three different relationships: (1) a department which is very closed in, (2) an affiliated relationship, or (3) an associated organization, which is inside the family but completely independent both physically and as to policy.

Our association at its convention in October opted for the third category beginning July 1, 1969.

MR. LIEBERMAN: You couldn't remain in that status and compete for members with the same purposes as NFA.

MR. MacRAE: Under their associated status they could.

MR. SMITH: This might give a choice between collective bargaining and the use of the faculty senate. There will be some competition, I am quite sure, but we're trying to keep it within limits.

ADJOURNMENT